Praise for
WAR'S END

"Makes you feel like you are in the plane alongside the crew
as they undertake their hazardous, breathtaking mission."
—U.S. Senator John McCain (Az.)

"A candid account, as authentic as it is arresting,
providing the ultimate insider's tale of this fateful mission."
—Historian James MacGregor Burns,
winner of the Pulitzer Prize and the National Book Award

"A most valuable addition to the history of World War II...
His book offers a wealth of information bearing on
the decisions and aftermath of the bombings. *War's End*
clears away a lot of the post-war recriminations about the
decision to drop the bombs."
—*The Patriot Ledger*

"Startling...masterful...dramatic...a riveting chronicle
written with a wit that is sometimes lacking in military
memoirs...[Sweeney] does a fine job of capturing the spirited
atmosphere of life on a wartime flight line...This memoir
should be required reading for all students of WWII."
—*Publishers Weekly* (*Starred Review*)

"An excellent book...
General Sweeney has done many uniformed people a favor."
—*Chattanooga Free Press*

"An inspiring story. I enjoyed *War's End* immensely."
—Dick Cheney

"Excellent...a masterpiece
of levelheaded yet impassioned prose."
—*Associated Press*

WAR'S END

E N D

An Eyewitness Account of America's Last Atomic Mission

MAJ. GEN. CHARLES W. SWEENEY, U.S.A.F. (Ret.)
with JAMES A. ANTONUCCI and MARION K. ANTONUCCI

AVON BOOKS NEW YORK

The photographs on pages 1 through 7 of the insert are courtesy of Maj. Gen. Charles W. Sweeney. The photograph of General Sweeney on page 8 of the insert is by James A. Antonucci.

AVON BOOKS, INC.
1350 Avenue of the Americas
New York, New York 10019

Cover photograph of the atomic explosion over Nagasaki courtesy of Maj. Gen. Charles W. Sweeney; inset photo of then Major Sweeney on Tinian, August 10, 1945, courtesy of Kinsale Enterprises, Inc., Malden, MA
Interior design by Kellan Peck
Published by arrangement with the authors
ISBN: 0-380-78874-8
www.avonbooks.com

Library of Congress Cataloging in Publication Data:
Sweeney, Charles W.
   War's end / Charles W. Sweeney and James A. Antonucci & Marion K. Antonucci.
      p.   cm.
   1. Sweeney, Charles W. 2. World War, 1939–1945—Aerial operations, American. 3. Atomic bomb—United States—Moral and ethical aspects. 4. United States. Army Air Forces—Biography. 5. World War, 1939–1945—Personal narratives, American. 6. Generals—United States—Biography. I. Antonucci, James A. II. Antonucci, Marion K. III. Title.
D790.S968   1997   96-48526
940.54'4973—dc21   CIP

First Avon Books Trade Paperback Printing: July 1999
First Avon Books Hardcover Printing: August 1997

AVON TRADEMARK REG. U.S. PAT. OFF. AND IN OTHER COUNTRIES, MARCA REGISTRADA, HECHO EN U.S.A.

Printed in the U.S.A.

OPM 10 9 8 7 6 5 4 3 2 1

★ ★

I dedicate this book to my children and grandchildren and to future generations of Americans who seek an understanding of their history.

ACKNOWLEDGMENTS

As the fiftieth anniversary of the end of World War II approached in 1995, hundreds of people of all ages sent me letters of well-wishing and newspaper articles about the war in the Pacific. Veterans often shared firsthand accounts of their experiences. Many of the veterans who wrote to me had been POWs in Japanese camps. I wish to thank all of the people who shared with me their interest in the facts about the war in the Pacific.

I also want to thank the late Kermit Beahan—whose notes about the mission I consulted—Fred Bock, and Jim Van Pelt. Jim passed away in 1995. When I needed to confirm a place or a date or an event, I could count on Fred and Jim to have what I needed. Some things never change, even after fifty years.

As I sat at breakfast on the last day of the 1995 reunion of the 509th Composite Group in Albuquerque, New Mexico, Don Mastick came over to my table and shared with me a remarkable incident he had witnessed shortly before my takeoff to Kokura when the Project Alberta technicians were assembling Fat Man. Later he graciously provided more detail, which I included in the book's opening chapter. I thank Don for sharing this experience with me.

My thanks also to our editor at Avon Books, Stephen S. Power, for recognizing the importance of this story, for vigorously championing its publication, and for shepherding it through the process to publication.

Finally, I offer a special tribute to General Paul W. Tibbets, one of our military's great leaders and the finest pilot I have ever met. I was honored that he chose me to participate in this extraordinary undertaking.

FOREWORD

When I was a kid in grammar school, I remember for the Armistice Day assembly they would drag in some poor old guys from the Spanish-American War to tell us about what they had experienced. Now I'm the old guy doing the telling.

The war is World War II. At twenty-five years of age, I was the only pilot who flew on both atomic missions—over Hiroshima and Nagasaki. I piloted the B-29 carrying the instruments to Hiroshima on the right wing of the *Enola Gay*. I watched as the *Enola Gay*'s bomb bay doors snapped opened and the 9,000-pound uranium bomb was released. As the bomb fell free, I thought, "It's too late now. There are no strings or cables attached. We can't get it back, whether it works or not. But if it works, it just might end the war." None of us, I remember, was entirely sure of what that bomb would do—to its target or to us.

Three days later, I commanded my first combat mission, to Nagasaki, this time carrying a live 10,300-pound plutonium bomb, a weapon that had never been tested free falling from an airplane before it was loaded into the bomb bay of the *Bock's Car* on the evening of August 8, 1945. The Japanese military surrendered six days later, and World War II came to an end.

It was as simple and as complicated as that.

We had a job to do, a war to end. I never questioned President Truman's decision to use every weapon at his disposal to end the bloody conflict—nor do I now. Nor did most people then, who lived through the escalating terror of that now-distant war in the Pacific. I remember press interviews after the war where reporters asked me, "What were the missions like?" "What problems did you run into during flight?" "How does it feel for the war to be over?" I was never asked whether I believed the bomb should have been dropped.

But that was over fifty years ago. For those fifty years I remained mostly silent about the war and President Truman's decision to use atomic weapons. In part this was because of my deep respect for and deference to General Paul Tibbets. I believed that as the leader of the 509th Composite Group, he should be spokesman for our crews and our missions. Nor did I want to take singular credit for events that were successful because of the efforts of thousands of people. Also, as I reflect upon the relative obscurity of the *Bock's Car*'s crew since the war ended, I believe that the deeply ingrained culture of secrecy that surrounded our missions every waking minute has remained instinctively with me—and with my crew. To this day, when our group gathers for its annual reunions, we never talk about the bomb.

Speaking out about our missions never struck me as an urgency. I did not doubt for a moment that the historical facts spoke for themselves. Who could question that the forces who had brought the war upon us were evil? Who could doubt that our actions vanquished foes who were guilty of unspeakable brutalities against humanity in the name of conquest, foes who refused to surrender even after unprecedented destruction was rained upon them from the skies in the unrelenting B-29 firebombing missions over Japanese cities?

Such persons emerged in the summer of 1994.

With the fiftieth anniversary of the war's end approaching, I found myself feeling outraged and betrayed when not only our national museum, the Smithsonian Institution, but some American historians as well attempted to change the history of the war in the Pacific. Suddenly I was hearing that Americans had been the aggressors and the Japanese had been the victims. The exhibit of the *Enola Gay* originally proposed by the Smithsonian—an exhibit that would be viewed by millions of Americans who would undoubtedly accept it as a factual representation of the war—was for me the final insult to the truth. To quote from the script of that planned exhibit: "For most Americans, this war . . . was a war of vengeance. For most Japanese, it was a war to defend their unique culture against Western imperialism."

I had occasion to read not only the original script of that planned exhibit but several of the rewrites that followed. They grossly minimized casualty estimates for an invasion of the Japanese mainland, one of the factors that had driven President Truman's decision to drop the bombs. They placed greater emphasis on alleged Allied racism against the Asians than, for example, on the hundreds of navy men who had been entombed in the USS *Arizona* at the bottom of Pearl Harbor. Some of those men were trapped for days before they died. Forty-nine photographs were to be exhibited showing the suffering Japanese victims of the war, and only three photographs of wounded Americans. This selection of exhibits was puzzling, given that the history of the war in the Pacific was also synonymous with Corregidor, Bataan, Iwo Jima, Okinawa, and Sai-

pan. It was a history of Japanese prisoner of war camps—
sites of unspeakable inhumanities—of kamikazes, and of the
infamous medical experiments conducted by Japanese doctors
on live prisoners of war. Were Americans, one might ask upon
learning all the facts, compelled to be brutalized until the Japanese were ready to say, We'll stop?

One day, those of us who fought the war—who were eye-
witnesses to it—will no longer be here to set the record straight.
What, then, will future generations be told about America's
role in the war in the Pacific? Who will be left to give an
accurate firsthand account?

The question is troubling: why would present-day historians
choose to minimize the sacrifices made by so many for all of
us and call into question the motives of the United States in
using atomic bombs to end the war? Is it to make the greater
point that nuclear weapons are a menace to the world? They
clearly are. But that truism does not excuse "reworking" the
war in the Pacific to accommodate and advance anyone's political philosophy. It does not justify bad scholarship's creating
pseudohistory.

I began to focus my outrage by speaking out against any
revision of events as they actually happened in the context of
the war. I decided to write this book. I've been asked, "Why
now?" "What's your purpose?"

My purpose in writing this book is not to chronicle an aging
veteran's memories about what a younger generation may see
as ancient history. Nor is it to recite the horrors of World War
II in the Pacific as a means of denigrating the Japanese people.
To the contrary, Japan has been a stable and valued ally of the
United States since the end of World War II. I believe it is in
our national interest to maintain that alliance and to strengthen
the economic and military ties that bind us together. But, while
doing so, it is equally important to recognize that Japan and the

world are better places today because Japanese fascism failed to conquer Asia, and that in victory, the United States was benevolent and not vengeful.

I certainly do not offer this book as a celebration of the use of nuclear weapons. It is my fervent hope that there will never be another atomic mission. The bombs we dropped in 1945 were primitive in comparison to nuclear weapons today. As the man who commanded the last atomic mission, I pray that I retain that singular distinction.

I am memorializing my story because I have learned that we who lived the events of history have an obligation to preserve and report upon the facts. The soul of a nation—its essence—is its history. It is that collective memory which defines what every generation thinks about itself and its country. It is a memory not to be tampered with, or recklessly revised, rewritten, or changed.

Fifty years ago we fought the empire of Japan, whose Imperial army and navy wrought suffering and death wherever they tread. Since that time—for more than half a century—the Japanese have ignored their culpability, brutality, and ultimate responsibility for the events that flowed from their conduct during World War II. An entire generation of Japanese are ignorant of their history in this regard. If we forget history, if we attempt to rewrite or distort history, we only contribute to the Japanese amnesia—to the detriment of both our nations and the world.

Unlike Germany, which acknowledged its responsibility for World War II and for the atrocities it committed during the war, Japan, with the aid of some American historians, persists in the fiction that it was the victim of circumstances. This mindset forecloses any genuine prospect that the deep wounds suffered by both nations and by Japan's Asian neighbors can be healed. Only the truth heals.

I thus offer this book, not only to future generations of

schoolchildren who will gather in assembly to learn about World War II, but also to the greater assembly. It is my eyewitness account. I hope it may add some meaning and context to the events that defined World War II.

Maj. Gen. Charles W. Sweeney, U.S.A.F. (Ret.)
June 1996

ONE

THE BOMB SAT in its cradle in the assembly hut, six inches off the concrete floor at its lowest point, sixty-six inches at its highest. Ensign Don Mastick walked into the hut and saw Arthur Machen straddling the rear end of the 10,300-pound plutonium weapon, working feverishly to file down a hole in the bomb's tail assembly, which was suspended in front of him from a block and tackle.

"Hey, cowboy, what the hell are you doing?" Mastick hollered to the bomb assembly technician.

Sweat poured down Machen's forehead, even though he was in the only air-conditioned building in the Pacific. He was racing against time, and filing through the .2-inch-thick aluminum plate was proving to be excruciatingly difficult. The *Bock's Car*, the B-29 that would carry this weapon to the target in its bomb bay, was scheduled to take off in a few hours.

The tension and exertion were taking their toll on the young scientists and technicians of Project Alberta who anxiously

1

watched Machen's progress. They were the representatives on Tinian Island from the Manhattan Project who were responsible for the assembly, arming, and loading of the weapon on board the *Bock's Car.* Any delay might cause the mission to be scrubbed, a prospect they did not want to entertain. Too many lives hung in the balance.

"Son of a bitch," whispered Machen as he wiped away the sweat, trying to keep his eyes clear. He didn't hear Mastick.

Earlier in the day, the delicate internal mechanism of the Fat Man had been carefully set into the bomb casing and the two spherical halves had been bolted together. Work had progressed slowly and methodically on this complicated nuclear weapon, which contained fifty-three hundred pounds of Composition B and Baratol, high-grade explosives, laid out in a precise configuration around an eleven-pound sphere of plutonium. This quantity of high explosives made Fat Man the most powerful bomb in the Pacific theater, even without the plutonium. A single spark could detonate the explosives, and in a flash, destroy the entire compound in which the assembly building sat.

The tail assembly—"the California parachute"—which would allow the bomb to drop on a predictable and stable trajectory, was about to be attached to the bomb's skin as the final step before transport of the bomb to the loading pit on the flight line. But as Machen had moved the tail section to jigger it into place, he was stunned to see that the upper hole on the tail didn't match its counterpart on the casing. They weren't aligned! Although the holes were off by only a fraction, maybe a hundredth of an inch, it was enough to keep the bolt from going through.

Maybe it was a mechanic's error. Or maybe the heat and humidity on Tinian had caused the metal to warp. But whatever the reason, after two billion dollars' worth of research by the best minds in the world, years of top secret military planning, and the combined efforts of hundreds of thousands of people, at the eleventh hour a technician was relying on a $1.98 rat-tail file and brute force to finish assembling the first plutonium bomb that would be dropped from an airplane.

This was to be the first of many surprises and near misses that would plague my mission to Nagasaki and test the dedication and skills of my flight crew and me.

I hadn't gotten much sleep since our return from Hiroshima on August 6. Colonel Paul Tibbets had told me on that evening that I would command the second atomic mission, on August 9, if a second drop was necessary. With barely enough time to recover from and reflect upon the Hiroshima mission, my crew would be flying another atomic strike in less than three days. It would be my first combat mission command.

I sat alone on a hilltop overlooking the massive runways on the northern tip of Tinian. The sky overhead was ink-black. Not a star was in sight. In a few hours we would be taking off from these runways. The men from Project Alberta were completing the final assembly of the Fat Man. This would be no concrete-filled "pumpkin" of the sort we had practice-dropped from our B-29s over the salt flats of Utah for the past several months. Our cargo would be live, with an expected explosive yield calculated to be equivalent to at least 46 million pounds of TNT.

This bomb would be the first weapons system ever used by the United States that had not been extensively field tested. Only one other plutonium bomb had ever been detonated, and that had been a static test in the middle of the desert in the Southwest with the bomb sitting secure on a tower, connected by wires to a command center several miles away near Alamogordo. In a few hours, we were going to drop a similar weapon from an airplane, where it would free-fall from 30,000 feet—with no wires attached. Although the scientists had ingeniously designed the physics package to fit within the confines of a bomb ten feet long and five feet across, none of them was sure exactly what the bomb would do. They expected it would be more powerful than the uranium bomb, the Little Boy, dropped over Hiroshima. But that was about it. How much more powerful? They weren't sure. Some thought it was possible our airplane would be blown out of the sky. Others speculated that a chain reaction that could destroy the world might be triggered. A few weren't even certain it would work.

I began going over in my mind every step of Colonel Tibbets's mission to Hiroshima. It had gone like clockwork. Perfect weather—not a cloud in the sky. Perfect execution—no fighter intercepts or antiaircraft fire at the target. Bomb away within seventeen seconds of the scheduled release—and a bull's-eye on the target. Then a flawless return to Tinian. It was up to me to live up to his expectations for this crucial second mission. He had chosen me to carry it out. I had to succeed.

"We must make the Japanese believe we can keep them coming every few days until they surrender," the colonel had told me. In truth, there was no third bomb behind us ready to go.

There had been no word of surrender from the Japanese after the bombing of Hiroshima, so I knew that our hope of quickly ending the war depended on this mission. After witnessing the blast at Hiroshima, I believed Japan would finally surrender. But her military seemed prepared to continue in a glorious and suicidal defense of the mainland. We were getting closer to the invasion of Japan, which was scheduled to begin on November 1, and the prospect of hundreds of thousands more American casualties in an invasion was not just some abstract concept to me—it was a sobering reality.

I focused on the steady flow of B-29s taking off from the runways below into the darkness for their firebombing missions over Japan. The burned-out hulks of the planes that never made it off the ground on earlier missions lay in the shadows of the runways. A lot of good men had died in them.

My mind drifted back to my last trip home in late 1944. By sheer coincidence, my friend Colonel Jim McDonald, with whom I had gone through flight school before the war, was home, too. Jim had just completed twenty-five B-17 missions over Europe with the Eighth Air Force. There were very few B-17 crews who survived the twenty-five-mission rotation. I knew that I would soon be going overseas, and since I had no combat experience, I was anxious to learn what advice my old pal might give me.

We met for dinner at the Parker House, on the corner of Tremont and School streets, on a snowy evening in downtown Boston. Jim was six years older than I. He had been just below the maximum age and I just over the minimum age when we entered flight school in the spring of 1941. Jim had advanced to become a lead pilot in Europe, which meant that he led the formations of bombers into the target. It was a job that required skill, courage, and maturity.

We were seated in the ornate, mahogany-paneled main dining room. Waiters in crisply starched aprons moved about on the thick carpets without a sound. Jim and I reminisced over drinks and sirloin steaks. At one point, I told him I would be going into combat with a bomb group. Secrecy precluded my mentioning anything other than conventional aerial warfare. I asked him what advice he could offer me. Anything special I should know? Any mistakes I should avoid?

He thought for a moment and then answered with a smile, "Promote your men as fast as you can."

We both laughed. Then he turned serious, leaned in toward

me, and in a precise, slow cadence said, "Never go over a target a second time. Never! If they didn't get you the first time, they'll get you the second time around with antiaircraft fire or fighters."

The activity on the runway below pulled me back. I caught sight of a B-29 lumbering down, laden with a full load of high-test aviation fuel and incendiary bombs. It appeared to be struggling to make it into the air. It was overloaded. It did get up for a moment, then hung in the air before plunging into the ocean. A burst of flames erupted in the darkness. The sounds of explosions punctuated the night.

Rescue boats stationed offshore sped instantaneously to the scene. Standby emergency vehicles moved in. There would be little they could do to stop the napalm spilling from the exploding ordnance from fueling the fire.

It was not the first or the last B-29 I would see crash on takeoff at Tinian. These ten Americans would be added to the statistics of the war—a war we had not started and did not want.

"No second runs," I murmured aloud, as if reciting instructions. But first things first. I'd have to get the plane into the air. In a few hours my crew and I would be rolling down one of these runways with a bomb and extra fuel that would put our airplane thousands of pounds over the manufacturer's specifications for maximum takeoff weight. With all that weight, we'd barely have enough runway to reach the proper air speed for liftoff.

Further complicating matters, our bomb, because of its complex detonation system, would be armed when it was loaded into our bomb bay, unlike the Little Boy, which had been unarmed on takeoff. The *Enola Gay* could have hit a brick wall and the bomb probably would not have detonated. For us, a crash on takeoff could vaporize my crew, Tinian, and me. But as I looked down on the runway, I had total confidence that I would get the airplane into the air and on to Kokura, Japan, our primary target.

I stood up to leave. At that moment I had no idea that my crew and I were about to confront a series of problems that would start at the moment of takeoff and continue until our forced emergency landing at an unplanned location ten hours later—any one of which could have doomed us and our mission and hundreds of thousands more in a prolonged war.

It was time to go.

TWO

THE SINGLE EVENT that changed my life happened on a sunny, cloudless Saturday afternoon in the summer of 1939 in Quincy, Massachusetts.

Like most of my generation, I didn't give much thought in 1939 to the troubles that were building "over there" in Europe and in Asia. The important pursuits of my life were in the U.S.A., which was secure and stable. For almost half of my twenty years, one man had been president. He was a reassuring presence who had brought us through the Great Depression. For this, he was idolized by my parents and their working-class friends and neighbors. His picture hung over our dining room buffet, next to the Sacred Heart of Jesus, where Mr. Roosevelt watched over our family dinners every Sunday afternoon. One day in the not-too-distant future, my mother would hang another picture on the opposite wall. She would cut it out of the *Boston Post,* and it would show five marines raising the American flag over Iwo Jima. But for the time being, "America First" was the refrain, which was fine with me. And even if worse came to worst on the Continent, I figured we could always shore up the English and French and let them fight their own war.

My friend Charlie McCauley had other ideas. He was twenty-one, and with the new peacetime draft, it was only a matter of time before he would receive personal greetings from President Roosevelt inviting him to a preinduction physical for the army. But Charlie didn't want to be a gravel scratcher. "I'm not going into the infantry," he insisted when we talked about the draft. "I'm going to be an air cadet."

Toward that goal, Charlie was planning to take his first ride in an airplane on that sunny afternoon in Quincy, and he wanted me to tag along. I sat on my front porch waiting for him to pick me up. Our two-story, wood-shingled house was not unlike most of the houses on our street. In our neighborhood, just ten miles south of Boston, almost everybody knew everybody else. Charlie lived two streets over. His brothers played with my brothers. During the summer, we all congregated on the street to play kick-the-can or to toss bubble gum cards from the curbstone after rubbing them with candle wax for added weight, investing in each toss all the gravity of a World Series game. I was watching just such a championship match across the street when Charlie pulled up in his father's car.

I hopped down the front steps and got into the passenger seat. Nice automobile. A shiny 1935 gray Plymouth four-door. Charlie had elbow-greased the shine as the price of borrowing the car. I noticed that he seemed a little nervous. "Hey," I thought, "maybe he's afraid of actually going up there."

"You know," Charlie said as we headed in the direction of Dennison Airport, "you really ought to think about being an air cadet, too. You've only got one year left." Because I was his best buddy, it seemed only right that Charlie would keep pushing me to enlist in the air corps with him.

But my priorities were elsewhere in 1939. The draft was not my immediate concern. It could be another year before I reached draft age, and a lot could happen in a year. Certainly the combined armies of England and France could stop Hitler. I'd read that France had the biggest and best-equipped army in the world. And the sun hadn't set on the British Empire yet, either. As for Japan, Asia was an even more distant place, six thousand miles away from the United States. How could Japan threaten us? Thus armed with the confidence of a twenty-year-old kid in safe and predictable surroundings, I encouraged my friend to fly. It would be an exciting way to spend his next few years.

I was working on my future, too. Since graduating from high school I had moved up in the wholesale leather business to become a salesman covering western Massachusetts and New York State. For an ambitious young man, it was a great job with limitless opportunities and good commissions. My boss, Jim Kelley, told me I was a born salesman. But I felt, really, I could be a born anything. All I had to do was keep focused on my goals, get along with people, and keep a sense of humor. To earn a bachelor's degree, I was taking evening business courses at Boston University and Burdett College. For now, I would learn my trade. Later, I would I have my own business. My life was on course.

"What do your parents think about you flying airplanes?" I asked Charlie as we approached the fence marking the outermost corner of the airport. Dennison was a private airport that adjoined the Squantum Naval Air Station. It was only a postage stamp with a half dozen or so open-cockpit airplanes.

"My dad said he doesn't know anything about flying,"

Charlie answered. "He said it looks dangerous to him. My mother is all upset."

When I'd told my father where Charlie and I were going, he'd just said "Be careful." Although he had never been in an airplane, I was sure he wouldn't be afraid of flying. He was confident. Even during the depth of the Depression he always found work. When everyone stopped building in 1929 he had to close his plumbing and heating business, but he managed to pick up odd jobs and do a little contracting until he was able to start up a business again. We weren't rich, but we weren't poor, either.

In 1926 we moved from a rented house near downtown Quincy into our own home. I was the second oldest of six children, five boys and one girl. Our home was dominated by Catholicism, patriotism, and belief in hard work and individual responsibility. Education was valued as a privilege. My mother and father encouraged us to be the best our abilities allowed. When I was a student at St. John's Elementary School, I won the Greater Boston Spelling Bee at Faneuil Hall three years in a row. I remember that my parents were so proud they showed my gold medals with the red, white, and blue ribbons to just about every Irish man and woman in Quincy. I still have and treasure those medals.

My father used our Sunday dinners, when he had a full audience and our undivided attention, to teach us life's lessons by quoting the Bible or telling us one of Aesop's fables. My favorite fable was the one where the wind and the sun were watching a man who was walking along wearing a heavy coat. The wind and the sun began arguing over which of them could make the man take the coat off. "I'll blow it off," the wind told the sun. But the harder the wind blew, the tighter the man held the coat to him. Then the sun tried. It smiled and shone. Soon the man began taking off his coat. "Now, learn your lesson accordingly," my father would say.

My father would also tell us about our great-grandfather, Jack Sweeney, who came to America from County Cork in 1850 with the wave of immigrants who were escaping the potato famine. "When young Jack Sweeney arrived in America," my father would say, "the owners of the giant Lawrence Textile Mill met him at the docks. They were looking for one hundred men to work in the mill. Grandfather worked six days a week, ten, twelve hours a day, for ten dollars." One winter afternoon Jack Sweeney decided to use his ten-minute break to run across the street for a quick beer. He rushed back to work and began to sweat in his union suit, the heavy woolen underwear he wore to ward off the cold and draftiness of the factory. A few weeks later he died of pneumonia, a young man. "He still owed money to the company store when he died," my father would say.

The city of Lawrence, Massachusetts, was named after the mill owners. The adjacent city of Lowell was named after the Lowell family, who also owned mills. I was born in Lowell on December 27, 1919, in the house of my maternal grandmother, Mary "Minnie" Murphy. In those days, young Irish brides didn't go to the hospitals to have their babies. They went home to their mothers' houses.

My first job, at the age of ten, was as a paper boy. We were all expected to work and contribute to the household. In no time I had a lock on all of the routes in our area and knew many of the families I delivered to. Around that time my father also started letting me go to work with him after school and on Saturdays as his "assistant." It was fun being with him. On the way to a job he would tell me about his father, Jack Sweeney. "Your grandfather was the best plumber in Massachusetts in his day," he would remind me. "He installed all of the plumbing and heating at Phillips Exeter Academy for Stone and Webster when the school was being built. Exeter," he explained, "is where the wealthy families send their sons to prepare for Harvard. He did such an outstanding job there, he was asked to do the same thing for Phillips Andover Academy." I was pretty impressed.

When I was fifteen I landed a plum job as a caddie at the Wollaston Golf Club. Wollaston was "the club" for the successful and politically connected Irish of the time. Excluded from the exclusive Brahman clubs, the Irish created their own clubs for men of accomplishment. The tribal character of Boston was very much alive then. For me, the tips were great, and I observed valuable lessons about the ways of business and life: being polite and courteous pays dividends; first impressions are lasting; trust is crucial to relationships.

I caddied for Massachusetts governor and former mayor of Boston James Michael Curley. He was a big tipper and a spellbinding raconteur who was always the center of every foursome. I also caddied for the future Francis Cardinal Spellman, a gracious and charming man. These men of prominence were heady company for a fifteen-year-old. The last time I saw Bishop Spellman at Wollaston was in 1935. Ten years later I would meet him again on Tinian Island in the Pacific.

Boston's leather district was only a thirteen-minute ride from Wollaston by steam commuter train from South Station, so quite a few leather company executives were members of the club. One vice president, Bill Kelley, offered me a job at his company after I finished high school. The problem was that his company, Salomon and Phillips, was headquartered in New York City. When I graduated from North Quincy High at seventeen, my mother wouldn't let me take the job. "New York is too fast a town for a young boy," she insisted, despite my pleas. So I didn't go. Luckily for me, though, about three

months later Bill's brother Jim set up a Boston branch and
offered me a job handling a few small accounts in Boston. I
was on my way.

Charlie pulled up to the road leading to the Squantum
Naval Air Station and turned at the entrance to Dennison Airport. A sign offered a five-minute airplane ride for two dollars.
We bought two tickets and headed toward the strip. A few
open-cockpit biplanes were parked along one side of the strip.
On the other side was a small wooden building where we found
the pilot. He was wearing overalls that looked like a flying suit,
a leather jacket (civilian), and a fitted leather helmet with goggles raised up on his head.

"Ready to go up?" he asked.

"Sure," Charlie answered.

We followed the pilot to an airplane that had yellow wings
and a blue body. There was a single seat for the pilot in the
rear and a seat wide enough for two people in the front.

The pilot asked us, almost as an afterthought, if we had
ever been in an airplane before. "Just relax. I'll take it nice
and easy," he said. "A few turns around the field, out toward
the ocean, and then back. Nothing to worry about," he assured us.

We climbed onto the wing and into the front seat. "Fasten
the belt," a voice called from the rear.

"How high are we going?" Charlie asked.

"About a thousand feet. We'll do eighty, ninety miles an
hour . . ."

"Wow."

The airplane taxied out to the center of the field and started
toward the other end, gaining speed. We lifted off the ground.

As we climbed up into the clear blue sky, a feeling of elation overwhelmed me. I felt the air rushing by. The sense of
breaking away from the bounds of the earth filled me with awe.

I looked left, then right. I had a wondrous perspective of the earth below. Familiar places were unfolding as a single whole. I could see it all. And we were still climbing into the space above. Effortlessly, the airplane banked gently to the left. My sense of place and being expanded. I was flying.

All too soon I felt the full weight of gravity pulling us back to the ground as the pilot brought the plane to a landing. I stepped onto the strip feeling weightless, feeling like I wanted to get back into the air. I looked up at the sky and knew my life would never be the same.

Charlie McCauley and I studied for four months to prepare for the air cadet entrance exams. English, history, physics, geometry, trigonometry. The physical and academic requirements were rigorous. All through school I had ranked in the top 10 percent of my college preparatory class. I had studied advanced mathematics and taken four years of Latin and French. The academic exams would take eighteen hours over two days. I felt I could handle them. As for the physical exam . . . I was six-feet-one, one hundred and eighty pounds, and I was in pretty good shape.

We arrived at the army base in South Boston in early October 1940 to take the exams, the first of many hurdles that were intended to weed out the majority of young men competing for wings. A lot had happened in a year. Hitler and Stalin had carved up Poland. Russia had invaded Finland. The Wehrmacht and Luftwaffe had swept through France, Belgium, the Netherlands, Norway, Denmark, Hungary, and Romania. England stood alone. The Battle of Britain raged as we read the daily accounts of the bravery of the Royal Air Force in beating back the Luftwaffe. Yet I still didn't think the United States would get involved, and neither did my friends or family. As I look back, I am amazed at how oblivious we all were.

A month later, I received a letter from the War Department informing me that I had been accepted into the Air Corps Flying Cadet Program and had scored in the top 10 percent. Some 50 percent of those taking the test hadn't passed, and of those who had, a few failed to meet the physical standards. Charlie McCauley had passed the exam but failed to meet the "sufficient weight" requirement. He was underweight. Since the army allowed one postponement of enrollment, I decided to wait until my pal and I could go together. I requested a postponement to April 1941. Ironically, Charlie never did meet the weight requirement and was eventually commissioned in the Army Signal Corps.

I wasn't twenty-one yet, so I needed my parents' signatures to join. My father signed, but my mother would not. I'm not sure whether she worried that we might go to war or whether she was terrified at the thought of my flying an airplane. She knew no one who flew. In fact, hardly anyone she knew had ever been in an airplane. I tried every approach to get her to agree. First I stressed the security of the military. Then I told her I'd have a prestigious position as a pilot—I'd be an officer and a gentleman. She didn't budge. Finally I told her that I had to fly. If I didn't, I would never be happy. Without another word, she signed the paper. Then, for the next few weeks, she cried every night at the kitchen table, questioning if she had done the right thing and pleading with me to reconsider.

On a cool April day in 1941, just before noon, my mother and father saw me off at Boston's Back Bay Station on Dartmouth Street. I was leaving for Tuscaloosa, Alabama. I had never been out of New England. I had bought a worsted wool double-breasted glen plaid suit at Hyman Brothers in Boston for the trip. My mother had picked out a sky-blue silk tie that, she said, matched the color of my eyes. I looked the height of style.

About thirty other cadets-to-be gathered on the platform, clustered in small groups with their families. Precisely at noon an army sergeant barked for us to listen up. The men formed around him in a loose semicircle. As he called our names, we stepped forward and were given a ticket. Surveying the mass of eager faces, he pointed to a man standing toward the rear of the group who seemed to be older than the rest of us.

"What's your name?" the sergeant demanded.

"Jim McDonald, sir." Jim was twenty-seven and soon to be my fast friend. Unbeknownst to us all, he would also soon complete almost as many bombing missions as he had years.

The sergeant grimaced. "Well, McDonald, you're in charge of this group. It's your job to make sure they all get back on the train at each stop."

"Yes, sir."

The sergeant grimaced again. "A piece of advice. Don't call me or any other noncom 'sir.' I'm no officer. I work for a living." With that he left the platform and disappeared into the recesses of the station. We boarded the train, headed for Alabama and Primary School.

The train stopped in Hartford, New York, Baltimore, and Washington. At each stop we picked up a few more cadets until our group numbered one hundred. Of this group, 50 percent would wash out of the program over the next several months. I felt excited, exhilarated, and fearful that I might fail. I thought nothing could be worse.

On Wednesday, a day and a half after we'd left Boston, we arrived at Van de Graaf Field in Tuscaloosa at nine P.M. A noncom went through the cars and rousted us onto the platform. Portable lights illuminated the area with a yellowish glare. As I stepped off the train, I was overcome by the acrid smell of sulfur coming from a local paper mill and the stifling humidity of the sultry Alabama night. Being dressed in a wool suit didn't help. But at least I would make a good first impression.

Three officers and several upperclassmen stood along the edge of the platform looking stern. A voice—I couldn't tell whose—ordered us to form a straight line and drop our bags to our left. A seemingly simple task for such intelligent fellows as us. However, a great deal of bumping and confusion ensued before we could stumble into something resembling a line— and a significant realization. We collectively recognized that we were in for something totally new. From that moment on, we would go everywhere in formation, we would do everything as a unit. Conformity would be expected, independence discouraged. This is the way of the military. It is a way that instills in every soldier the truth that all our lives are dependent on each other—that we are engaged in a serious business with serious consequences.

As instructed, I had brought only the clothes on my back and a change of underwear. Picking up the small overnight bag, I was marched with my unit to the barbers. In a matter of moments I looked remarkably like every other cadet. We were quickly marched to our barracks and tucked away for the night. So far I thought I was doing pretty good. As was my habit, I had no trouble drifting into a deep sleep.

At five A.M. we were startled out of our slumber. "Move, move, move!" reverberated throughout the barracks. There was a heaviness in the air even at that early hour that promised another hot, humid day. Standing in the first light of dawn, I got my bearings. There were four one-story wooden barracks, each accommodating fifty double-bunked cadets, our group and a group of one hundred upperclassmen. Each barracks had only five toilets, with the result that many of us did not get a chance to visit those facilities on that first morning before being herded outside. We learned to solve this problem through cooperation and order—which was the intent of the exercise.

Each barracks appeared to have been newly constructed and was spick-and-span. We were on a civilian field under contract to the army. Because the army had very few experienced pilots, and certainly not enough to train and evaluate cadets at Primary School, our instructors would also be contract civilian pilots. What we were unknowingly part of was a major buildup of the military orchestrated by General George Marshall. He, in contrast to most of his contemporaries, recognized the inevitable.

Unlike military bases and airfields, this civilian airfield had no supply depot. We would be required to purchase our uniforms—two sets of khakis, a hat, socks, underwear, and a pair of shoes—from a local purveyor recommended by the lieutenant in charge, who happened to be a local boy and a cousin of the store's owner. For the next three days, however, we would drill in our civilian clothes. For me this meant marching around in the hot Alabama sun in a worsted wool double-breasted suit.

As we stood in formation, the sergeant walked slowly down the line. He stopped by me. Leaning in close, in barely a whisper, he asked in a soothing voice, "Isn't that outfit a bit warm?"

"Yes, sergeant, it is."

"Take it off!" he bellowed.

I slipped off the jacket and held it. But the sergeant meant I was to get rid of it. The thought of dropping my brand-new jacket onto the dusty field caused me to hesitate. The wrong reaction. After a barrage of invective that froze me in place, the jacket slipped from my grasp.

The sergeant stepped back and surveyed the scene. There I stood, navy blue suspenders holding up my pants.

"Son, are you some kind of jackass or are you just dressed up like one?"

Before I could respond, he barked that I take the suspenders off. Now my beautiful new suit jacket and my stylish suspenders lay in a heap beside me. My transition to military life was getting off to a rocky start. I'd wanted to get noticed—and so I had.

The seemingly endless, monotonous marching began on the airfield ramp in the blazing sun. We were harassed without letup. As I marched, my pants kept falling down. Each time I grabbed them the drill instructor yelled for me to put my hands by my sides. Somehow I managed to keep my hands beside me and still hold up my pants.

I knew we were being tested, that it would be tough. It was part of the ongoing ritual of weeding out those who couldn't cut it. But I was going to be a pilot.

On Saturday afternoon we purchased our uniforms. When we arrived back at the field, we were issued our flying suits. We would begin flight training Monday morning.

Primary School was the place to find out if a cadet had the aptitude and temperament to be a pilot. Some cadets would wash out immediately. Others might not wash out until after a substantial amount of flight time. We were being evaluated at every stage. Some of the criteria were objective and easy to understand. Some of them were highly subjective on the part of the instructors. They were looking for pilots—for a quality that can't be quantified or even explained. Some guys had it and others didn't. Being a pilot is what you are, not what you do.

On Monday morning I reported to my flight instructor as ordered. He and I walked out to an open tandem-cockpit Stearman PT-17. The pilot sat up front, the student in the rear.

There were dual controls in the front and rear cockpits. A gosport allowed the pilot to talk to the student, but the student couldn't speak to the pilot. There was no radio in the airplane, no means of communicating with the ground. Strict adherence to air discipline was required. All airplanes in that area had to maintain defined traffic patterns of precise position and altitude, particularly on takeoff and landing.

My instructor went through the basics in a clipped and mechanical manner. He might have been a civilian, but in his attitude and bearing he was identical to the drill instructors. There were no reassuring words or pleasantries, just the unspoken imperative: Pay attention; your future here, not to mention your life, depends on it. This would be the first time since Charlie's and my flight at Dennison that I would be airborne.

It was a wild ride, and I loved it—even though I didn't know whether I was afoot or on horseback, as the expression goes. I had no idea where we were in the air. I just saw trees and fields and hills. The airplane dipped and rose and dived and banked. My reverie was suddenly broken by the instructor's voice coming through the gosport. "Sweeney," he commanded, "take us back to the field."

Take us back to the field? I didn't know where the hell we were and this guy wanted me to take him back to the field? Not to mention that I had no idea what to do with the controls in front of me.

Again: "Sweeney, don't you know where you are?"

Then without warning he flipped the airplane upside down. "Look down, you stupid bastard. The field's right below us."

This was part of the routine. In the beginning they harassed us. Later they would be more soothing, wanting to bring along any cadets they thought had promise. For the next ten weeks the cadets flew in the morning and attended ground school in the afternoon. It was totally up to the instructor how fast to move a cadet along. In my case, advancement came rapidly.

Surrounding the main airstrip, in the neighboring country-side, were four auxiliary airfields—well, not exactly airfields. They were open pastures the government had rented from local farmers. Over these fields I practiced takeoffs and landings, flew traffic patterns, and perfected other basic flying maneuvers—like the Immelman. Named after a German pilot, this maneuver required sudden acceleration, then a turn up over the top so that the plane was upside down, and then a roll out, bringing the airplane quickly right side up again. For the split S, I rolled the plane on its back and took it down through a maneuver that brought me heading in the opposite direction.

Two weeks into my training, the instructor flew to an auxiliary field, where we landed. As was their practice, the pilots never told cadets when their first solo flight would be. For me, that was the day. The instructor stepped out and told me to take the controls up front. I was exhilarated. The idea that I would be on my own didn't concern me. I concentrated on the task ahead. The instructor carefully explained what I was to do. Take off. Make a series of banking turns around the field in a particular pattern. Make an approach and watch for him.

Sitting at the controls, I aimed the airplane in the proper direction and eased the throttle forward. I reminded myself to focus on the patterns and my airspeed, to watch the throttle setting and my approach speed. I lifted off. I was flying! I went through the designated patterns and made my approach. The instructor waved me off and gave me the signal to do it again. Then he waved me off two more times. He was letting me fly.

On my landing, he greeted me with a big grin and a hand-shake. Later, as a sort of graduation present, he took me on my wildest ride to date. He introduced me to what real pilots are—ironically, not conformists, but thinking individuals who push themselves and their airplanes. It's a strange dichotomy in the military that the very qualities that make a great pilot chafe against the rigidity of the military structure. We flew six feet off the ground, through trees, under bridges. None of this was approved army procedure.

Our ranks were thinning out. Some guys never got over or learned how to control the nausea they experienced in the air. Others couldn't master the basics of flight. And others, in the opinion of the instructors, just didn't have it in them to be pilots. The training got more intense.

I made it through Primary School and was shipped off to Basic Training at Gunter Field in Montgomery, Alabama. We received the government-issue slate-blue uniforms flying cadets wore. We now looked, thought and acted like military men. I received my first "command"; I was appointed sergeant major for my squadron. My duties were to maintain discipline within the sixty-man group and act as the implementor of the orders and commands of the squadron officers.

The Basic Training intensified—relentless marching, physical conditioning, and military tactics. The upperclassmen tormented us constantly. They were worse than the drill instructors. This was understandable, because although they had gone through the same training and, you might assume, would have some empathy for us, they now considered themselves to be part of an elite group that wanted to maintain its elitism.

Our first day at Gunter was memorable. We were all in great physical condition and pretty sure of ourselves. Perhaps to disabuse us of this idea, the drill instructor took us out onto the parade grounds. Under the blazing summer sun, we marched and drilled in close formation for hours. Some men passed out and were taken to the infirmary. Yet our shared exhaustion and communal suffering were drawing us closer together. Everything we did was precise and undertaken as a unit, not because we thought about it but because we now were one. That night I ached like I'd never ached before. The pain in my joints and muscles was extreme. It was the worst night of my life. But I still had no reservations that this was precisely where I wanted to be. These trials and tribulations would make me stronger.

The flying was heaven. We got to fly the Vultee BT-13, a much heavier airplane with a closed two-seat tandem cockpit, a radio, and above all else, speed. Our study of aviation became more advanced and detailed. Night training was the most exciting. The first time up, we went with the instructor. After that, we were on our own. Sent up into the blackness, we bored holes in the sky in predesignated zones to get comfortable flying without reference to visible landmarks or a horizon.

Ten weeks came and went in a flash. More of our comrades washed out. A common problem for some was the occurrence of "ground loops." In a ground loop, the pilot lands, everything has gone right, but he has a lapse in attention and assumes that the flight is over, when, in fact, the props are still turning. He lets up ever so slightly on the controls, and the airplane spins about one hundred degrees. If he's lucky, that's all that happens. More often than not, he might catch a wing on the ground and damage the aircraft. Ground loops are gross errors of coordination.

My Advanced Flight Training took place at Barksdale Field in Shreveport, Louisiana. Barksdale was a multiengine school. About 25 percent of the cadets were assigned to multiengine schools (bombers) and the rest to single-engine schools (fighters). The extent of the overall military buildup was now obvious. Having survived ten weeks at Primary and ten weeks at Basic, I now had the luxury of being able to observe my surroundings. Everywhere I looked was a beehive of activity.

Barksdale had been created to meet the training demands

for new pilots, as had Gunter and Van de Graaf. Up to this time the army had had three training facilities scattered in the West. Of course, the army still wasn't sure what to do with airplanes, but even the most hardened soldier thought they might be useful.

Barksdale was a regular army air corps field, complete with permanent housing, a golf course, clubs, and commissaries. There was an active bomber wing assigned to the field. We were still part of the military—the formations, strict schedules, and military discipline—but the harassment, tormenting, and tribulations subsided. We had made it. All that remained was completion of Advanced Training and a commission in the Air Corps Reserve.

Although we were still cadets, the world looked on us as pilots—and all that that implied. With a reputation as "sports," cadets were offered deals by local car salesmen on high-performance convertibles—twenty-five dollars down and seventy-five dollars a month. The parking lot at the field was a sea of brand-new convertibles.

We trained in B-10s, B-12s, and B-18s—all obsolete. But mostly we flew the Lockheed Hudson, a state-of-the-art patrol plane with an unusual design, manufactured in Long Beach, California. All the systems in the Lockheed Hudson had been designed to British specifications. The planes were delivered to us, we logged three hundred hours of flight time in each one, and then they were flown to the Northeast for shipment to Canada and then to England. The reason we flew the planes before shipment was simple. Congress had not authorized the sale of weapons to Britain. Under Roosevelt's Lend-Lease Program, only used war matériel could be legally delivered. Once we put three hundred hours on the Hudsons, it was legal to give the "used" airplanes to the British via Canada. It was a "happy coincidence" that the instrumentation and systems were of British design.

Halfway through training I received my assignment for after graduation. I would be a ferry pilot. I would take delivery of Hudsons and A-20s, the "Boston Bombers," at the Lockheed and Douglas factories on the West Coast and fly them to shipping points in the Northeast. It was a cream puff assignment. I would be a commissioned officer in the army air corps, share an apartment in Laguna Beach, and fly around the country, getting paid for what I loved to do. I couldn't have asked for more. I must admit a certain swagger crept into my gait.

My class was scheduled to graduate in five days. For the first time, the officers' golf course was open to us. After Sunday mass and breakfast, a group of us played a round. It was early afternoon when we walked into the lounge. We could immediately see that something was wrong. The conversation at the bar was animated as a tight cluster of officers crowded around a radio. I couldn't make out what the announcer was saying. An officer noticed my group standing there and said, "The Japs bombed Pearl Harbor."

I was stunned. I instantly visualized Hawaii, sitting in the middle of the Pacific. The Japs might attack the Philippines. That would make sense. But not Pearl Harbor.

Reality quickly set in. We were at war. No one at the field knew exactly what to do. Each of us was issued a weapon and assigned guard duty. Sabotage became the main concern. Anything was possible, even an attack on Shreveport. Security at the field was increased. A panic initially gripped the country. Rumors spread and multiplied. Phone lines were jammed. It took me a day to reach my mother, in Boston. She was terrified. Although an invasion on the West Coast seemed more likely, one rumor had a German bomber force heading for the East Coast to wipe out major cities. It seemed far-fetched that any airplane would have that range. But who knew? Maybe the Germans had been working on a secret airplane.

Reports of actual damage at Pearl were sketchy. It would be several weeks before the government acknowledged the actual calamity that had taken place. Most of our Pacific fleet and thousands of sailors lay at the bottom of the harbor. Some navy men had been entombed in their ships where they could not be reached. Their clanging, a sign they were still alive, lasted for seven or eight days before it was silenced. Only three aircraft carriers were left between Japan and the West Coast. And with each passing day the news grew worse as the Japanese moved against our forces in the Philippines.

On December 12, 1941, my class graduated as scheduled. My earlier orders were canceled. One other classmate and I were assigned to the Jefferson Proving Grounds in Madison, Indiana. The rest of my class was assigned to units preparing for overseas duty. On the morning of December 14, with a single gold bar on my right collar and a shiny set of wings on my chest, I boarded a train to start the war in the cornfields of Indiana.

THREE

JEFFERSON PROVING GROUNDS was a brand-new state-of-the-art facility situated near the banks of the Ohio River. It was designed for the testing of conventional iron bombs, rockets, fire bombs, and howitzer shells—heavy ordnance that was fired from big guns or dropped from aircraft. A one-hundred-square-mile reservation, the base employed about 950 civilians from the neighboring towns and transferees from Aberdeen Testing Grounds in Maryland. Fifty ordnance officers and enlisted men ran the firing and drop ranges. The ordnance officers were all reserve officers who had been commissioned during the 1920s and 1930s. The captain in charge of the airborne testing was recall reserve. He was about forty-five years old and had served in the army air corps during World War I. He was a fine fellow, but, to put it politely, he was out of touch with the advances in aircraft, not unlike most of the army in 1942. He would be replaced by Major John Waugh, who was a career pilot officer.

Jefferson was under the overall command of Colonel Cabell, a West Pointer from a distinguished military family. He
had supervised the construction of every detail of the proving
grounds. As part of the general buildup of the military, the
army had purchased the land in this area long before Pearl
Harbor, and Colonel Cabell had been directed to build a modern facility to supplement the famous Aberdeen Testing
Grounds. The newest and best equipment and the latest safety
features were incorporated into every detail of the reservation.

Because the army had bought not only the land but everything that stood on it, there were several beautiful houses scattered about the base. Colonel Cabell selected thirty of the more
outstanding homes and moved them to a part of the reservation
that would become the residence area for its officers. He laid
out the houses in a horseshoe design and created a perfectly
manicured neighborhood that could have rivaled any exclusive
neighborhood in the country.

This was a comfortable place to be. Five other officers and
I shared one of these homes. Our accommodations were vastly
different from the conditions most of our friends and classmates
were experiencing. But as a second lieutenant, I had no choice
of assignment. In fact, I was glad to have an assignment that
meant I could do my part for the war effort. Someone had
decided this was where I belonged.

Bob Van Dusen, of Rochester, New York, my classmate
from Advanced Training, and I were the only test pilots at
Jefferson. This meant we were about to get a lot of flight time
in advanced aircraft—B-24s, B-25s, A-20 bombers, and P-47
fighters, and Major Waugh left it mostly up to us to run the
tests. His only command was, "So you boys know what you're
doing?" We assured him we did and went on our way.

The procedure for testing was simple. Random samples of
munitions were taken from the production lines at the factories

by government inspectors and were shipped to us. Civilian technicians assigned to the proving grounds or representatives from the manufacturers briefed us about the specifications and characteristics of what we'd be testing. The samples were then loaded into the appropriate aircraft or racked under the wings, depending on the nature of the ordnance. The civilian technicians would proceed to the observation area adjoining the drop range. Bob or I took up the load and dropped or fired it as briefed.

The flight testing ensured proof of function of ordnance already extensively tested prior to full-scale production. Our job was to demonstrate that, straight off a mass-production line, the ordnance would perform as intended, detonate when expected, and produce a blast yield within specification. Of special concern was premature detonation in or under the aircraft, which might signal a design or manufacturing defect. Fortunately, that never happened at the proving grounds while I was there.

Given our rigorous and thorough testing of every type of bomb that might be used by an American pilot, it would have been incomprehensible to me in 1942 that in three and a half years, on an island in the Pacific, I would take off in an airplane carrying the largest bomb ever dropped in a free fall by the United States military that had never once been tested from an airplane prior to its planned detonation.

When we weren't testing ordnance, I would take every opportunity to get into an airplane and just fly. For a pilot there are two states of being—when he's flying and when he's not. In the air, all things are possible. There's a sense of invincibility. You seem at times to be free of the laws of gravity. You live to challenge yourself and take your machine to the limit. This may appear reckless to the uninitiated. And it is reckless to be careless, or to make mistakes because of a lapse in judgment. But it is not reckless to push the envelope in a calculated way. Like an artist, a pilot not only uses the necessary physical and mental skills for his craft, he is also driven by intuition.

I guess it was intuition that drew me under the Madison Milton Bridge. The air corps' main matériel depot was located in Dayton, fifty miles north of the Ohio River. I flew there regularly. On the hundred-mile stretch of the Ohio between Cincinnati and Louisville, I would see a single bridge crossing the river at Madison, Indiana. It stood out like a beacon. One afternoon, as I approached the bridge from five thousand feet on my way to Dayton, I took my A-17 into a dive. My airspeed picked up nicely to 170 miles an hour. Approaching the bridge, I gauged there was maybe a fifty-foot clearance above the water, give or take a few feet. I flew under the bridge with room to spare, and immediately took the airplane into a sharp climb to about three thousand feet. That bridge had been just calling out to me. Joy is the only word to describe my response.

But one man's joy can be another man's terror. The civilians who were on the bridge at the time didn't experience the same life-affirming thrill I did, and they made that clear to the base commander.

Colonel Cabell cut straight to the point. "If you kill yourself that's a loss for the army, which invested a good amount of money and time in training you. But we'll get over that loss. If you kill Mom and Pop and the kiddos driving over a heavily traveled bridge in Ohio, your death will pale in comparison. Do I make myself clear, Lieutenant?"

It was, under the circumstances, a mild reprimand. Nothing went into my service record, and I was still flying. And for a time I did stop. But the temptation would occasionally overcome me and—*whoosh*—I'd be under that damn bridge again. After a while, either the townsfolk got used to it or the colonel accepted this idiosyncratic behavior of one of his pilots.

I believed that our work with all of the bombers and fighters at our disposal was making a significant contribution that would save the lives of airmen. That was until Bob Van Dusen came in one afternoon to tell me he had heard that one of our classmates had been killed in a B-17 over the Pacific. It wasn't certain whether Frank Sullivan had died in combat or in an accident. There were no details. Frank had been from the Bronx, a great fellow. We'd bunked next to each other at Barksdale. He'd been a natural flyer—outgoing, fun-loving. Although I had been aware of the mounting casualties in the Philippines as MacArthur tried vainly to blunt the Japanese assault, I could now put a face and a name on the finality of it. My pal Frank Sullivan was dead.

Living and working in Indiana didn't seem enough anymore. It didn't feel right. I had been at the proving grounds for three months. And even though second lieutenants are the lowest form of life in the military food chain, I decided to petition my immediate superior, Major Waugh, for a combat assignment. He listened patiently to my request for reassignment to a combat wing and to the reasons why I thought it was a wise use of my skills. He promised me he would look into it. A week later he called me back in and told me I had been promoted to first lieutenant. Everyone at the proving grounds thought I was doing a superior job. They couldn't afford to lose me. As for a transfer, now was not a good time. With that, he dismissed me.

I'm not sure to this day if my promotion was related to my request for reassignment, but eight months later I made the same request and was promoted to captain.

I concentrated on my duties. My experience with aircraft and the subtle techniques required to milk the most out of each of them grew daily. The flying business is always dangerous. But if I made a mistake in flight, chances were I could learn from it. For my friends and classmates overseas, a mistake could be fatal. Casualties among our air crews in Europe were approaching staggering proportions, among them more and more of friends and airmen I knew and cared for.

Fate stepped in. During my eighteen months at Jefferson, I had become friendly with the major. He was being reassigned to Eglin Field in Florida to become director of operations for the Aircraft Weapons System Testing Grounds. Eglin was a busy, bustling central command. Pilots and crews getting ready to go to Europe, and many of those returning, were cleared through it. I figured that if I could get to Eglin as a test pilot, I would have more opportunities to turn that role into a combat assignment.

Major Waugh said he understood completely and would let me know if an opening presented itself. Within two months he called me. "Chuck," he said, "they need a base operations officer. You want it?" It took me one second to say yes.

In June 1943, as the war raged on in Europe and the Pacific, I drove down to Florida in my 1929 Studebaker, which I'd bought from Major Waugh for fifty dollars, and discovered a place that dwarfed Jefferson in every way. Eglin Field sprawled from horizon to horizon. Its scale was immense. It sat on what had once been a vast swampland, which the Army Corps of Engineers had filled in. I learned later that a powerful congressman from that district had been instrumental in convincing the military that this was valuable real estate, even though most of it then sat under several feet of water.

I was in command of the main field and the nine auxiliary fields that ringed it. All aircraft not assigned to a specific section were under my direct control. I had at my disposal a huge staff to handle the administrative duties of managing the operation.

At the age of twenty-three, I had been given a great deal of authority.

I struck up a friendship with Major Bernie Swartz. Bernie had been around for a while and was in command of the maintenance subdepot. This may not sound impressive, but believe me, he held the keys to the kingdom. Under his direct control were what the military classifies as "third-echelon aircraft." These are aircraft that need substantial maintenance beyond the skills and tools of the flight line crew chief, or repairs requiring a machine shop. You name it, Bernie had it: B-17s, B-24s, B-25s, P-51s. If it was in the army air corps inventory, it eventually found its way to Bernie's shop.

I negotiated a little bargain with Bernie. Someone would have to test the aircraft after the repairs were completed—a test pilot assigned to him for that purpose. I heard he had a girl-friend down in New Orleans he liked to visit monthly. I'd arrange for him to be on one of my airplanes going that way whenever the spirit moved him, and he'd give me carte blanche to test any aircraft that came off the maintenance line before it was returned to service.

It was always the same greeting: "Bernie, what do ya have today?" He'd hand me his inventory list and I'd look for an aircraft I hadn't flown before. I never bothered with any lengthy instructions. The prescribed procedure before any pilot could take the controls of an airplane would be for him to be checked out by someone qualified to fly that particular airplane. I dispensed with the formal checkout. All I needed was someone to tell me where the throttle was and I'd figure out the rest.

Our arrangement fell way outside the usual organizational chart, but it worked great for Bernie and me. He spent time with the love of his life, and I spent time doing what I loved— flying everything I could get my hands on. It was unheard of that a pilot could accumulate substantial flight time in all kinds of aircraft—two- and four-engine bombers and fighters—and be rated to fly them, but by the summer of 1944, I was rated to fly every airplane in the army air corps inventory.

I also made myself available to the fighter section, which was short of pilots. As problems, either real or expected, with a particular airplane were identified, it was necessary to stress the aircraft, that is, take it up and fly it for a prescribed number of hours to push the airplane and its systems to their specifications. I volunteered, and so I got to accumulate even more time in these airplanes. The experience was priceless, and the word got around: If you need someone to fly something, call Chuck Sweeney. It doesn't matter what it is as long as it has wings.

One of my duties was to assemble and deploy crash investigation teams when an airplane went down in our sector. What most civilians don't realize is that even during peacetime the military is a dangerous place. Thousands of men are in close proximity to weapons and explosives. With airplanes, the daily risks are greater. War only exacerbates the state of that risk. I witnessed a test P-38 go into a vertical dive, lose its tail, and plunge straight into the earth, leaving nothing but a crater filled with an indistinguishable mix of human remains and metal debris. I saw explosions in midair kill an entire crew in a flash. I witnessed crashes on takeoff and landing. Sometimes we learned why, sometimes the reason remained a mystery. But the first time I went to a crash scene left the most lasting impression.

It was July 1943. A call came into my office. A twin-engine Lockheed had gone in shortly after takeoff from one of our auxiliary fields. Fire trucks and ambulances were en route. No details of casualties were available.

I ordered my aide to alert the emergency team—Judge Advocate General (JAG) officer, chaplain, photographer, maintenance chief, and technical officer. A small airplane was parked right outside, and I flew it directly to the crash site.

Fire and ambulance personnel were there when I arrived, but there was little for them to do. I was immediately struck by the smell of burning flesh. The airplane had come down in a grove. The left wing had been shorn off and lay next to a tree. It appeared that the airplane had then skidded sideways for about sixty or seventy yards through a clearing. The fuselage had come to rest in a heap of rubble in a stand of cypress.

I walked through the clearing, noting bits and pieces of the aircraft strewn around. Here and there I saw a flight bag, a cap, unrecognizable dismembered bodies of men thrown from the airplane. Smoke was rising from the wreckage. I reached the fuselage, which had been blackened by the fire. Its left side had been sheared back like the lid of a sardine can. I looked directly into the cockpit. The pilot, copilot, and flight engineer were still strapped in. The pilot's hands were contracted in a tight grip on the wheel. All the bodies were charred and smoldering, the smoke and stench of their burning flesh drifting toward me. But the true horror was that they had not been burned beyond recognition. I could still make out their features. The pilot's head was tilted back oddly, at a forty-five-degree angle. His face was taut, his teeth bared, his eyes still open. I couldn't move.

A voice broke in behind me. "Captain, the manifest shows six passengers. The controller at the tower said after takeoff they went into a violent left turn and then a stall."

I had to fight my nausea and try to reconstruct the crash. I peered again into the cockpit and scanned the interior. A violent left turn before the crash. It was too obvious to be right. But there it was. The trim tab setting on the center post was set all the way to the left. The trim tab assists the pilot in steering the aircraft. On takeoff, the setting must be in the neutral position. With the trim tab set to the left, once the plane is airborne it will veer sharply left regardless of what the pilot does. It will fail to gain altitude and airspeed. It will stall and crash. The ground chief is supposed to check the trim tab before turning the airplane over. But the final responsibility is always with the pilot.

The investigative board determined that the trim tab was the cause of the crash. An experienced combat pilot who had survived countless missions over Europe made the fundamental mistake of not using his checklist. This mistake killed him and his crew.

In the summer of 1943 a two-star general arrived from Washington. He was forming a B-25 wing to go to India, and he needed pilots. The British and Chinese were anxious for the United States to fulfill its commitment to intensify a campaign from India to harass the Japanese in Burma and Thailand. It was no secret that within the overall scheme of things this mission had a low military priority. The real action was in Europe.

I suspected that the war couldn't last that much longer and that it was now or never. I met with the general, explained my desire to volunteer, and was accepted. Orders were cut for me to transit to India by troop ship via the Mediterranean, through the Suez Canal, to my new base. The trip would take two months. I wasn't used to this type of slow transport, and the thought of being crammed onto a troop carrier did not suit me at all. But I would finally get into the war. I was to report to Newport News, Virginia, for debarkation at the end of the year.

I would have a few months to wrap up my duties at Eglin and prepare to depart, but fate would step in again. Out of the blue, my military career was to veer in a totally unexpected direction.

FOUR

AN OLD BROMIDE observes that chance favors the prepared. On what started out as an otherwise uneventful day in September 1943, chance swooped down and favored me.

It was highly unusual for an aide to a commanding general, such as General Grandison Gardner, to come to my office. If the general wanted to speak to a captain, the captain was summoned. Yet there was the general's aide standing in front of my desk. The well-scrubbed major wasted no time. "Captain, the old man wants extra military police out at hangar seventeen this afternoon," he stated precisely. "A B-29's coming in from Seattle. The area will be cordoned off and no unauthorized personnel are to be within three hundred feet of that airplane."

I assured the major that I would take care of everything. What I didn't tell him was that I had no idea what a B-29 was, which certainly piqued my interest. If it had wings and belonged to the air force, I knew about it. I told my staff sergeant to pull the technical orders on it. At all airfields, operational manuals called technical orders are on file for every aircraft in the military inventory. They provide detailed information on the operation and maintenance of each aircraft. The sergeant returned a few minutes later and told me there were no technical orders for a B-29. No one had ever heard of such an airplane.

Shortly before two P.M. I went up in the control tower and scanned the sky in the direction of the approach. Off in the distance I saw a small silver dot. As it drew closer, it grew into the largest airplane I had ever seen, and it had four huge engines. On its final approach, I quickly made some rough mental calculations: wingspan, 150 feet; length, 100 feet. This thing was massive.

The gleaming silver fuselage glided in like a feather. A single puff of dust kicked up as the wheels touched down. Rolling down the runway, it dwarfed any other olive drab airplane of the time. It was twice as large as the B-17, the Flying Fortress, the largest heavy bomber then in service. It could have come from another planet, its size and appearance were so radically different from the combat aircraft known to me. It was the most beautiful thing I had ever seen in flight. Its majesty on landing took my breath away.

I ran down the tower, hopped into a jeep, and drove over to where this magnificent airplane would come to rest. A perimeter guard had already formed as instructed. The MPs waved me through, and for a moment I stood alone as the B-29 taxied to a stop within a few feet of me. Fifty years later, I can still feel the awe I experienced as I stood in front of that polished, shiny silver behemoth. Its nose canopy gleamed with Plexiglas. I could easily view where the pilot, the copilot, and the bombardier would sit in flight—in this glass bubble with 180-degree unobstructed visibility. I would later learn that this area was designated the "greenhouse" by the engineers. It was the first time the pilot, the copilot, and the bombardier were all in the same compartment. As the airplane turned and came to a stop, I could make out two large bomb bays under the belly, one forward of the wings and the other aft. Another first. This airplane was special in every way.

I stood on the tarmac looking up. The plane was like a beacon sending a single message, and sending it specifically to me: Fly me. Whether it was youthful exuberance or just ego, I knew for sure it was just my size, and come hell or high water, I was going to fly it.

Staff cars pulled up, and General Gardner and Major Waugh joined me. From beneath the forward compartment, out stepped a handsome, jaunty lieutenant colonel dressed in a perfectly fitted flying suit. My first reaction was that he must be special if he had been selected to command this imposing airplane. The rear bomb bay doors opened and an elevator let down four Cushman scooters and members of the crew. Unbelievable. They carried their own transportation.

Pleasantries were exchanged with the general while the colonel introduced himself to the group as Paul Tibbets. His manner was reserved and soft-spoken, yet he projected an air of professionalism and self-assurance. I stuck out my hand. "Colonel Tibbets," I said, "I'm Chuck Sweeney, Base Operations Officer. Anything you need, just let me know. We have staff cars waiting here for your use."

Colonel Tibbets replied politely, "We'll use our scooters, Captain. Thank you. We'll need the usual refueling arrangements. And I want security maintained as long as this aircraft is here."

As I observed the rest of the crew, it became clear that they held this man in high regard. There was an unmistakable crispness in their manner that conveyed their pride in being part of his crew. He was a star, no doubt. I resolved to get on his team.

As the group dispersed and Colonel Tibbets departed, I hung back. The copilot was finishing up a conversation with the flight engineer, who disappeared back into the airplane. The copilot, Captain Bob Lewis, walked in my direction. Lewis was a bear of a man. At six feet tall, he had broad shoulders, blond hair, and a stocky build. He was physically imposing, one of those people who fully occupies the space he's in. In sharp contrast to Tibbets, Lewis had an air of arrogance that fit perfectly with his physical appearance. I decided to play to his ego to perhaps learn a bit more about the airplane and the colonel.

"Captain, Chuck Sweeney. Any chance I can get a closer look?" I asked, gesturing toward the airplane.

"Not if my mother's life depended on it," Lewis replied, giving me a look of disdain and annoyance. He was a man who had important things to do.

I had no intention of pressing the point, although, as the base operations officer responsible for the security detail, I could have. What I wanted from this arrogant SOB was information, not a fight. I continued calmly. "Some kind of airplane. You guys must be the very best we've got to fly this monster." That injection of flattery hit the mark. We were now talking about him.

"I was handpicked," he responded. "There's a whole wing of B-29s forming at Smoky Hill Air Base, Kansas. Me and the old bull are in charge of the entire testing program with Boeing," he concluded, nodding his head in the direction in which Tibbets had gone.

An entire wing of B-29s! Up until two hours before then I hadn't even known this grand airplane existed, and this guy was telling me an entire wing was forming in Kansas. How do you form an entire wing without anyone knowing? My interest in Tibbets was growing stronger by the minute. "That's quite a job, I imagine. So what do you have to do to get into this outfit?"

"Don't even give it a second thought, Captain," he answered dismissingly. "To start with, you need a degree in aeronautical engineering and at least four hundred hours in four-engine airplanes." He paused for effect and to give me a patronizing, sympathetic look.

I thought to myself, "This guy must be one hell of a pilot, because he wouldn't win any popularity contests."

But my reconnoitering had yielded some good intelligence.

In wartime, everything is possible. Perhaps there was a way around the requirements mandated for pilots in this project. I didn't know what Tibbets was doing, or what his aircraft had been designed to do, but I knew chance might favor me if I acted. If I could hitch my wagon to Paul Tibbets's star, there was no telling how high or far I could go.

That night Tibbets came into the officers' club unaccompanied. I had already resolved to act, and then was as good a time as any. In fact, if I hesitated, I could squander the only opportunity I might have for a one-on-one discussion of my plans with the colonel in a relaxed social setting. I walked over to him and asked, "Colonel, would you care to join me for dinner?"

To my happy relief, he answered, "Yes."

We took a table at the far end of the club. My first impression was confirmed. He was a man who knew exactly where he wanted to go. His speech and demeanor were low-key and measured. He talked about his combat experiences over Europe, but not in the usual pilot's bravado about close calls or spectacular successes. Rather, he talked about the nuts and bolts of flying— the art of it, his respect for airplanes, and his knowledge of the machines he flew. He knew flying. Not just the how, but the essence of it. His love of flying struck a sympathetic chord in me. He asked about my background, and I gave him the Reader's Digest version of what I'd done for the past few years, stressing the experience I had had with different types of aircraft.

He turned the conversation to his assignment at Eglin. The B-29 he'd flown in on was one of two prototypes being tested by Boeing. The other B-29 would be delivered shortly. I had come pretty close in my estimates of its size. The actual wingspan was 141 feet, 3 inches; length, 99 feet; range, 3,800 miles with a full bomb load. It was the first airplane with a pressurized cabin that could really operate at 30,000 feet carrying a full bomb load of ten tons—forty iron bombs weighing an average of 500 pounds each. By comparison, the B-17 could carry only six 500-pounders. Over Europe, the B-17 Flying Fortress was theoretically capable of operating at 30,000 feet, but practically, it performed at peak at about 23,000 feet, fully loaded. And at these altitudes in unpressurized cabins, the crews were forced to wear bulky flight suits and oxygen masks while working in temperatures of 40 to 50 degrees below zero. Add to these conditions the ferocious pursuit of the Luftwaffe and the withering antiaircraft fire over France and Germany, and casualties among airmen in the air over Europe were climbing into the tens of thousands.

Tibbets explained that he was at Eglin to test a central fire control gunnery system for the B-29 using two prototypes—the XB-29 and the YB-29, each having a competing system. In the XB-29 the central gunnery system had been manufactured by Sperry; the YB-29 used a General Electric system. The air corps needed data on the performance of each in order to determine which one to purchase. As with everything else on the airplane, central fire control was revolutionary. In earlier planes, each gunner manually controlled and aimed just one set of guns.

With the B-29, a single gunner could control several turrets with one sight and be able to direct all the fire on a single target. The guns would slave to the sight.

Although Tibbets's testing had been given a top priority, pilots were still a precious commodity as the war intensified. To carry out his assignment he needed pilots to fly target tow airplanes, the XB-29 and the YB-29 that was coming in soon. Here was a chance for me. I made no effort to hide my enthusiasm to join his unit.

"I would love to get into your outfit, Colonel," I offered directly. "I understand there may be special requirements, but I know I can fly."

In a manner that was to become familiar to me, he sat back, thought for a moment, and said matter-of-factly, "That's a possibility."

I then realized that I had left out one minor point. "Colonel, I should have mentioned that I have orders to report to India with the Tenth Air Force."

"That's no problem," he said without hesitation.

No problem? I didn't believe that in this military my orders could be canceled by any colonel on God's green earth, even a colonel who obviously was part of something big. In James Michael Curley's Boston . . . no problem. In the United States Army . . . highly doubtful. But from the way Tibbets answered, I got the feeling he had the juice to do it. I didn't need to get into the details, and the colonel wasn't giving me any.

As we left the dining hall that night, I could not have imagined that in a few weeks I would become responsible for the entire B-29 central control gunnery systems testing program while Colonel Tibbets attended to other matters.

Tibbets called me a few days later. He needed an airplane to go up to his administrative offices in Marietta, Georgia, and

then on to the Boeing plant in Wichita, Kansas. I told him I'd
make the arrangements and meet him on the ramp in an hour.

"I'll go as your copilot," I offered. Here was an opportunity
to spend some time with him in the environment I loved most,
maybe show him what I could do.

"Fine," he replied.

I took a look at the aircraft roster. We had a Martin B-26
available immediately. It would not have been my first choice,
but that's what we had. The B-26 was derisively known as the
"flying prostitute" because it had no visible means of support.
It had a very short wingspan, which gave it a lot of speed but
a small lift ratio. Even for experienced pilots the Martin was a
tricky airplane to fly. I had flown it only once before.

While the Martin was being fueled I went to the weather
office. The noncom on duty started in, "Captain, we got zero-
zero in fog. I'd suggest you wait until it burns off."

I asked to see the report. The fog topped out at about four
to six hundred feet up. Above, clear skies. There would be no
real danger taking off. Landing, however, would be a different matter.

"Captain, I'd strongly urge you to give it a couple of hours.
Should burn off by ten or eleven," the sergeant offered again
apprehensively.

I knew one thing for sure, Tibbets wanted to go, and he'd
asked me to arrange it. Therefore, we were going. Period. End
of discussion. This was an opportunity I wasn't going to blow
because of some early-morning fog.

Uncharacteristically, I snapped at the startled noncom.
"Sergeant, your job is to hand me the weather report. My job
is to make the decisions about flying. So I'll make the decision
and you can go back to your work."

It was an overreaction I regretted the moment the words
left my mouth.

Colonel Tibbets was waiting for me at the airplane in the company of three Boeing civilian technicians who were hitching a ride back to Wichita. It was a gloomy, thick, humid Florida morning. We made our walk-around, accompanied by the crew chief.

Deferring to rank and my own limited experience with this airplane, I said, "Sir, why don't you go ahead and fly it."

"Sure," he responded. "I've never flown one."

This was going to be interesting. Our combined experience with this airplane approached zero. We climbed into the cockpit. There was an awkward silence. Neither of us knew how to start it. Thank God for the crew chief. As if it were normal operating procedure, he offered, "Let me turn this over for you, gentlemen," and started it up.

Once we were off the ground, Tibbets lit his pipe and settled in, pouring himself a cup of coffee from the thermos.

My job was to navigate, his was to fly. He said very little. Even though I was anxious to learn more about him, the B-29, and whether he really could cancel my impending ocean cruise to India, I followed his lead and didn't try to engage him in conversation. Looking over occasionally, I saw him puffing away, eyes on the horizon, the picture of contentment.

We touched down in Marietta. Tibbets asked me to stay with the airplane. Thirty minutes later he was back. We taxied out and took off. As we completed our climb and banked toward the west and on to Wichita he said, "Your orders to India have been canceled. You're assigned to my unit."

That was it. My orders had been canceled. I didn't know where this would lead me, but I was certain I was going to be part of something special. I wanted to hoot, but I responded simply and directly. "Thank you, sir," I said.

We cruised at 8,000 feet. I set us on ADF—automatic direction finding. ADF locks on to a radio frequency and the pilot flies to the source of the transmission. It could be a commercial station or a published FAA frequency. This was the standard navigational technique in those days. As we approached the Mississippi, the skies became undercast at about 6,000 feet. My guess was that the clouds bottomed out at maybe 4,000 feet. We couldn't see the ground. No big deal.

Then I looked down at the ADF. It was out.

I flipped the switch off, on, off, on; nothing. The unit was dead. The question hit my brain and stomach at the exact same instant—how long had it been out? Five minutes? Ten? When had I last looked at it? As my brain raced and my stomach turned, I sorted out the options. If I could judge when the ADF had gone out, I could fix our last known location and figure out where we were by using the time/distance formula. Some copilot. The only job I had was to sit there and navigate—to keep my eye on the ADF. Damn it. I didn't even know what the wind speed was. I was trying to impress Tibbets, and the first time out I got us lost.

Reaching over to get out the maps, I steadied myself and informed him in a flat tone, "Boss, the ADF is out. I'm trying to get a fix on our position."

"How long's it been out?" he said, and resumed puffing away on his pipe.

Here it comes. "I'm not sure."

What a picture I must have struck studying the map. Taking a sideways glance at Tibbets, I saw him sitting there unperturbed, puffing on his pipe. Not a sign of anger or concern.

"Why don't I take it down for a look?" he asked calmly.

We came out from the undercast at about 3,500 feet. Below, the landscape offered few clues. We could have been over Kansas or Oklahoma or Nebraska. It was certain we were lost as hell, and it was my fault. Scanning the terrain and considering the options, I guessed that we had drifted south and could be in Oklahoma. I offered a suggestion that we fly due north.

Tibbets nodded, and we proceeded north. In the distance, I picked up a set of railroad tracks and a water tower. Descending to 100 feet, we made a slow pass. The letters painted on the tower told us we were in Iowa. Strike two. Navigation was proving to be my weak suit. I was positive that my new future with Paul Tibbets was going up in flames. But if he was upset, he was doing a superb job of hiding it.

He broke the silence. "Now we know where we are."

We changed course. It was getting dark. What should have been a three-hour flight had evolved into a six-hour odyssey through the Midwest. We hugged the bottom edge of the cloud cover. On our new course we reached Kansas. Another water tower sat on the horizon, and we went down to 200 feet to verify. Close but no cigar. Painted in big block letters on its side was "Independence."

For two experienced pilots, we weren't having a good day. Yet Tibbets was still relying on and taking my suggestions.

We had just started our climb back up to 500 feet when it happened: our right engine started sputtering. The oil gauge indicated we were rapidly losing oil pressure in that engine. The Martin was difficult to fly with two good engines. If we lost the right engine at this altitude, the airplane could drop like a rock with no room to maneuver. For the first time I felt the urge to take the controls. I had great confidence in Tibbets, but in this situation, like any pilot, I wanted to be in control. I told our passengers in the back to buckle up and sit tight.

With a final gasp, the right engine quit. On a single engine, Tibbets gradually nursed the Martin up to 1,500 feet. It was the first of many flying feats I would witness him perform. My uneasiness about not being at the controls subsided. I noticed that he didn't have his safety belt on.

"Boss, why don't you let me fly it, just hold it for thirty seconds while you put your safety belt on? If the left engine cuts out we're going to catch a cornfield."

As he buckled up I told him the closest airfield was Kansas City, presuming he'd want to land this beast as soon as possible.

"Nah. We'll press on to Wichita," he said nonchalantly, taking back the wheel.

I ran the situation through my mind. We were flying on one engine in an airplane that was hard to control even with both engines. Neither of us had much experience in a Martin B-26, except for this flight. And I wasn't at the controls. But I did have confidence in this man. If I wasn't flying, then the only other pilot I'd want at the controls would be Paul Tibbets. Of course, I was also the guy who'd gotten us into this mess, so my vote probably didn't count for much.

"Boss, whatever you want," I replied matter-of-factly. I understood the gravity of our situation, but it would be a waste of energy to get rattled or even to express doubt. The situation would not improve by my getting upset. We were professionals. Staying cool and focused were the primary tools necessary to fly through this problem.

Darkness was now swallowing the last light of dusk. Approaching Wichita, Tibbets took the airplane up to 2,500 feet for our final approach and started the run at about six miles out instead of the normal two. We would start out high and long to give us a little more margin on the approach. The tower was alerted that we were coming in on one engine. In sight of the field, he let up on the power a little, throttled back, and cranked in some right trim to help compensate for the lost engine as we came in. I let down the landing gear. The airplane rattled slightly as Colonel Tibbets gradually eased it down, making continuous minute adjustments on the descent. This

was it. Long, short, or just right, we had one shot. He held
the nose up and kept it steady. In the last light remaining of
the day, the ground was coming up to meet us. A few final
slight adjustments on the stick and we were over the runway
and settling down.

He had made a perfect landing. The B-26 couldn't taxi on
one engine, so he let it roll to the end of the runway. Fire
trucks rushed to each side of the aircraft. Men came clambering
out and onto the runway ready to douse the airplane with
foam. I opened the hatch, and Tibbets climbed down, followed
quickly by the three white-faced civilian technicians, who
spilled out onto the tarmac.

"Boss, you hitch a ride into town and take care of your
business and I'll stay with the airplane and have the engine
changed or repaired," I recommended, believing that my days
with Paul Tibbets had come to an abrupt end. No sense
inconveniencing him more.

He bid me a good evening and disappeared into the night
as I stood in the darkness next to the crippled Martin B-26. I
was devastated. I had wanted to make an impression—and I
had. My failure to pay attention to the ADF had led to a series
of problems that could have gotten us killed. My navigational
skills had been reduced to leaning out the window at 200 feet
to read the printing on water tanks and making judgments
about our location by the type of soil below: "Too sandy to be
corn country, so we must be in Oklahoma." I wondered if my
orders to India could be reinstated.

The next morning the colonel met me at breakfast. "Chuck,
we're taking the YB-29 back to Eglin. Make the arrangements
to have the Martin ferried back; you'll fly with me," he said.

"Oh, God. This is beautiful," I thought. "I'll be his copilot
in a brand new B-29." I was still okay.

Tibbets never mentioned the flight to Wichita. Reflecting

on the previous afternoon, I considered that he might have seen that I had kept my cool, stayed focused, and reacted professionally under difficult circumstances. Making mistakes was human. The pilot's skill was in rapid, effective reaction. I concluded that my conduct during the emergency actually might have helped boost my standing with him.

We walked over to the Boeing ramp. In a few brief days I had gone from fantasizing about getting into a B-29 to actually climbing up into the flight deck of the sparkling YB-29, settling into the brand-new leather seat, and preparing to conduct a preflight check with Paul Tibbets. The only other crew member was a flight engineer from Boeing who introduced me to the operating procedures of the Superfortress.

The flight back to Eglin was both uneventful and exhilarating—although I did make one interesting observation. When Tibbets flew, he never left the pilot's seat. During our six-hour flight to Wichita the day before, I'd thought he stayed in the seat because we were in a tenuous situation. But on this day, for the next three hours he drank coffee, puffed on his pipe, said very little, and never got up to stretch or use the toilet facilities on board. I like to occasionally move around on long flights in a bomber. But again, I followed his lead and stayed put, much to the regret of my aching bladder.

FIVE

Our headquarters at Eglin for Tibbets's operation was a converted truck trailer backed up against an isolated hangar. Inside, we had a small office and supply room. I was working on the details of securing B-17s and B-26s to tow the targets that would be used in testing the new central gunnery control systems in the B-29s, and on developing schedules for the missions. A third B-29 was on its way to Eglin, and our pilots would soon begin testing the competing General Electric and Sperry systems. The problem I was running into was that we didn't have enough pilots to accommodate the demanding timetable Tibbets had been given.

I assigned Captains Don Albury, Bob Love, and Bob Lewis to the B-29s. We would have to borrow copilots for them, as well as pilots and copilots for the tow ships. I scheduled myself to fly the tow ships. This seemed reasonable since I had no experience in piloting a B-29. In fact, I hadn't even made the transition from the right seat to the left. Since our return from

Wichita, I had been relegated to observing from the copilot's seat or from a jump seat in the rear of the cockpit. For a pilot, this was worse than being grounded. It was like being handcuffed, especially since I had grown accustomed to flying any airplane on the base I wanted. But I paid attention and kept my growing frustration to myself. Paul Tibbets never mentioned when, or even if, I'd ever sit in the left seat.

One afternoon a group of us was sitting at a table on the officers' club terrace enjoying a few cocktails before the evening meal when Colonel Tibbets came over and asked to speak with me. As we walked away from the table together, he said, matter-of-factly, "Chuck, why don't you take it up tomorrow? We have to test fire the system on each airplane before we start the target runs. It's got to be done tomorrow, and I'll be gone for the day."

I was elated. In little more than twelve hours I'd be in command of a B-29. It was the biggest event of my life.

"Yes, sir," I replied.

"We can go over your report when I get back."

I hurried back to the table to share the news with my friends, who were anxious to learn what the conference had been about. "Hooo-eee," one of the guys shouted, and he patted me on the shoulder. I was being asked to take over a job that Tibbets would have done if he were there!

I had no idea that afternoon what Tibbets might have had in mind for me as the war grew more bloody in the Pacific.

We were scheduled for takeoff at eight A.M. I filed my flight plan, checked the weather, and prepared to taxi out at 7:45. I settled into the left-hand seat. In my excitement, I hadn't considered that I had never piloted a B-29 for takeoff. My copilot was equally inexperienced. In theory, if one points an airplane down the runway, gives it full power, gains airspeed, and eases back on the stick, the plane should go airborne. I taxied out. The visibility from the greenhouse was extraordinary.

I was sitting in a technological marvel, an example of the supremacy of American science and engineering. The B-29 was not just a collection of incremental improvements to existing aircraft design, a simple step in the evolutionary progress of any technology. Incorporating scores of revolutionary advances, it was a quantum leap into the future. The B-29 had the first fully pressurized cabin. It had four giant, thirty-six-cylinder Wright R-3350 engines, and the first central gunnery fire control. It was capable of carrying ten-ton payloads. At 30,000 feet, it could cruise easily at a ground speed of over three hundred miles an hour. It contained hundreds of less dramatic, but equally important, innovations. And with its payload capacity and range, the airplane was about to become a truly independent strategic weapon capable of projecting American military action anywhere on the globe. Unbeknownst to the died-in-the-wool army and navy devotees, who viewed the airplane as a novelty, the modern air force had taken a major step toward independence.

In the fall of 1943, production of the B-29 was progressing on the fast track even before all of the quirks and problems associated with any new aircraft had been worked out. The famous test pilot Eddie Allen and his entire crew had died a year earlier in the very first XB-29; an engine fire had sent it crashing into a suburb of Seattle. The details of the crash were classified top secret and not released until after the war. However, the army air corps was committed to the B-29, and production proceeded even in the absence of a totally satisfactory flight test program.

For a twenty-three-year-old captain sitting at the controls for the first time, the geopolitical ramifications of the B-29 that were swirling around the upper echelons of the military were of little significance. My job was to fly. Many of the problems with the B-29 would be addressed by the testing and training coordinated by Paul Tibbets and our unit at Eglin and later at Grand Island, Nebraska. On this morning, I would conduct a defined two-hour mission to test fire the central gunnery system over the Gulf of Mexico.

I didn't know then that the airplane I was flying was not only a high-altitude, long-range heavy bomber but it was also the necessary vehicle to deliver a fearsome weapon, a weapon our scientists in the Manhattan Project were laboring against the clock to develop before Hitler could. The project, after all, had begun after President Roosevelt received a letter from Albert Einstein urging the United States to develop an atomic weapon before the German scientists did. If the B-29 had not already been in development, it would have had to have been created to accommodate the physical realities of the atomic bomb. No B-29 . . . no delivery system. It has always been a curious coincidence to me that the bomb and the B-29, which together would have such a profound effect on the war and the course of history, developed independently of each other.

With the airplane pointed down the runway and clearance from the tower, and with partial flaps, I advanced the throttles to takeoff power, 2,600 rpm. I released the brakes, and we rolled forward, picking up speed. Sixty knots . . . eighty knots. I eased up on the controls and the laws of aerodynamics kicked in. I felt her lift off the ground. At about 300 feet, with airspeed at 140 miles per hour, I ordered, "Gear up, flaps up easy," keeping my eyes on the horizon ahead. As we gained altitude I decreased power to climbing speed. When we reached 8,000 feet, we leveled off and cruised at 200 miles per hour. It was the easiest airplane I had ever flown, behaving like a B-25. After I synchronized the manifold pressure and the propellers, I turned the airplane over to my copilot.

With everything in order and the props turning at 2,000 rpm, I relaxed at the controls and enjoyed the thrill of flight in this magnificent flying machine. It was the biggest, heaviest, and most powerful airplane I had ever flown. Yet it responded beautifully, with a gentle and precise handling of the controls. From an open-cockpit Stearman PT-17 to this, I thought, in what seemed like the snap of a finger. I wondered at my good fortune.

At 30,000 feet in a fully pressurized cabin, we sat in total comfort in our shirtsleeves, much like sitting in a commercial jet today. I lit up a cigar. The gunners were stationed in their Plexiglas blisters, from which they would sight and fire their weapons by remote control. At the appointed position over the gulf, I ordered the gunners, "Okay to test fire." Unlike the deafening staccato *rat-a-tat-tat* of the .50-caliber machine gun turrets in the unpressurized B-17, the sound inside our artificial shirtsleeve environment no longer blotted out the ambient hum generated by the engines. I looked over to my left and could see the tracers trailing away. The bombardier, who had a gun sight, and the two aft fuselage gunners, reported all firing systems normal. Our mission over the gulf was completed, and I started home.

It was time to consider how to land this son of a gun. Although the laws of aerodynamics had "magically" lifted us off the ground, I had a deeper respect for the immutable laws of gravity, which on our final approach, would be pulling us back to earth. My instincts about this airplane had been right so far, so, I reasoned, I'd just aim it at the runway, make sure the wheels were down, reduce speed, and it should land.

On our final approach I ordered the gear and flaps down. We touched down and the nose slowly settled forward. It might not have been a picture-perfect landing, but it sure felt like one.

Those twenty hours observing had paid off. From this point on, the B-29 was my airplane. I would fly it every chance I got.

The details of managing any testing program can be mind numbing. The aircraft, support personnel, ordnance, maintenance, record keeping, and pilots all present multiple problems that have to be juggled, coordinated, and, if necessary, massaged. In the military, redundancy is built into even the most mundane task. Triplicate is not a measure, it is a mind-set. Paperwork becomes an end in itself. And as in private industry, the boss must have a loyal and competent number-two guy to see to the details. I became that number-two guy.

Tibbets was often traveling to Marietta or Wichita or somewhere. If he had had to be tied to the administrative minutia of the testing program, his trips would have seriously hampered his ability to manage the program itself. Seeing an opportunity to make myself valuable and to demonstrate my loyalty to him, I just assumed the day-to-day administration of the gunnery testing program. As the base operations officer, I had the experience, knew the players at the base, and knew where to get what we needed with the least amount of red tape. The more weight I could take off the colonel's shoulders, the easier I could make his life. And the more necessary I would be to him.

The purpose of the new General Electric and Sperry central gunnery control systems was for a single gunner to control and direct the fire from several turrets on a single target at the same time. Prior to this innovation, a single gunner fired at a target from only one turret. The testing protocol was simple. A tow plane lined up on the runway. The ground crews spread out a five-foot-wide, forty-foot-long, waxed-mesh fabric sleeve with a target painted in black in the center. The tow aircraft would drag a cable attached to the mesh sleeve through the sky, and the target would trail behind. Aboard the B-29s, each gun turret was loaded with ammunition having different colored tips. The B-29s and the tow plane would rendezvous over the Gulf of Mexico. After each run, the target was examined to determine which turrets had hit it and at what proficiency. The rate and accuracy of hits on the target from the different turrets was used to evaluate the competing systems.

We had one XB-29 and two YB-29s for the testing. As the person scheduling the flights, I had complete discretion as to who flew which aircraft. This was a perk I took full advantage of. Although I would take out a tow plane every once in a while, I was now flying B-29s almost exclusively and accumulating considerable time in them. Eventually I would have more flight time in the B-29 than any other pilot in the army air force.

To keep up with the tempo of the war, the B-29 program was moving fast. In December, Tibbets pulled me off the testing program for three weeks and sent me to Birmingham, Alabama, accompanied by a flight engineer. In Birmingham, the Bechtel McCone Modification Center was engaged in adding improvements to the B-29s once they were completed in Marietta according to their original blueprints. The problem for the center was that it had a backlog of upgraded B-29s and no pilots to test them. Bechtel McCone's pilots were only skilled in flying B-24s. Boeing was training Bechtel's civilian pilots in Wichita, but the clock was ticking. In three weeks I tested fifteen new modified B-29s out of Alabama. My crew would record any problems, the center would fix the problems, and the airplanes would be shipped to combat units.

When I returned to Eglin, the pace for completing the gunnery system testing was requiring our group of pilots to average 150 hours a month in the air, well above the desired military maximum of 100 hours. To stay on schedule and minimize stress, we set up a rotation allowing pilots of the B-29s and the tow ships to alternate as pilots and copilots on a continuing basis. We could have used more help.

But as quickly as young men graduated from flight school, they were assigned to combat school for special training. Even though our project had top priority, the need for pilots throughout the theaters of operation in Europe and the Pacific was of more immediate urgency. Allied air crews over Europe were suffering steady and staggering losses. Replacements were a priceless commodity in the economics of war.

I asked Colonel Tibbets for more pilots, explaining that our crews' continuous schedule could lead to fatigue and might ultimately affect performance.

"If I try to go through channels," he answered, "the war will be over by the time the pencil pushers make a decision." He decided, "I'm going to call an old friend who has a ready source of highly trained pilots who could be assigned to us without going through the chain of command."

How could there be a cache of highly trained pilots anywhere? I wondered, but I didn't ask.

Tibbets picked up the phone, had a brief conversation, and announced, "How about five copilots for the tow airplanes? That should take the pressure off the guys and give them some relief."

"That's great, boss," I replied. "We could sure use the help. Thank you."

I learned what was coming, but the others did not. I simply told them that the five new pilots, who were recent graduates of flight school, would relieve them for some flights in the right seat of the tow aircraft. On the day the C-47 carrying the new pilots arrived, a few of us waited at the ramp to greet them. Out stepped five woman—trim, neat, and spit-and-polished in their blue Eisenhower jackets and slacks. To say my fellow pilots looked confused would be an understatement.

With the vast majority of men in uniform, most of them either in Europe or in the Pacific, the military had begun to more effectively use the skills of its women, who were not permitted by law to engage in combat. Pilots were needed for stateside duty to ferry aircraft from the plants to airfields and from one field to another. So the Women's Auxiliary Service Pilots was created under the leadership of Jackie Cochrane. Jackie, a famous aviatrix before the war and a pioneer in aviation, recruited both experienced women pilots and those who wanted to learn to fly. She oversaw a demanding course in which no special favors were requested or extended. The program was as rigorous as the men's and it produced some of the finest pilots in the country. The WASPs flew in all kinds of conditions to carry out their assignments, and many lost their lives in the line of duty. Their contribution to the war effort has never been fully appreciated—or, for that matter, even known—by the public. This remains a great injustice to the pilots and their families.

Some of my pilots might have initially harbored lingering doubts fed by their own preconceived view of what was proper for a woman to do, but in short order these proficient, dedicated, and brave pilots proved invaluable to the successful completion of our testing program. I would later learn firsthand in an almost fatal incident at Denver just how proficient our new pilots were.

The testing proceeded through the winter, and we accumulated a mountain of data on the relative efficiencies of each system. Although others would do the detailed analysis of our data, it became clear to the pilots that the General Electric system had the edge, a conclusion that would be confirmed when G.E. received the production contract. The B-29 itself, however, was getting a reputation among some pilots as being unreliable and dangerous. A colonel who commanded a group of B-29s in training at Clovis, New Mexico, had called Tibbets to ask his advice about the growing hesitancy of his pilots to fly the airplane. Engine fires, in particular, had become commonplace. The psychological effect of the pilots' lack of confidence was feeding on itself.

Tibbets had an idea. He selected two WASPs in our unit and took them in a B-29 to an unused airfield in Anniston, Alabama. It was important that word not get out. He trained them to fly the B-29. When he was satisfied that they were ready, he sent them on their way with orders to land at Clovis. Word spread quickly throughout the flying community about what happened next. When the B-29 arrived at Clovis, it taxied to the ramp, parked, and out from the front wheel well stepped the two women pilots, smiling and exuding confidence. The message was clear. If women could fly this monster, then men should have no trouble either. True, it was a sexist thing to do, but it was a remarkably simple way of solving the problem. The colonel at Clovis had no more complaints from his men, and we had two more pilots qualified to fly the B-29.

My own personal experience with our women pilots is forever fixed in an incident that occurred at Denver. I had taken a B-29 to a modification center—a mod shop—at Stapleton Field in Denver to have an adjustment made. During the war several companies had been under contract to make repairs and modifications to military aircraft at such centers. As my copilot, I took one of the WASPs, Helen Gosnell. We arrived at the Denver airfield on a clear, sunny day and delivered the airplane to the maintenance crew. I had also been experiencing trouble with the PITOT system, which measured airspeed and rate of climb, especially critical for an instrument takeoff or landing. The PITOT system was not the reason I took the plane to the shop, but as long as I was there, I asked the maintenance chief to take a look at it.

When we arrived back at the field that evening it had started snowing. I went over the repair log, and everything was checked off and in order, including the PITOT system. By the time we were taxiing out, the snow was coming down pretty hard and the backwash from our props made it appear from the cockpit that there was a blizzard outside. Visibility was close to zero. We would make an instrument takeoff and head north. Because the land rose in that direction, we had to pay careful attention to our rate of climb or we might run into the ground.

We rolled down the runway at full power. As we picked up speed, the visibility became even worse. The snow was whipping about the nose, creating a total whiteout. I quickly glanced over at the copilot's airspeed indicator and saw that its reading was different from mine. At that instant I realized that the PITOT system had not been properly repaired. It was not working, nor was my rate-of-climb gauge working. Without these readings, I couldn't tell on an instrument takeoff whether I was climbing or diving once I left the ground. I sensed that our airspeed was passing probably eighty knots. We were committed. In the space of a second we were airborne. If I maintained full power and pulled back on the stick, I might stall and crash into the ground, which might be rushing up to meet us because of the rise in the terrain. Standard procedure is to call for power position two and throttle back while the wheels are retracting. Reflexively, I did what I had been trained to do. "Power position two," I commanded. The words had barely left my lips when my instincts bypassed my conscious brain and told me that our rate of climb was shallow. I yelled, "Full power!" But we were still at full power. Helen had hesitated just long enough for me to realize what was happening. It was a beautiful maneuver. The whole incident lasted maybe ten seconds, but in that time we might not have recovered if she had reduced power as I had ordered. I can't say for certain we would have crashed. But I am certain it was my good fortune to have a copilot whose instincts and presence of mind rendered the question moot.

Fifty years ago I wasn't thinking about the women's movement or civil rights. I was thinking about completing the job Paul Tibbets had given me. But in retrospect, my experience in working with women pilots reflects, I believe, a noteworthy aspect of military service. That is: When a soldier finds himself or herself in a difficult situation, which is the nature of the business, he or she quickly learns that all that counts in a partner is competence, courage, and the ability to work together.

One morning at Eglin in mid-January 1944, I came face-to-face with my childhood hero. Charles Lindbergh arrived on the base, accompanied by a Boeing vice president. He was there to find out about the B-29. "Hap" Arnold, commanding general of the army air forces, wanted his opinion. Charles Lindbergh was an American icon, the first international celebrity, more famous at that time than any other living person. The base was buzzing.

I had been assigned to take Colonel Lindbergh for his B-29 ride. I was, of course, in awe of the man. I met him at lunch at the officers' club, after which we headed to the flight line. The airplane was ready when we arrived. I conducted my preflight walk-around inspection as I had done so many times before. But it was the first time I was walking around a B-29 with a living legend. Still, at that moment we were just two pilots doing what all pilots do before takeoff, visually inspecting the integrity of the nuts and bolts that collectively make up an airplane.

I gestured toward the forward wheel well. "After you, sir," I said. I followed him up the ladder and waited on the top rung. I remember he turned around and looked down at me and asked, "Which seat shall I take?"

"Take the left seat, sir," I replied. I figured if his unfamiliarity with the plane caused any problems, which I sincerely doubted, I could still fly from the right-hand side if necessary.

On board with us was the Boeing vice president, who, together with me, provided Lindbergh with an in-flight narrative of the capabilities of the B-29. We flew for about forty-five minutes to an hour. On our approach back to Eglin I advised him that the B-29 handled identically to the B-25, which I knew he had flown.

He brought the big bird in with no trouble. As he walked away from the airplane, he extended his hand and thanked me for the ride. I said it had been an honor for me.

When one is in the company of someone famous, there is a tendency not to fully enjoy the moment until it has gone. Before, during, and after the flight, I had wanted to ask him about his solo flight over the Atlantic. I had wanted to tell him it was a feat of extraordinary skill and heroism. But I knew my job that day was to assist him in any way I could in learning about the B-29. I was happy I had been given that opportunity. It's not every day one gets to meet his childhood hero.

It was spring 1944. Our testing project had been completed and we were out of a job. We were in the middle of a world war, unassigned. No one seemed quite sure what to do with us.

Colonel Tibbets decided to call another friend of his, General Frank Armstrong, who would later be immortalized in a novel and a movie, *Twelve O'Clock High,* for his exploits commanding the Eighth Air Force in Britain. General Armstrong was preparing a wing of B-29s for deployment to the Pacific, and Tibbets thought he might perhaps have a mission for us.

SIX

■ WAS BACK in the heartland of America with a new title, director of standardization. From the cornfields of Indiana to the cornfields of Nebraska.

Paul Tibbets had been named director of plans for General Frank Armstrong at Grand Island, Nebraska. Once the military had ordered production of sixteen hundred B-29s even as the bugs were still being worked out, the need for flight instructors to train the pilots to fly them was pressing. General Armstrong assigned Tibbets to oversee the development of a flight instructors' school. I would identify and standardize all procedures for the operation of the aircraft.

By that time it was the summer of 1944, and the tides of war in Europe had shifted to our advantage. The Allied forces who had landed at Normandy were pushing forward into France without serious opposition. Victory seemed certain. Some thought it would come soon. But the world would soon learn, at the Battle of the Bulge, that the Germans were still formidable. Underestimating the will of the German army would prove to be a tragic miscalculation, paid for with the lives of tens of thousands of young American boys. Much suffering lay ahead, especially as our full attention turned to the war in the Pacific.

For our new assignment, I had a staff of assistants responsible for each of the operational areas of the aircraft: pilot, navigator, flight engineer, bombardier, gunners. Every operational step required to fly the B-29 had to be identified, broken down into its constituent parts, and standardized so that crew members could be interchangeable from one B-29 to another or from squadron to squadron. The work allowed me to continue racking up hours in the B-29 and to develop a detailed knowledge of every nut, bolt, and weld in the airplane. By this time, when I was at the controls I felt like I was part of the airplane—as if it were my second skin.

Life at Grand Island was uneventful. My wife, Dorothy, and I had an apartment downtown. We socialized with some of the guys who had come up from Eglin, but Paul Tibbets and I saw very little of each other. Our duties kept us both busy.

I had met Dorothy at Eglin. She was a nurse at the base hospital—and coincidentally was from Woburn, Massachusetts. We were introduced by the senior chaplain for the base, Father Harrington, who was also from Massachusetts—Waverly. The Massachusetts connection was perhaps a sign, although our initial meeting was a bit strained.

One day Father Harrington invited me to accompany him to the nurses' quarters at Eglin to get the altar linens, which the nurses laundered every week for the chapels. As we approached the laundry room, a group of nurses came walking toward us from the ward across the way. Having the genetic wit of any Irishman, Father Harrington decided it would be good fun to introduce me as "Father Sweeney," a newly arrived priest. Perhaps in deference to the good father, or because my propeller insignia resembled a cross, the group seemed to accept his introduction.

"Good evening, Father," they greeted me in unison.

What attracts one person to another is often a mystery. For whatever reason, my attention was immediately drawn to Dorothy McEleney. Maybe it was the sparkle in her bright blue eyes, or her warm, shy smile. But there I was, speaking to her in the person of Father Sweeney.

"Wait a moment. If I may, I'd like to ask you a question," I said, jumping into my new role with a most solicitous tone.

"Yes, Father?" she responded.

"Do you write to your mother every day?" I queried, wondering to myself where I'd come up with that one.

"Why . . . almost every day, Father."

"Good. Good. And where are you going tonight?" I probed.

"To the movies," she answered quietly.

"Do you have a date?" I pressed.

"Yes," she said, now less certain.

"Is he Catholic?" I asked in a serious but benevolent tone.

She stammered nervously for an instant and then confessed, "I don't know, Father . . . But he's very nice—"

I held up my hand as if to calm her concern and said, piously, "Well, you be careful." She nodded and promptly took the first chance she got to gracefully flee from my presence.

Happily, she was a good sport and quite forgiving when we started to date. I eventually proposed marriage and she accepted, but with one proviso—she wanted to be married at home. In wartime most couples got married at the base chapel because getting leave to go home was difficult. With both of us in the army, the chance of our getting leave at the same time was nil. But Dorothy was insistent that she wanted to get married with her family and friends in the church she grew up in.

I spoke to Colonel Waugh.

"I can't give you any leave, Chuck. There's a war on," he said.

"Sir," I offered, "I'm scheduled for more navigational training flights." Since routine training was required, it should make no difference if I bored holes in the sky over the Deep South or in a northerly direction.

The colonel shook his head, and with a barely visible smile said, "Go ahead."

I gassed up a B-25, filed my training flight plan, arranged to place a certain nurse on the crew for the mission, and off we went to Boston. Dorothy was married in a flowing white wedding gown with her friends and family in attendance.

I'll wager, though, that she was the first woman to ever spend her honeymoon on board a military aircraft.

At Grand Island, Colonel Tibbets's guiding hand was always evident. Shortly after arriving there, he recommended to General Armstrong that I be promoted to major. Armstrong endorsed the recommendation and sent it along to the Second Air Force at Colorado Springs for approval. It was promptly returned "Denied," because the quota for majors in the entire Second Air Force had been filled.

The denial sent Armstrong into a spin. He knew that within the army there was a barely concealed antipathy—jealousy, even—toward the air corps. One manifestation of the attitude had been an aversion to promoting pilots. Theater commanders like MacArthur were notorious for routinely denying promotions to airmen. For the general officers who'd risen through the ranks in the age of the cavalry, the air corps was an intruding burr in their saddle. They had never grasped the strategic value of airpower. In Europe, Eisenhower ordered LeMay to bomb railroad trains while LeMay argued that he should be bombing the factories where the locomotives were manufactured. It was a battle of wills that would not be resolved until the air corps became independent of the army after the war.

So for Armstrong, more was at stake than my little promotion. He had the reputation—and the power—to throw his weight around. A member of his staff told me later that he personally called the War Department and made it clear that in the future if he sent a recommendation for promotion, he expected it to be approved. Period. My promotion was summarily approved.

The issue again surfaced when two seasoned combat pilots returned from the Pacific and joined my staff. Those guys had extraordinary flight experience and had been in some pretty heavy combat. Yet each had been frozen in rank as a first lieutenant while other army officers raced past them up the chain of command. It was a disgrace that these combat veterans had been repeatedly denied promotion within General MacArthur's theater. I brought the problem to Tibbets's attention and, with his permission, to General Armstrong's group operations officer.

Armstrong promoted them both to captain on the spot, waited a week, and then promoted them to major. Bing. Bing. The army might have thought the flying machine was not there to stay, but Armstrong was making it clear that a new day was coming for the airplane and the men who flew it.

Up to this point, my two and a half years in the military had been a series of assignments unencumbered by excessive supervision from above. Each posting I had been given was just slightly outside the usual chain of command, allowing me extraordinary freedom to carry out my assignments. I knew without question this was because I was part of Paul Tibbets's team. I felt a bond with Paul Tibbets and a true sense of loyalty to him, which he reciprocated. He extended me respect and understanding and confidence. The time we had spent together at Eglin became the foundation of our relationship, which would carry me with him toward Hiroshima and Nagasaki.

After we relocated to Grand Island, Colonel Tibbets and I lost our utility airplanes which we had so inconspicuously acquired at Eglin. While we were working at Eglin, Tibbets had been ever resourceful. One late afternoon I greeted him on his return there from one of his many trips to Marietta, where his administrative offices were located. He taxied up in a brand-new, twin-engine, ten-passenger Lockheed Vega B-34, a fast, versatile airplane.

"Nice airplane, boss," I said, and then added as a joke, "You think I could get one, too?"

"If you're a good boy, I'll see what I can do," he responded jokingly.

"I'll see that it gets logged on our inventory," I said to save him the trouble of doing the paperwork. All aircraft in the military must be accounted for by being officially placed on the inventory of aircraft located at every base. The airplane then is assigned at each base to a wing or squadron.

"Chuck, I think we want to keep this one off inventory for a while. I'm going to use it as my utility airplane, and it would be simpler if we leave it unassigned," he replied in a most convincing manner.

Translation: I don't want to share this airplane with anyone, and I want to use it whenever I want.

"No problem, boss."

In about a week Colonel Tibbets called me in and told me he had located a B-26 in Dayton that I could get. This one would also be off the inventory. In short order we became the only pilots in the military then or now, to my knowledge, to have control of our own utility airplanes.

This gave me unprecedented freedom of movement, a privilege I was careful not to abuse, but our testing at Eglin was winding down and we had free time. I asked Tibbets if I could take some time off and fly to Boston . . . on another training flight. As is the custom, I let it be known that anyone who needed a lift going in that direction was welcome. Dorothy managed to get a couple of days' leave, and so we, two officers, and three enlisted men from the Boston area headed home.

I stopped at Philadelphia and then at Mitchell Field on Long Island. The weather on the way up the coast was perfect. After leaving Mitchell, we received a weather advisory of a surprise nor'easter in the Boston area. Prudence dictated a return to New York or maybe landing in Hartford. But I was at that stage in my life when I believed a little bad weather sure as hell wasn't going to stop me from getting home. Many pilots with this mind-set suffer from a fatal affliction known as "gethomeitis."

Over my radio came the order to return to Mitchell. I did what any pilot who is full of himself would do. I pressed the throat microphone close to my neck and responded, "Do not copy. Say again." They said it again as clear as a bell, but my "gethomeitis" was now affecting my hearing. I turned the radio off.

I proceeded toward New Haven. The weather was getting worse real fast. Ice began to build up on my wings. The airplane had no de-icers; it had been intended for local use in Florida. The solution to my problem was either to climb higher to drier air, which would rid the wings of the ice, or to swoop down to below 1,000 feet, where the temperature was warmer. I was locked into a preset FAA altitude that precluded me from

climbing in this very busy air corridor where other assigned
military and civilian aircraft were flying. Going below 1,000
feet at two hundred miles an hour in visibility of less than half
a mile presented the prospect of catching a steeple or maybe
running into a hill.

Down I went. Because of reduced visibility and my maneuvers to free the wings of ice, I was no longer sure of my location and I was positive air traffic controllers had lost me. The
best I could do was hold a compass bearing that I knew would
get me to Boston Harbor. The visibility grew worse as the snow
picked up in the stiff northeasterly winds. At rooftop level, I
pressed on toward home. Out of the haze I saw the harbor.
The closest airfields were the naval air station at Squantum or
Logan Air Field, which in those days was the size of the old
Dennison Airport—a postage stamp. B-26s were specifically
prohibited from landing at Logan because of its short runway.
So Logan was out. Squantum wasn't any better lengthwise—it
was only four thousand feet long. For obvious reasons, the
Navy didn't believe in long runways. I located Wollaston Bay
and the Wollaston Yacht Club, which led me right to the
Squantum Naval Air Station. Without clearance, I took it in.
As we touched down on the ice-encrusted tarmac, I knew we
were going to use every inch of the available runway. We didn't
go into the bay, but if we had gotten any closer to the end, a
swift kick would have tipped the airplane into the water.

I had needed the grace of God—and some great good
luck—and both came through. Or, as a true pilot would say to
his buddies over a few beers, "Superior skill and cunning saved
the day."

I had, in fact, done a superb job of flying. But the need for
such skill had been the result of a poor decision born of supreme arrogance in my ability as a pilot. The truth is, I could

have been a small headline in the local newspaper the next morning, another statistic of pilot error.

Everyone at Squantum knew me. I had flown in there often. They all thought I had done a great job, an opinion that was not universally shared at that moment. As soon as I walked into the operations hut, the officer of the day handed me the phone. On the line was the military detachment officer, a captain, in charge of Logan. His tone and attitude were frostier than the weather beyond the snow-whipped windows.

After formally identifying himself and getting some particulars on who I was, he proceeded to lay me out in lavender. "You ignored a direct order to return to New York," he bellowed at me. "Civilian traffic has been tied up for over an hour. Everything's been stopped because of you. You had no clearance. We had no idea where you were." *Rat-a-tat-tat* . . .

He was, of course, 100 percent right. But I was so glad to be alive that I remained unshaken as his invectives escalated; this seemed to infuriate him further.

"I'm filing a report on you," he said, spitting out the ultimate threat. I still didn't respond, only because I had no plausible excuse.

Then he said something that triggered an ill-timed attempt at humor on my part.

"I know you came up to see your girlfriend." His voice dripped with sarcasm.

"No sir. I did not. I brought my girlfriend with me on the airplane," I said evenly. It was the absolute truth.

That did it. "Captain," he said, "enjoy your flight home, because if I have anything to say about it, you won't ever fly again." Then he hung up.

The next two days at home were heaven. I put the unpleasant military detachment officer from Logan out of my mind.

On the way back to Eglin, I made one stop at White Plains,

New York, where Dorothy and I hoped to visit with my old friend Bill Kelley. But he had left for Miami to catch a flight to Buenos Aires on business. His wife asked if there was any way I could see him off. I assured her I would try.

When I arrived back at Eglin, I found that Colonel Tibbets had gone up to Marietta. I wanted to check in and let him know everything was fine and ask for some more time off so that I could see my buddy off in Miami.

I got him on the phone and we engaged in some general conversation. Then I popped the question, expecting a perfunctory yes, having totally forgotten about the unpleasant incident with the captain from Logan.

"Chuck, I have in my hand a five-page report detailing multiple violations," he said. Without pausing, he proceeded to read the entire report to me, word for word.

I'm not sure if he expected a defense of some kind, but I thought a direct and simple response would save a lot time. "Boss, he didn't leave a thing out. It's one hundred percent accurate."

The silence on the other end of the line remained fixed. I decided to press on. "Boss, that night reminded me of the time you and I were coming around Stone Mountain in that storm, trying to land at Marietta without clearance. Remember how mad they were when you—"

"All right. All right," he relented. He even added that I could go down to Miami.

Without trying to engage in a lot of amateur psychological analysis, I must say that I believe Tibbets respected my flying ability under those trying circumstances while at the same time recognizing the foolishness of my actions. But that very foolishness had a flip side, the quality of being able to overcome a problem, do the unconventional, and succeed. In combat, that quality can make the difference between success and failure.

What is foolish in peacetime can become a virtue in war. I believe the incident helped solidify his belief in me as a pilot.

When we left Eglin, Tibbets and I brought our two utility airplanes to Grand Island, where we naturally expected to keep using them. Sometime after we arrived, however, the base commander inquired of his operations officer why two airplanes were always at his base even though he had no records for them. Taking the judicious course, Tibbets suggested that we turn in our utility airplanes while the turning in was good.

In a few short months, however, we would have our own private air force.

My most memorable encounter at Grand Island occurred when I was assigned to give General Curtis LeMay a complete course in the B-29. The reputations of some men precede them in the same way the fear of a typhoon or other force of nature precedes the cataclysmic event. LeMay was such a man— tough, brilliant, and demanding. He expected perfection and tolerated nothing less from his subordinates. As with all such large personalities, stories circulate from person to person that are part myth and part truth. In my opinion, the most insightful story, whether true or not, went like this:

General LeMay was never without a cigar clenched in his teeth. Smoking is not permitted near a parked airplane; any open flame or spark could potentially set off an explosion. One day LeMay was inspecting aircraft on the flight line. He hadn't bothered to extinguish his cigar as he approached one of the parked airplanes. The crew chief responsible for this airplane politely reminded LeMay that his cigar might cause the airplane to explode. In his usual gruff tone, LeMay barked, "It wouldn't dare," then proceeded to conduct his inspection, confident that the laws of nature didn't apply to him.

Paul Tibbets rang me up at home late on a Friday evening

to tell me that LeMay would be at the base on Monday morning. "He's preparing to take command of the Twentieth Air Force, which is in the Marianas, to start missions against mainland Japan. I want you to take him through the training course personally," he said. "Meet him at the airplane at oh-eight-hundred."

As I hung up, I didn't quite focus on the task being assigned as much as on the fact that Paul Tibbets had once again selected me to carry out an important assignment. But then the enormity of training Curtis LeMay hit me. At eight A.M. Monday the typhoon would strike.

I arrived at the flight line very early. The crew chief was already there, and as he and I walked around the airplane, my crew started to assemble. I lined them up in anticipation of a formal inspection by General LeMay; such an inspection would be customary for a senior officer. At precisely 0800 the army staff car pulled up to the airplane. An aide jumped out of the front passenger side and in a single flowing movement he opened the back door and snapped to attention. I called my men to attention.

Grabbing a handle on the door with one hand and the door jamb with the other, the general lunged out, cigar first. LeMay was a beefy man, but quite agile. After taking a few steps toward me, he stopped and placed both hands on his hips, ignoring the salute all of us present held as we awaited his response. He surveyed his surroundings, his round face set in a scowl. His eyes were narrowed as if focused on some offending matter. He returned a perfunctory salute.

He removed the cigar from his mouth, and his gaze came to rest on me. Military protocol dictated that I speak. "General, my crew is ready for inspection."

"You got any airplanes in that hangar?" he rasped.

"Yes, sir," I replied smartly.

"Good. Dismiss your crew. We're not going to fly today. We're going to sit in the cockpit and you're going to tell me everything you know about this airplane—every nut, bolt, gauge, and rivet," he commanded in a loud, clear tone.

I was in shock. I had expected to take him up and demonstrate the capabilities of the B-29. I was totally at home in the air. In the hangar, one-on-one with LeMay, I wasn't so sure. I had never conducted an extemporaneous lecture on the B-29 while sitting on the ground. And LeMay was legendary for reaming subordinates who were ill prepared.

"And bring the flight engineer," he added, moving past me into the hangar.

We settled into the cockpit of a B-29 sitting in the hangar, LeMay taking the left seat. For the next three hours he peppered me with an endless stream of questions: "How many generators are on each engine?" "Where are they?" "How does the fuel feed into the cylinders?" "How does the cooling system work?" "What about the hydraulics? . . . the brakes . . . ?" A short break for lunch and then three more hours. He didn't want me to tell him how to fly this airplane, he wanted to know this airplane, to understand the finite mechanics of the multiple systems that when put together made it what it was. I respected his insight. As commander of the Twentieth Air Force, if he were to use the B-29 effectively, he had to know it.

I was amazed at how much I knew about the plane's inner workings. LeMay never said anything one way or the other about my performance. He didn't compliment or criticize. I didn't know if I was alive or dead with him. I concluded that I must have done a good job. He hadn't thrown me out of the airplane. And his last words of the day were, "Tomorrow we go up."

The next morning, perhaps out of some sense of following

protocol with his instructor, he asked me, "Where do you want me to sit?"

I confidently replied, "Sir, take your choice." As if there had been any doubt, he settled into the left-hand seat. I knew I could fly the plane from either the pilot's or copilot's seat, so my relative position wasn't important—to me.

On this day we would fly two three-hour missions, one in the morning and one in the evening. As we went through various maneuvers, LeMay listened to my commentary and instructions with little or no comment. He was all business. I couldn't tell what he was thinking, but I could almost hear the gears in his mind whirring.

The day before, as we'd sat in a B-29 cockpit on the ground, looking out the nose canopy, I'd explained to the general a phenomenon known as parallax. On a B-29, unlike other aircraft of the time, the pilot looked out through the curved Plexiglas that surrounded the entire cockpit instead of through the conventional flat windshield. This curve caused a distortion for the pilot in which images appeared a little to the left of where they actually were, especially on the approach when landing. If the pilot failed to compensate, he'd actually land off center from where he thought he'd touch down. The parallax was even more pronounced at night, when the pilot was relying on boundary lights to fix his point of touchdown. But until a pilot experienced parallax, it was a hard concept to grasp.

At the conclusion of the morning mission LeMay landed without incident, a little off the center line, but nothing to comment on.

As we completed our night mission, the general began his approach. In the distance ahead we could see the landing beacons and the boundary lights on each side of the runway. To me, it was obvious he was making the same mistake every pilot makes the first time he experiences parallax at night. The closer we came to the runway, the more apparent it became that he would be off center and would end up landing half on the runway and half in the mud. But he wasn't making any adjustment. As the instructor, I could have stepped in or even taken over the controls. But I didn't. I let him continue to make his own mistake to allow him—and me—to see how he'd react.

We were at a critical moment. In a few seconds we'd be committed and would not be able to pull out. I surreptitiously moved my hands on the controls, ready to take over. I wanted him to benefit from this error, but not to the extent of risking a crash on touchdown.

I'll be a son of a gun if LeMay, when he realized a problem had developed, opted to give it full throttle, pulled out, and retracted the gear. He did the smartest thing a pilot can do. It is an old flying maxim: When in doubt, go around. But so many pilots ignore that simple truth and fly themselves into the ground.

Around we went, and on the second approach he landed dead center on the runway. Although he didn't say so, I believe he appreciated my letting him learn from the mistake rather than stepping in and correcting it.

On our last day he ordered up three B-29s to do some formation flying, which was something that would be of great importance to him during operations against the Japanese mainland. We did fast climbs to 30,000 feet, descents, and banking maneuvers. He wanted to get a feel for what this massive airplane could do under stressful conditions in flight with similarly massive airplanes in formation.

It was moments after a rapid climb from 8,000 to 30,000 feet that an explosive sound ripped through the fuselage. A rear window had blown out due to some minor breach in the integrity of a seal or perhaps a crack in the window. Whatever it was, the internal pressure blew out the window with explosive force. Everything that wasn't nailed down in the cabin was sucked out the hole: paper, cushions, equipment, upholstery on the walls, everything. It was fortunate that the entire crew had their safety belts on. The sudden decompression could suck a man out if he wasn't strapped in securely.

I immediately knew what had happened. Reaching for my oxygen mask, I looked over toward LeMay, who was also strapping on his mask. No questions, no hesitation, no panic. He was dealing with the situation as if he'd been born inside a B-29. Gradually he descended to a lower altitude.

After landing, I offered some comment about what a pleasure and an honor it had been to fly with him, and I wished him good luck. In usual form, he grunted something that sounded like "All right, kid" and walked off.

I took it as a high compliment, indeed.

In a few weeks, General LeMay would commence operations with an air force of eight hundred to one thousand B-29s that would culminate in the spring and summer of 1945 in massive firebombings of Japanese cities in an attempt to force the Japanese to surrender.

Thus, I fully expected that I would finish the war tucked away in Nebraska or in some other equally uneventful place. So I didn't make much of it when Paul Tibbets went down to Colorado Springs to report to General Ent. Maybe we'd get another assignment to test more B-29s or train more pilots somewhere.

SEVEN

COLONEL TIBBETS TOLD us nothing about his new assignment when he returned on September 1, 1944, except that the base he would be going to was desolate and, even by military standards, primitive. He made it clear that any of us who preferred to stay with General Armstrong's wing at Grand Island, Nebraska, was free to do so. Those who wanted to go with him were welcome. Tibbets and I worked closely together during the past year testing the capabilities of the B-29. I had developed a great respect for him as an officer and a pilot. I didn't need to think about it. I wanted to go.

On September 11, I arrived at Wendover Field in Utah. It was desolate and primitive, all right. He could have added that it was also in the middle of nowhere. Bob Hope called it Leftover, Utah. On one side was the Great Salt Lake and on the other an endless expanse of desert. The base itself was surrounded for miles in all directions by stretches of barren salt flats. Our quarters were simple tar paper huts and cement block buildings squatting on concrete slabs. The temperature would change from scorching heat during the day to bone-chilling cold at night. When we arrived, the closest town had a bustling population of 103. The next nearest town was one hundred miles away.

Captain Albury, Master Sergeant John Kuharek, and a few others and I were among a small nucleus who were the first arrivals of a group that was to become fifteen hundred men. What caught my attention immediately was that security at the base was pervasive. Restricted areas were set up and military police were posted everywhere. Barbed wire cordoned off sections of the field. Signs were prominently posted warning of the importance of secrecy. At one end of the flight line there was a missile-testing project, its missiles similar to the V-2 rockets being used by the Germans. Soon I would learn that this project was a cover. The true purpose of this base had nothing to do with rockets.

After I attended an early-morning mass on my first Sunday at Wendover, a uniformed security officer, Captain McClanahan, came to my quarters and invited me to take a ride with him. In the military, it was the kind of invitation you know is an order. We drove out into the desert. The conversation was all popcorn talk: sports, the weather, stuff that mattered little to either of us at the moment but that filled the time until he got around to telling me what this was really about. We drove deeper into the vast expanse of the desert, farther from any remnant of civilization.

It was a brilliant, sunny morning. The sun's glare bleached the landscape. Nothing was moving, there were no signs of life, just the endless desert. I had to wonder what two fairly intelligent human beings were doing out there in the rising heat.

The jeep slowed and McClanahan surveyed our surroundings. Satisfied that this was the spot he was looking for, he stopped. He got out and so did I. We walked a short distance. He stopped and faced me. A faint whistle of wind was the only sound.

"Did you ever read about Einstein's theory of relativity?" he asked in a flat, matter-of-fact way.

By pure coincidence, I had read an article about the theory that had appeared in the *Saturday Evening Post* in 1939. I had been fascinated by the idea that unlimited quantities of pure energy could be generated from tiny particles of matter like those in a piece of wood or rock.

I answered, "Yes," and explained the article as I understood it.

He reached down and picked up a handful of the brownish, grainy desert dirt and held it as he spoke. He told me that our scientists were working on a new weapon, a weapon using Einstein's theory. The weapon would be twenty thousand times more powerful than any existing bomb.

He never took his eyes from mine as he spoke. He said, "One bomb will reduce an entire city to this." He tossed the handful of dirt into the air. I watched as it scattered in the wind.

There are some moments in life that stay indelibly embedded in your memory. This was one of those moments. I knew I would not forget—not a single detail. One plane. One bomb. One city.

I didn't understand the physics (I would later learn that few people really did), but I certainly understood the implications. I knew of the terrible losses being sustained by our air crews in Europe while flying what amounted to suicide missions trying to knock out German industries. Many of the men in those air crews were my friends, classmates, and neighbors. All were my countrymen. And tens of thousands of them were dying. Thousands of planes had been lost. Thousands of iron bombs

had been dropped. But they could not destroy an entire city—
reduce it to dust.

Now there was McClanahan telling me that what those
brave men could not do, this one bomb could. If he was right,
I knew we could shorten the war and end the killing. Maybe
he was crazy. Maybe he wasn't. It didn't matter. We were
working on a bigger, better bomb. That was all I needed to
understand. Any weapon that could bring victory and save
American lives was worth trying.

My instincts told me not to ask a lot of questions, although
I had a lot. I felt I should just let him keep coming to me,
telling me what he wanted me to know. He let the silence sit,
perhaps looking for some reaction. I said nothing and tried to
give no reaction.

The silence seemed to last a long time, although it was
probably only a few seconds. He went on, "You are being told
this because Colonel Tibbets has chosen you to train the crews
in the tactics and procedures necessary to safely drop this new
weapon. To do your job you need to know the nature of the
weapon."

Again he paused. Again I said nothing.

"The key problem will be to get the aircraft as far away as
possible as fast as possible. No one's quite sure how powerful
this weapon will be or what the blast will do."

For the past year at Eglin Field and then at Grand Island
I had been testing the capabilities of the B-29. I had more flight
time in the airplane than any other pilot in the air corps. It was
a magnificent airplane. But it had some disturbing operational
problems. It could carry a heavy bomb load safely—sixteen to
twenty thousand pounds—but at high altitudes with these loads
on long missions, the engines frequently overheated and the
superchargers stalled, greatly reducing the big bird's performance. And I would learn that, in spite of these problems, the

scientists, who were anything but certain of the power of the bomb, had calculated that the aircraft must get to at least eight miles from the blast in less than one minute.

I asked my first question. "How heavy is the bomb?"

"Colonel Tibbets will brief you on the information you need to know. And never refer to it as a 'bomb.' Call it a 'gimmick' or a 'gadget,' but never a 'bomb.' " McClanahan emphasized the word *never*.

He stressed that security would be strict beyond any previously known measures. There would be many security people, some in uniform, some in civilian clothes. Agents would be placed within the various units. No one would know who they were. I was not to assume that anyone else knew about the project, not even Colonel Tibbets. Even if he and I were alone in a car or an airplane—anywhere—we could never discuss it. If I had a training question or a problem that related to the weapon, I could discuss it with the colonel in one isolated, debugged building on the base—and only in the presence of a security officer. Any breach of security would result in immediate removal. No questions asked, no explanations given— "You'll be out of here and never heard from again."

There would later be a dramatic incident at Wendover that would drive this point home to everyone and make it clear that no matter what your rank or position, a breach of security, no matter how minor, would be dealt with quickly and harshly.

Also, my mother would tell me later that our neighbors had been visited by some very nice men from the FBI asking lots of questions about me. She thought I might be in some kind of trouble. I told her it was nothing, just the usual background check for all pilots. To this day I wonder what kind of answers my neighbors gave, particularly as I search my memory for any youthful transgressions I might have inflicted on the neighborhood.

We started back to the jeep. As we walked, McClanahan said, "The code name for the development of the weapon is Manhattan Project. Your unit code name will be Silverplate. Never use these two code names together under any circumstances."

He didn't ask me if I had any questions, and I knew not to ask any. He just motioned me to get into the jeep. That was the first and last time he ever spoke to me about the "gimmick." Even on the ride back our conversation was popcorn talk.

The next day I met with Colonel Tibbets. There was no discussion of my "ride" with McClanahan. We proceeded to an isolated building at the far end of the field. Inside was a table, a few chairs—all standard military issue, functional and uncomfortable—and a single phone on the wall.

A captain, whom I assumed to be a security officer, stood silently throughout our meeting. No notes were taken. In fact, there were no writing implements in the room. I clearly understood without being told that what we discussed in this room was not to be recorded in any manner. This would become standard procedure for many aspects of our training.

In his usual, low-key, taciturn style, Colonel Tibbets began by explaining that he had been given broad authority to create an entire organization that would be outside the usual military chain of command. He would form a composite group that would be almost totally self-supporting. It would have its own bomber, transport, military police, matériel, ordnance, engineering, air service, and base service squadrons. I knew he could requisition any equipment, matériel, or personnel he wanted from any source anywhere, without any questions being asked. This was unheard of for the military, with its rigid bureaucracy. What was even more incredible was that a lieutenant colonel had this power, which most generals only dream of.

There was one slight problem. By invoking the unit code name Silverplate, Colonel Tibbets had complete authority to select any personnel from any command in the military, and he had decided to take an entire combat-ready bomber squadron, the 393rd, from the 504th Group, based in Harvard, Nebraska. These crews would be understandably suspicious of, and even upset by, their removal from their own group just as it was preparing for transfer overseas and their reassignment to the Middle of Nowhere, U.S.A., with no explanation of what they would be training to do. Even though Tibbets had the power to order what he wanted, he had the insight to know that his success depended on the loyalty of the men under his command. That loyalty in turn required his respect for the strengths and weaknesses of highly competitive men working together under trying circumstances. If I was to be in charge of the training, the unusual position I should hold would be squadron commander of the bombers. But the 393rd already had a well-liked commander, Lieutenant Colonel Tom Classen, whom the men respected and trusted. If Classen were replaced after they arrived at Wendover, it could destroy the morale of these highly skilled crews.

The Colonel had made it clear that I could have any position I wanted to carry out my assignment. But I think he knew that my loyalty was to him and that I would recognize the difficulty of the situation. We talked it through. One solution was for me to assume the position of deputy squadron commander. But this posed two new problems. It would be highly unusual for the deputy to take over the training of the crews from the squadron commander, and it might even be seen as undermining Tom Classen's authority within the squadron. Second, replacing the current deputy, James Hopkins, might create the same morale problem as replacing the commander. We looked at the organizational chart. I noticed that a newly created transport squadron, the 320th, was awaiting assignment of a permanent commander.

The 320th Transport Squadron existed on the organizational chart only. Unlike the 393rd, this unit was to be created out of thin air by Colonel Tibbets, who would requisition men and matériel to form the squadron. So that the unit could be officially activated, Major Hubert Konopacki would serve as the interim commander until a permanent one was appointed.

"Well, boss, what if I take the transport squadron?" I asked. "But for it to work," I quickly added, "I'll need one B-29 and its crew assigned to me so that I can conduct the squadron training. This shouldn't ruffle too many feathers, especially if it's sold as very specialized training for a top secret mission." This arrangement would be incomprehensively strange to a military observer.

The colonel gave me that thin, reassuring smile of his.

And so I became the only officer in the air corps ever to command a transport squadron and at the same time have an assignment to a bomb squadron.

It became painfully obvious that we had a limited amount of time to perfect the tactics of delivery, even while the scientists were working feverishly to complete development of a functioning bomb. Although we knew roughly what the bomb would look like and weigh, it was still far from certain that the scientists would be able to fit a working "physics package" into the predetermined shape of the bomb. And, of course, the physical limitations of the B-29 left little room for last-minute adjustments. We would be training for months in total isolation to accomplish a mission that might never happen. It was one thing to have a controlled chain reaction in a pile of uranium the size of a room, and quite another to achieve the same result within the limited confines of a globally shaped bomb that was intended to free fall from 30,000 feet. But our job was only to be ready to deliver the "gimmick." The rest was out of our control.

From the beginning we learned as we went. We had no ballistic tables for a bomb of this weight and shape. No carrying hooks to hold its ten-thousand-pound weight. No reliable fuses to trigger the complicated firing mechanism for a plutonium device. No experience in the precise, high-speed, high-altitude, sharp-banking turns critical to our survival after the release of the bomb. No reliable data on what the bomb would do, or even if it would do anything at all.

As we went along, we would also be redesigning the B-29 itself to accommodate the requirements of this special mission. Those changes would ultimately prove essential to the successful completion of my mission on the second atomic strike and contribute to saving the lives of my crew and me.

The force that Albert Einstein had set in motion with his urgent plea to President Roosevelt in 1939, warning that Germany possessed the ability and resources to develop a bomb of unimaginable destructive power and that any nation that had such a weapon could rule the world, was now hurtling toward reality. The science had gone beyond theory to fulfillment. An atomic bomb was no longer "possible" but "probable." The Germans and the Japanese were both working on atomic weapons, and before long the Russians, Hitler's former ally, would also possess the basic science.

I hoped to God we would have the weapon first.

EIGHT

IT SAT ON a dolly beside a parked reconfigured prototype of a B-29 in the bomb-loading area, in an isolated corner of Wendover. A lieutenant in coveralls was engaged in a discussion with several other men in coveralls. It was about ten feet long, maybe five feet in diameter, and was painted mustard-yellow. We would soon refer to it and the scores of duplicates we received later as "pumpkins" because of their shape and color. The pumpkin was a concrete-filled ten-thousand-pound replica of the final exterior design of the first plutonium bomb. In eleven months, after considerable refinements to its interior at Los Alamos, New Mexico, the real thing would take mankind across the threshold from theoretical physics into the nuclear age.

The parked B-29 was both a reminder of the dual tracks on which our scientists in the Manhattan Project were proceeding and a testament to the uncertainty of how best to proceed. Originally the bomb was to have been a fairly primitive design using a uranium core at the end of a long gun barrel. A particle of uranium would be fired down the barrel and hit the uranium core, initiating a chain reaction. It was basic atomic physics. At the beginning, the gun barrel design seemed the most practical. However, the scientists were still working out the minimum dimensions into which they could build a working uranium bomb. To accommodate the final design and provide a yardstick for the scientists, the center section of the belly of this B-29 had been cut out from the front of the forward bomb bay to the rear of its aft bomb bay, creating a single bomb bay that allowed for a bomb with a maximum length of twenty-eight feet. Ultimately, the scientists would get the package for the uranium bomb down to ten feet, which could be loaded into the forward bomb bay. Only one untested uranium bomb would ever be made, and Paul Tibbets would drop it over Hiroshima.

Later, the scientists solved the technical problems of a much more sophisticated plutonium implosion device that made the uranium bomb instantly obsolete. But for all the complex physics and sublime engineering represented by the pumpkin, there was a simple and as yet unsolved mystery facing us that morning. How would we get that oversized boulder into the airplane? No one had thought about this rather basic principle: the bomb had to be put into the plane before it could be dropped. A two-billion-dollar weapons system suddenly depended on a group of army officers and enlisted men who, although they were crackerjack ordnance men, didn't know the difference between a neutron and an electron.

I introduced myself to the lieutenant and then took a few minutes to assess the situation. Inside the forward bomb bay, a truss had been rigged up to the shelves at the bottom of the bay with stanchions extending upward. At the top, crossbars had been welded diagonally from corner to corner with a hook in the center to hold the bomb on its side by an eyelet. Electric motors had been set into the four corners at the top of the stanchions, to which cables would be attached running from smaller hooks welded to four points on the pumpkin. Assuming that we could get the pumpkin into position under the bomb bay, I had some questions about the integrity of this system and the reliability of the hook. But first things first.

Because of the pumpkin's five-foot diameter, we couldn't roll it under the bomb bay with the bay doors open. Nor could we get it past the nosewheel to roll it into place down to the bomb bay. Either way, we didn't have a five-foot clearance. The lieutenant and I came to a consensus that the only possible solution for the moment was to lift the nose off the ground and roll the pumpkin into place below the bomb bay. The ground crew found a large tarpaulin, which they draped over the vertical stabilizer on the tail section, being careful not to damage the elevators on the horizontal stabilizer. With the wheels securely chocked in place to prevent the airplane from rolling, six or eight men on either side of the tail pulled down on the ends of the tarp, the body of the aircraft pivoting on the wheels, the nose rising. Another group rolled the dolly with the pumpkin under the nose section and down to the forward bomb bay. The nose was then lowered, with the pumpkin positioned under the bomb bay. Rube Goldberg would have been proud.

Success, however, was far from certain. We still had to get the pumpkin up and connected to the hook. Each of the four motors at the corners of the stanchions had its own control. To lift this ten-thousand-pound globe, the four motors would have to lift simultaneously and at the same rate of speed in order to keep the pumpkin's weight balanced. On our first try, a cable snapped in midair and the pumpkin went crashing to the ground. Laboriously, we repositioned the pumpkin and

tried again. Finally we got it attached in the bomb bay. At this
rate, it would be more efficient to roll the bomb to the target.

The solution was to build a concrete-lined pit with a hy-
draulic lift, like the lift at a gas station. The pumpkin would
be loaded onto the lift and lowered into the pit. The airplane
would be backed over the pit and the pumpkin would then be
lifted up into the bomb bay. We made an emergency request
to the Army Corps of Engineers to construct a pit to our specifications. It would be late November—approximately two
months—before the pit was ready. In the meantime, I proceeded with my assignment to fly test drops of the pumpkins,
and the ground crews became most adept at loading them with
the system they had developed.

In late September, the crews of the 393rd bomber squadron
found themselves in the middle of the Utah salt flats without
a mission and with just one B-29 available to them. Tibbets
briefed the crews, telling them that they were part of a highly
secret project that could bring the war to a speedy end. He
gave them no details about what that project was. Because
there were no airplanes for them to fly yet, Colonel Tibbets
immediately gave them ten days' leave to go home. He told
them this would be their last leave for a very long time, and
he left them with one absolute rule—not now or ever were they
to discuss the base, the airplanes, the training, or the fact that
they were working on a project with anyone—including their
families. Absolutely no one. Security was the single most
important responsibility they had. It was also best if they didn't
ask too many questions. Any violation would be dealt with
summarily and decisively.

It was already clear at that point that the defining character-
istic of the project would be that nothing proceeded in orderly
sequence. There was so much to do in such a limited time that

details had to be worked out on a rolling basis. In fact, the official orders activating the top secret 509th Composite Group weren't even issued until December 17, 1944. The breadth and complexity of the project and the time constraints were almost numbing. Organizational details were moving ahead on their own.

Wendover Field was ill equipped for the massive influx of men and machines that was under way. The field and its ancillary services, designed for a small contingent of fighters, were unsuitable for the demands of a heavy bomber group. By December, over eight hundred officers and other personnel had crowded into the existing facilities, and by the end of January 1945 the number had ballooned to over fifteen hundred. Colonel Tibbets had to create an entire self-contained and self-sustaining unit overnight—security, communications, staff support, armament, weather, photography, personnel, intelligence, cooks, bakers, and candlestick makers. Supplies had to be brought in and maintenance and facility improvements had to be made on an ongoing basis. All of this quickly made getting the 509th into operational shape a monumental challenge.

Then, once the organization had been put into motion and staffed, Tibbets had to select the crews, develop unique tactics for delivering an untested weapon that might never come to be, train the crews in the new tactics—and in the B-29, which was still undergoing design changes—develop a strategy to get the weapon to a target, and coordinate with scientists who were unsure if a functioning weapon could be delivered in time.

The clock was ticking, and the Japanese killing machine was continuing to inflict unimaginable horrors on American soldiers, marines, airmen, and sailors struggling in the Pacific at places like Guadalcanal, Bougainville, Tarawa, Saipan, Guam, Palau, and Leyte Gulf. Back at Wendover, we would hear of the atrocities our Allied prisoners of war were enduring. General Sherman's oft-quoted "War is hell" failed to convey the depth of the horror. A more appropriate metaphor would have been Dante's Inferno.

Failure for us, then, was simply not an option. Helping to end the war was the single focus of our entire effort.

A small group of civilian technicians and scientists operating under the code name Project Alberta were already at Wendover when I arrived. They served as liaison between Silverplate and the Manhattan Engineering District, a nondescript official designation for the Manhattan Project. The task of these civilians at this stage was to compile data on the flying characteristics of the pumpkin and test various fuses being developed at Los Alamos.

No ballistic tables for a bomb of this shape and weight yet existed. Thus it would be critical to measure the pumpkin's flight after release to develop ballistic tables for bombing accuracy. If the bomb wobbled or tumbled in flight, no one would be certain where it would land. Such a problem could be solved by refining the design of the fins to assure a true and predictable arc after release. But the refinements could be determined only after repetitive drops on targets had been observed by the scientists. They could then calibrate not only the accuracy of the intended target but also the bomb's flight through the air under varying conditions.

We had three bombing ranges: Target A, at Tonopah, Nevada, near the California border; Target B, at the Salton Sea in Southern California, about one hundred miles east of San Diego, where a large white raft was anchored at the southern end of an oval-shaped lake that ran north and south; and Target C, an abandoned army air corps range near Wendover. Observation posts were set up at each range incorporating photographic cameras using high-speed film and motion picture cameras to record the arc and speed of the bombs' descent to the target. Perfecting the aerodynamics for a bomb of this weight and shape was difficult at first, especially because changes were being made to the interior and exterior tail section that affected the pumpkin's shape and weight. Accurately dropping a ten-thousand-pound globular-shaped object from 30,000 feet presented its own set of technical barriers for those trying to harness the forces of the atom. A standard joke was that the safest place to set up the cameras and the observation crews was right on the bull's-eye because that was the last place the pumpkin would hit.

After each drop, the Project Alberta staff would study the results and make incremental changes in the drop protocol or the fin design. Colonel Tibbets or a technician at the bomb-loading area would communicate to me the changes the scientists wanted us to make. They might request a new altitude at which to release the pumpkin or a change in our approach to the target—such as "up sun," "down sun," or "cross sun"—to allow for better observation. Mathematical data from these ballistic tests would be preloaded into the Norden bombsight tables for every speed and altitude of the B-29, allowing the bombardier to accurately drop the bomb. (When the time came to carry out live bomb drops, scientists would be on the planes over Hiroshima and Nagasaki to confirm the accuracy of the data they had compiled from these tests.)

During the months of October and November we also tested the fuses for the bomb. As any air crew would, my crew and I would have to have a perfect fuse. Nothing is more unsettling than a premature explosion of a conventional iron bomb under an aircraft. Of course, I was the only one on board who knew this was not going be anything close to a conventional bomb.

Shortly after we began the test drops, the scientists started to hang fuses on the pumpkin. The results were not encouraging. Sometimes the fuses worked, sometimes they didn't. Unlike perfecting a stable flying configuration for the bomb itself, perfecting the fuses would remain a nagging problem right up to the day of my mission to Nagasaki. One incident occurred when I was on approach to Target C, still within visual range of the base. My bombardier, Captain Kermit Beahan, released the pumpkin at the aiming point for the designated target. The fuse detonated under the plane. If we had been carrying even a conventional bomb, we'd have been blown out of the sky.

My crew and I were at the pick-and-shovel level. We had barely any contact with the Alberta people, even after hours. I thought they were billeted in a hotel in Wendover, because I never saw them at the officers' club or at any social functions on or off the base. I don't know if this was by design or chance, but as I told my crew on day one, "This is something new we're trying and that's all the conversation there will be. Just do your jobs."

The atmosphere of secrecy permeated every level of activity at the base. My crew never engaged in any conversation about the pumpkin. No one commented on it—not even innocuous comments about its size, shape, weight, what it might be, or where it might be used. This level of secrecy was very unusual for any group of men working together so closely. All incoming and outgoing mail and phone calls were monitored and censored by intelligence officers, regardless of anyone's rank or position. Reminders of security were everywhere, from a poetic sign admonishing,

What You Hear Here
What You See Here
When You Leave Here
Let It STAY HERE!

to the less subtly posted restricted areas patrolled by heavily armed military police who conveyed a simple and potentially lethal message: Stay out unless you're authorized to be here. The existence of our own military police company was, in fact, unheard of within a bomb group in the air force and added to the atmosphere of secrecy. They provided a very visible show of security, armed not only with standard-issue sidearms and Garand carbines but also with Thompson submachine guns and jeep-mounted .30-caliber machine guns. They weren't there to break up barroom brawls.

As the influx of men and material continued through January 1945, barbed wire sprouted from the ground like tumbleweed that blew across the vast desert expanse that had become our home. More and more portions of the base became restricted areas, open only to authorized personnel bearing proper identification.

The only totally secure communications link with Los Alamos was by a single telephone line strung directly from Wendover to Los Alamos over the mountains. There was no regular telephone exchange. The line was patrolled by heavily armed security police. God help the fool who wandered near that line. The phone itself was the single phone in the secure, debugged room on the base. I later learned that the room had been lined with lead to prevent bugging or eavesdropping and that the phone was rarely unattended. Neither Wendover nor Los Alamos was ever referred to by name. Wendover was "Site K" and Los Alamos was "Site Y." Scientists and our personnel going from Wendover to Los Alamos or to Wendover from Los Alamos never traveled directly. They would fly to Albuquerque and then go on to their destination by car or truck. Whenever our personnel went to Los Alamos via Albuquerque, they removed all insignia identifying them as army air corps and replaced it with Corps of Engineer insignia. Neither the

casual observer nor a trained spy could draw any outward connection between the air force and the people at Los Alamos.

The B-29s wouldn't arrive until December. By mid-October,
B-17s were coming in so that the crews of the 393rd could
begin practice bombing and navigational missions to keep their
skills honed and be introduced to the demands of long-range
navigation. Our actual B-29 missions could involve a three-
thousand-mile round-trip flight over water, so navigational
training became a high priority. Even a minute miscalculation
could result in missing the intended destination by many miles,
given the distances to target. By then it was pretty clear that if
the mission were ever flown, it would be flown against the
Japanese. The Germans were collapsing on both the western
and eastern fronts in Europe.

Because of the suicidal defense the Japanese were mounting
at each island assault, it was uncertain how close to Japan our
base of operation would be. While General Eisenhower was
beginning his breakout from the Normandy beachhead in
France in June 1944, Admiral Nimitz was launching the invasion of Saipan, another stepping-stone drawing American
ground and air forces closer to Japan. Of the 32,000 Japanese
soldiers defending the island, 28,000 died in a futile attempt to
beat back the overwhelming invasion force. Repeated suicidal
banzai attacks by the Japanese inflicted massive casualties on
the American forces—16,000 casualties, including 3,426 dead.
When the battle was lost, hundreds of Japanese soldiers and
civilians committed suicide rather than surrender and bring dis-
honor to themselves, their families, and their country. A month
later, a few hundred more marines died in a nine-day battle
taking a flyspeck of rock in the Mariana Islands called Tinian.

Later the marines and the army, supported by the navy,
would take the strategic island of Iwo Jima, just 770 miles off

the coast of Japan, at a cost of 27,000 American casualties, including over 6,000 dead. Hundreds of B-29 crews owed their lives to those marines and soldiers and sailors because disabled B-29s returning from missions over mainland Japan were able to make emergency landings at Iwo.

Shortly after my arrival at Wendover, Colonel Tibbets asked me to join him for a briefing he was to receive from operations analyst E. J. Workman, then president of the University of New Mexico. Dr. Workman had been developing a profile of Japanese fighter capabilities at high altitudes. Inside the secure room, Tibbets, the ever-present security officer, and I listened as Workman detailed the mathematical calculations and proofs that showed that at 30,000 feet, the Japanese Zero had a very limited capability to attack a target and fire accurately. After getting up that high, based on various aerodynamic principles, a Zero could make only one pass at a B-29 before being unable to maintain its altitude—in pilots' terms, the fighter would literally run out of air to support the aircraft and fall out of the sky for not having sufficient lift. By the time the Zero could recover and make a second climb, the B-29, with its IAS (indicated airspeed) of over 250 miles an hour, would be long gone. The total time that the Zero would be on target would be less than one second, assuming the B-29 took no evasive action. To take evasive action would require maximum speed, maneuverability, and altitude. In other words, less weight. If we could make the airplane lighter, we could fly higher, faster, and with more maneuverability.

After the briefing Tibbets remarked in typical fashion, "Any pilot who can't get out of the way for one second doesn't belong in this outfit."

After Dr. Workman left, the colonel asked my opinion about removing all the armament from the B-29—the turrets, guns, and ammunition—and leaving in just the 20mm cannon in the tail. He explained that the airplane would then be lighter by about seven thousand pounds, which would get us the increased speed, maneuverability, and altitude. This would be much more valuable to the safety of the crews than the guns. I told him I thought it was a terrific idea. Knowing the predisposition of bomber crews to rely on their guns against enemy fighters, Tibbets wondered what I thought the crews' reaction would be.

"If you explain your reasoning," I answered, "I'm sure they'll see the advantages."

He then asked me to meet with the pilots and "sell the idea to them." I would be the stalking horse. If the men didn't respond well, Tibbets would still be left with the option of trying another approach without having been directly confronted by dissent from the crews.

The 393rd had been reorganized into fifteen crews with three flight commanders in charge of five crews each. All of the pilots were intelligent men, and I believed that once they understood the science they would embrace the idea of removing the armament. I also believed that even at this early stage they respected Paul Tibbets's ability and would accept the changes if he thought they were important. Tibbets could simply have ordered the changes made, but in this case, he was asking them to accept something radical and wanted them included in the process. In the end, the armaments would have to be removed if the mission were to have every chance for success.

From a personal standpoint I loved the idea because it would get rid of the forward gun turret, which took up a lot of space in the cockpit. As big as the cockpit was, the thought of its being more spacious and comfortable was music to my ears. Unlike Colonel Tibbets, I liked to move around during flight.

I decided that instead of calling a meeting of all fifteen pilots, a better approach would be to call together the three flight commanders. If they could be won over, they could take the idea back to their pilots. At first they hesitated. "How do we know what capability the Zero will have in the future?" "If they make the high-altitude improvements before our mission, we'll be sitting ducks. Big sitting ducks."

I let the conversation and debate continue so that everyone could get his thoughts out on the table. Then I set out the two key considerations.

"First, our mission could very well end the war," I offered. "Removing the guns is just one of many risks we'll be facing. Our job will be to get to the target, whatever and wherever it might be. If taking the armament off increases our chances, then based on what we know today, it's the right decision." No questions.

"Second," I continued, "no one is a better strategist about the use of airplanes in combat than Colonel Tibbets. If he thinks this is a good idea, then we owe him the loyalty to make it work." That pretty much ended the discussion—except for a unanimous vote.

Now that Tibbets had jumped that hurdle and avoided any reduction of confidence within the crews, he needed to determine if we could remove the turrets ourselves and patch the holes without ordering new airplanes. I had our engineering squadron remove the forward turret and make the necessary repair to the hole in the fuselage. Then I needed to test the strength of the patch when the cabin was pressurized at high altitudes. Taking the plane up to 30,000 feet could be both inconclusive and dangerous. Inconclusive because, even if we stayed up for hours, it would not mean that the patch was secure; we would need to stress the patch for an uninterrupted and extensive period of time. Dangerous because if it did blow, it could rip off a substantial piece of the fuselage.

The nearest modification center that had pressurization equipment was in Denver. I flew the B-29 to Denver, cruising at a minimum safe altitude, unpressurized. At Denver, the workers inserted hoses, sealed off all the doors and openings, and pressurized the interior of the airplane, bringing the pressure up to the equivalent of what it would be at 30,000 feet. In a few minutes the patch blew. End of experiment.

Tibbets decided that new airplanes would have to be manufactured with the turrets removed and other design changes built in on the assembly line. As long as new airplanes were going to be ordered, he wanted them equipped with the new Curtis Electric reversible propellers that would allow the plane to stop in a shorter distance on landing, with pneumatic bomb bay doors that snapped open and shut, thus decreasing air drag on the airplane, and with fuel injection for better fuel economy. These changes would prove to be critically important in helping me successfully complete my mission over Nagasaki and in saving the lives of my crew and me.

Having made the decision, Colonel Tibbets invoked "Silverplate" and asked Dayton to order twenty-five brand-new redesigned B-29s from Boeing. Boeing selected the Martin plant in Omaha for this production. Engineers worked around the clock to design the changes. When they were completed, Boeing inserted the new design into its assembly line.

The decision confirmed the total independence of the 509th for anyone who had any lingering question about it. Like General Frank Armstrong. On the military organizational chart, the 509th was "attached" to the 315th Bomb Wing under the command of General Armstrong, who had moved from Grand Island to Colorado Springs. The reality was that General Armstrong had no authority over the 509th and didn't even know what it was training to do. When word of the redesign order got to his attention, he immediately injected himself and made it clear that he was going to Wendover to find out what "those guys" were doing. Given his experience with the Eighth Air Force in England and the losses sustained by his bomber command at the hands of the Luftwaffe's Messerschmitts, the idea of removing the armament from the B-29s must have seemed insane. In short order he was unceremoniously told that he could not go to Wendover under any circumstances. And that was the end of that.

Except for two 20mm cannons in the tail, the 509th would go to war unarmed.

NINE

THE TARGET WAS a circle with a diameter of three hundred feet painted on the ground. We were expected to drop the pumpkin into this dot from an altitude of 30,000 feet with an accuracy of impact no more than two hundred feet from the center of the target. All things considered, this was the easy part.

The problem was: once the pumpkin was replaced by the bomb, would we have enough time to get out of there after we released? Without knowing the exact explosive force that would be unleashed or even the true nature of the explosion, the scientists at Los Alamos offered their best estimate. To survive we would have to get the airplane a *minimum* of eight miles away from the blast.

It was left to Colonel Tibbets to figure out how to accomplish such a maneuver. From 30,000 feet, the bomb would detonate forty-three seconds after we released it. Conventional wisdom dictated that it was physically impossible for the B-29, traveling at 320 miles an hour ground speed, to be eight miles away in forty-three seconds. If the plane were to continue in a straight line after release of the bomb, given the speed of the B-29, we would be approximately five miles away from the blast in forty-three seconds. Not enough. We could be blown out of the sky.

Tibbets's answer to the problem was brilliant. The bomb, of course, would be released *before* we were over the center of the target. On release, it would initially travel at the same speed as the airplane, approximately 320 miles per hour ground speed, then fall in a trajectory toward the target. Tibbets used a classic geometric formula we all learned in junior high school, a gift from the ancient Egyptians and Greeks, that calculates the distance from a point on a tangent to a semicircle. If, immediately upon release, we banked the B-29 into a sharp, rapid, diving 155-degree turn—going back in the same direction we came from in a tight arc, or a tangent to a semicircle—we could take the airplane eight slant-range miles or more away from the blast in forty-three seconds, even though the maneuver would reduce our altitude by about seventeen hundred feet.

It was a totally unheard-of tactic for bomber pilots trained to fly in tight formations into and away from the target. But once Tibbets had devised it, it was up to the pilots to execute it. There were no training schools or manuals on this one. We would have to train ourselves.

The irony was that once we perfected the maneuver and got the airplane up to twelve miles away in time, the scientists were still not completely sure that that would be enough. This was to be the first bomb used in combat that had not been tested live from an airplane. We would never know for sure what would happen until after the atomic bomb was actually dropped.

With the arrival of the B-29s in November, Tibbets wanted

intense practice to begin for bombing accuracy and perfection of the evasive maneuver. The first of our new redesigned airplanes would not be delivered until the spring of 1945, but the B-29s available to us would serve the immediate task at hand. Tibbets and his crew and my crew and I led by example in executing the maneuver. Day after day the crews ran missions over our three bombing ranges in the desert and on the Salton Sea. Pilots who failed to master the technique were given additional special training. The pressure was there to milk the very best each man could deliver. All elements of the groups—engineering, support, and air crews—worked tirelessly and sometimes around the clock. It had to be picture-perfect right. Although all the crews made good progress in improved proficiency, of the fifteen crews, three began to emerge with the best overall results: Colonel Tibbets's crew, Captain Claude Eatherly's crew, and my crew.

The nucleus of the 509th had been formed when Tibbets invited pilots Don Albury and Bob Lewis, flight engineer John Kuharek, and me to join him at Wendover. He specifically requested three combat veterans be assigned to him: Tom Ferebee, his bombardier; Dutch Van Kirk, his navigator; and bombardier Kermit Beahan, all of whom had served with him in North Africa and England. Another highly experienced navigator, Jim Van Pelt, was brought along on the recommendation of Ferebee and Van Kirk. From this core group Tibbets formed two crews, one for himself and the other for me. His crew consisted of Lewis as his copilot, Ferebee, and Van Kirk. My crew had Albury as copilot, Kuharek, Van Pelt, and Beahan. The rest of the crews would soon be filled out by Tibbets based on recommendations received from his key people. When he or I was not flying as airplane commander, our copilots, Lewis and Albury, took command of our crews, an arrangement unique to Tibbets and me.

Our past experience with testing the B-29 over an extended period of time gave our crews an advantage over other highly qualified pilots who came through in the training exercises. Pilots are by nature competitive. Intensifying this natural tendency were the isolation of Wendover, the relentlessness of the training, and the uncertainty about what we were training to do. For the most part the competition was good-natured and the degree of cooperation among all the personnel was exemplary. A sense of common cause bound us together in this desolate place to train for an ultrasecret mission that might end the war.

Although, as with any group, problems and conflicts would arise, the colonel kept his focus squarely on one object: deliver the weapon to a target. To meet this goal he would suffer fools—to a point, overlook indiscretions—if they were small, and even tolerate odd behavior—but only if the skills of the men involved justified keeping them.

Being encapsulated in this isolated place under heavy guard and constant surveillance was wearing not only on the men but also on their families who had joined them. Dorothy and I had driven to Wendover from Grand Island in a beat-up 1938 eight-cylinder Pontiac coupe I had bought in Florida for $250. Don Albury and his wife, Roberta, had driven in tandem with us in their car. The first night out we pulled into Cheyenne, Wyoming. Dorothy was ill with a high fever, and our car was on its last legs, having struggled up the Rocky Mountains to Cheyenne. I recommended to Dorothy a time-tested remedy—a glass of warm milk with two shots of straight 100-proof bourbon. She went out like a light and the next morning was feeling fine.

The Pontiac was another matter. A mechanic at the local service station confirmed what I had already suspected: the compression in the engine was at about 28 percent of what it should have been. Since the rest of the trip would be less arduous, I asked him to do what he could just to get me to Salt Lake. He poured some elixir into the crankcase and off we went, this time descending toward the Great American Desert and Wendover. Whatever he put in there worked. The Pontiac limped into Rock Spring, Wyoming, that afternoon, the next day into Salt Lake City, and finally, on the fourth day, into Wendover.

Living accommodations at the base were Spartan and in short supply. Priority for base housing was given to civilian personnel with critically needed skills. As an officer, I was entitled to accommodations at the bachelor officers' quarters. Military dependents, however, had to fend for themselves. Dorothy had resigned her commission after we were married and was now a civilian nurse at the base, which qualified us for base housing. Our first house was a two-room, twenty-foot-by-twenty-foot concrete block structure with a concrete slab floor, which was how all housing at Wendover was constructed. We had a bedroom and an all-purpose living room, kitchen, rest room, you name it. Later, Colonel Tibbets arranged for us to move into a larger four-room house with two bedrooms, a living room, a kitchen, and a bath. We had two coal stoves, one potbelly for heat and the other for cooking. It was, by comparison, palatial.

For Dorothy and all the other wives life was particularly tough at Wendover. The men at least had their military responsibilities, as difficult as those jobs might be. But the women had been plunked down in a barren outpost to cope with endless sand, dust, mice, rats, bitter cold, wilting heat, and isolation. The isolation was made more palpable because we couldn't tell our families anything about what we were doing. This kind of secrecy would invite strains for any married couple. The base wives also had to live every day with the reality that their husbands might be sent overseas and killed. Dorothy never complained or pressed me about why I had volunteered to bring her to this place or what I was doing there. Instead, she dedicated herself to her job as a civilian nurse at the base hospital.

Fortunately, we were young and resilient. We found a way to make our own fun and entertainment. Dorothy and I invited our friends over for dinner, and they us. We ran dances and other events at the officers' club. This drew us all together in confronting our common condition.

When we ventured outside of the base, even the town itself reminded no one of home. Wendover had a split personality. It sits dead center on the line dividing Nevada and Utah, equidistant between Elko, Nevada, 125 miles to the west, and Salt Lake City, 125 miles to the east at the southern tip of the Great Salt Lake. Half the town was Mormon dry and the other half was wide-open, no holds barred, freewheeling Nevada wet. When we dined at the local State Line Hotel, one half of the dining room served us cocktails with our meal, but the other side could not. To our left, wine, women, and song—not to mention unrestricted gambling. To our right, buttoned-up restraint. These two cities in one location could have been on different planets.

The combination of our living conditions and our training drew the crews closer together. Like most airplane commanders, I tended to spend much of my time with my crew. Each man brought a unique but complementary strength to our common cause. As a unit, we developed unquestioning faith in the character, ability, and judgment of each other.

Captain Don Albury and I had worked together since the testing program at Eglin. He was a steady, unflappable, even-tempered professional—and a skilled pilot. I knew that I could count on him without question, regardless of the situation. Captain Jim Van Pelt, assigned to me by Tibbets, excelled as a navigator. With a man like Jim on my team I had the luxury of not worrying about anything except flying the airplane. Jim would guide me to where I was supposed to be and get me home on a true and efficient course. John Kuharek, my flight engineer at Eglin, was reliable and resourceful. He knew how to get the most out of the airplane and was a second pair of eyes for me in monitoring the various aircraft systems in flight.

And finally there was Kermit Beahan, my bombardier. Of all the men I knew during the war, he was the most generous, engaging, and full of life. He had an enthusiasm for life, a zest for living—not in any flamboyant or overbearing way, but with a genuine joy that attracted people to him. People liked being around Kermit. With his slow, southeast Texas drawl, he made you feel at ease. Kermit was a true artist with a bombsight. If it was possible to deliver a bomb to its intended target, he was the man to do it. When we named our B-29, I decided to let the crew offer ideas and then vote on it. The name that emerged as the unanimous favorite was, in honor of Kermit, *The Great Artiste*. It was a double entendre. Kermit was not only an artiste with the Norden bombsight, he was also an artiste with the ladies. His charm and sense of humor attracted women. They loved him.

But Kermit was far more than a skilled technician or a charmer. He had survived extensive combat in North Africa and Europe, had been shot down four times in combat, and had once survived a crash landing in the African desert that killed his pilot and copilot. The only residue of these experiences was a slight stutter, a reminder of the trauma that followed most of the airmen who survived the meat grinder of the air war in Europe. It was therefore extraordinary to me how steadily and calmly he carried out his duties. When Kermit leaned over the bombsight, it was as if he closed off the entire world around him. He concentrated on the target with single-mindedness, regardless of what was happening around him. His steady hand made the minute adjustments that meant the difference between hitting the target or hitting something unintended. In those days, we had no laser-guided smart bombs, just the skill of men working together.

It was Kermit whom Colonel Tibbets chose in December 1944 to go to England to consult with the Royal Air Force about a carrying hook for our bomb. The RAF was dropping ten-thousand-pound conventional iron bombs, and Tibbets wanted an assessment of whether their hook could accommodate the pumpkins we were dropping. Based on what Kermit learned, we requisitioned sample hooks and blueprints from the British. With some modification, this is what we used.

I should note this trip was no vacation. During Kermit's visit, the Germans were showering London with V-2 rockets. For all its starkness, Wendover was at least safe.

Claude Eatherly had come in with the 393rd. He was a charmer of a different stripe. A good-looking guy, in the mold of a hotshot pilot, he was flamboyant, erratic, impulsive, and at times, reckless. Claude liked to gamble and was not averse to getting embroiled in fights with the local constabulary and our security people. Our outfit's Sergeant Bilko, he always had one scheme or another brewing. He lived life big. He was also a guy you couldn't resist. No matter what he did, the guys couldn't stay upset at him. I liked him. He was a fun guy to be around, to have a beer with, and he always had an original tall tale to tell. But above all else, Claude was a seasoned and experienced pilot. He had the ability to fly with great precision; during our training sessions, he handled every type of simulated emergency situation I threw at him with competence and cool.

After the missions over Hiroshima and Nagasaki had been

completed, and while we were still on Tinian, Claude would often remark that he was going to make a ton of money off the atomic bombings after the war. I believe he came close. He is the one who fabricated the story that he had witnessed the dropping of the atomic bomb over Hiroshima and that seeing the blast made such an impact on him he went crazy. The story emerged in Texas after the war. It was part of his successful insanity defense in federal district court. Claude had been arrested in Texas and tried in federal court for armed robbery of a general store that happened to house a United States Post Office. He beat the rap and gained notoriety for a while. The press, naturally, picked up his story without ever verifying it. And year after year the story gained more acceptance with each reprinting in the newspapers. If any reporters had bothered to check, they would have learned that Claude not only didn't witness the atomic blast, he had, in fact, flown one of the weather planes on August 6 that was nowhere near Hiroshima at the time of the blast. But once in print the story took on a life of its own that persists to this day. Claude did indeed have a sad time after the war. But his tale about witnessing the blast is not true. In true Eatherly style, however, it did get him out of a jam.

Then there was Bob Lewis. Bob had been with Tibbets from the start of the B-29 testing program back at Eglin. He was one of the most experienced and capable B-29 pilots in the air force, having benefited from Tibbets's guiding hand. But unlike Tibbets, who was reserved and self-assured, Lewis seemed driven to establish an aura about himself as a fearless bomber pilot. Competition among the crews to score high in their proficiency ratings was healthy and always collegial. For Bob Lewis, however, it was more. He wanted to be the best so he could stand apart from all the other pilots. His style wore thin with many in our squadron.

As Colonel Tibbets became more enmeshed in the overall management of the 509th, Lewis lost what he thought was a special one-to-one relationship with him. He compensated, I suspect, by a more outward show of odd behavior. Over time, his behavior became more erratic. Once he took an airplane for an unauthorized trip home for Christmas. As time passed at Wendover, and later on Tinian, Lewis became a more and more disagreeable fellow. As incredible as it sounds, he believed that he, and not Paul Tibbets, would command the strike airplane when the mission we were training for was flown.

Lewis, like Eatherly, also added to the popular myths that have surrounded the atomic missions and the men who flew them. To my knowledge, they are the only two from the crews of the 393rd who, to pursue their own agendas, distorted the historical record. Sometime after the war, Lewis attracted a lot of press attention when he reported that upon seeing the explosion over Hiroshima he'd entered in his log, "My God, what have we done!" A reflective, remorseful, and dramatic remark by Paul Tibbets's copilot. Unfortunately, it didn't happen that way. Not only would such a statement have been totally out of character for Bob Lewis, but, in fact, he said quite the opposite at the time. As heard by members of the crew on the flight deck, and told to me many times thereafter, what Bob actually said was, "My God, look at that son of a bitch go!" His written entry in the log says only "My God." What I can say directly is that, after the flight, Lewis was excited and elated that the mission had been a success, as was everyone else. There were no expressions of doubt or remorse. We had done our job.

The training continued through November and into December. All the crews were becoming more comfortable with carrying the ten-thousand-pound pumpkin and gaining more confidence in executing the quick banking maneuver. Meanwhile, more personnel were pouring into Wendover. An endless stream of civilian and military liaisons with the Manhattan Project were coming and going. Each visit of scientists brought some further refinement or new idea to facilitate our mission. This, of course, only added to the difficulties of those in the 509th who would be required to make those changes. It seemed that, not unlike our surroundings, we were operating on a base of shifting sands.

During the latter part of December, after Beahan had been dispatched to England, an ordnance officer assigned to Project Alberta arrived to test a new fuse. For this test, Tom Ferebee would fly with me in Kermit's absence. The ordnance officer, a major, sat behind Albury and me. The officer had briefed Tom earlier in the day about the fuse. My first impression was that this major seemed to think we were at his disposal, particularly in the way he spoke to Tom before and during the flight.

Tom took his position as bombardier in the front of the canopy, sitting over the bombsight. Reaching the initial point, the IP, which is where we would begin a bomb run, Tom and I made our final adjustments. We approached the AP, or aiming point, where Tom would release the bomb. Prior to arriving at the AP, Tom had set the series of switches necessary to activate the electrical circuits to release the bomb. With the aiming point in his crosshairs, he said, "Bomb away."

I immediately took the airplane into a 155-degree turn as quickly as I could. Tom looked over his shoulder and said, "Chuck, the bomb didn't release."

He'd barely gotten the words out when the ordnance officer, with some expression of disgust, moved clumsily past me, reached over Tom's shoulder, and pushed the backup manual release lever, causing the bomb to fall from the bomb bay while we were still in a steep turn. Luckily, the bomb cleared the doors and the side of the airplane and fell free. It could just as easily have struck the doors or side of the airplane while we were banking to the right and damaged the airplane. Five tons of concrete striking the plane at this angle could have had catastrophic results.

I rarely get angry in flight, but at that moment I could hardly control my rage. The stupidity of what he had done deeply offended me. After all we had gone through without an incident, this stranger, a guest on my airplane, could have doomed us all. Under no circumstances should he have interfered with the bombardier—or, for that matter, with any other member of the crew or the equipment on board. The proper procedure in such a situation would be to check the circuits and go around again. Whatever had possessed this dolt to do such a knuckleheaded thing was beyond me. I don't recall all the adjectives that gushed forth, but I know there was little I didn't call this guy.

When we landed, I chased him out of the airplane and continued my harangue on the tarmac in front of a gathering crowd. This was the first and only time during our project that I lost my temper, and in so public a way. Tibbets and some other brass had come running down to the flight line because something had obviously gone wrong with the test. I made it clear to them and everyone within earshot that I never wanted this guy near me, my crew, or any aircraft I ever flew again. Having spent my outrage, I glanced over at Tibbets to see if I had perhaps gone too far. But I could see that wry smile breaking and the atta-boy look. Not surprisingly, although this major remained at Wendover for a while, he never came near me again.

TEN

TWO SIGNIFICANT EVENTS coincided on January 6, 1945. I officially took command of the 320th Troop Carrier Squadron, my first official command, and advance elements of a small contingent from the 509th were en route to the warmer climes of Cuba.

Because of the need to move men and top secret matériel around quickly to top secret locations, Paul Tibbets included in his organization an independent transport squadron under his direct command. His organic fleet of C-46s, C-47s, and four-engine C-54s freed him from having to rely on any other commander or justify his transport requirements. This unusual arrangement added to the aura of the 509th as something mysterious and special. As with everything else we did, it was a level of independence unheard of in the army air force. Tibbets's transports ferried scientists to and from Los Alamos via Albuquerque and provided him with flexibility going to and from Wendover, Colorado Springs, Los Alamos, and Washington, D.C. Being independent also facilitated our filing of false flight plans to conceal where we were actually going, which prevented prying eyes from being able to draw any conclusions or make any connections. The transport squadron proved indispensable to moving our operations and the bomb components to Tinian rapidly and to continuing ferry services between the United States and Tinian, Guam, and Saipan. It became known as the Green Hornet Airlines.

The transport squadron had been activated on December 17, 1944, and remained under the temporary command of Major Hubert Konopacki until I assumed the post. At five A.M. on the previous day, in the dense and fog-shrouded forest of the Ardennes in Belgium, eight German Panzer divisions suddenly and furiously sliced through Allied lines along a seventy-mile front. Having concluded that the German army had no ability to wage an offensive, General Eisenhower and his intelligence staff had gravely underestimated both the fanatical resolve of Hitler to fight on, in spite of the obvious futility of continuing the war, and the will of the Wehrmacht to fight for their Führer and the Fatherland.

The high command, believing the war in Europe was just about over, transported seasoned troops to the Pacific theater and replaced them along the front in the Ardennes forest with green recruits. These young recruits ultimately faced Hitler's most combat-hardened units, including the infamous Death Squads of the Waffen SS. The Germans moved a quarter of a million men to within a few hundred feet of the American forward positions without being detected.

Although the offensive was finally halted before the Wehrmacht could split the Allied forces and reach the sea, the Allies regained the lost territory only after a bitter, barbaric, and costly counteroffensive. Foot by foot they pushed back the Germans for the next month. In the end, more American soldiers were killed and wounded in the Battle of the Bulge than at Gettysburg, which until then had been the bloodiest battle in American history. It was a tragic miscalculation of the nature of the enemy for which ten of thousands of young Americans paid the ultimate price. As reports filtered back to us about the extent of the battle and the desperate situation, which could prolong the war in Europe, the thought crossed my mind that maybe our group might be called upon to deliver a final blow to the Nazis to stem the onslaught.

Prior to taking command of the transport squadron, I was busy training the bomber crews and testing the pumpkins. A key element of the training in the air had yet to be addressed: long-range overwater navigation. Winter had arrived early to the salt flats, and November and December had been bone-chilling. I discussed with Tibbets a plan to start long-range flights over the ocean. We would take off from Wendover and head toward—not to—Anchorage, then turn southwest toward—not to—Hawaii, and finally turn northeast back to Wendover, forming a three-thousand-mile round-trip in the shape of a triangle. The exercise would provide the necessary training for the navigators.

Tibbets listened to my plan and asked if we couldn't accomplish the same purpose with exercises over the Caribbean. I understood immediately. If we had to train over water, why not find a warm, more pleasant base of operation to fly from? It was a master stroke by an officer concerned about the well-being of the men in his command. Tensions had been building within the unit. More and more of the guys were blowing off steam in the local bars in Wendover and Salt Lake. Fights, disputes, and general ill will were becoming more prevalent, a sure sign that the crews needed some release, some reward for their hard work. A change of scenery to the south would fill the bill. Tibbets found a way to reduce the stress and still keep the high-intensity training for the project on track.

Plans were made to take a cadre of five crews to Batista Field in Cuba, together with a small contingent of support personnel. Colonel Tibbets arrived at Batista Field by transport ahead of the units. Before he settled in, he saw to it that quarters were assigned for every man and that meals were ready on their arrival. Late into the night he was seen helping make beds. It was the kind of thing an enlisted man wouldn't soon forget.

Havana was a party town, and the locals had longtime experience with people who took their reveling seriously: tourists, businessmen, politicians, mobsters. The 509th rose to the occasion. For a month, when off duty, our crews partied, swam, gambled in the casinos, took in the shows, dined, and all in all made the most of this island paradise. Some left behind stories for the locals to tell long after we were gone. This experience also had the benefit of solidifying a sense of pride among the men that they were part of the 509th Composite Group. Sprung from their penitentiary-style life at Wendover, now out and about in the general population, they saw themselves for what they were, a special and elite military unit. A corner had been turned in unit cohesion. The 509th now meant something to the men.

In January 1945 Curtis LeMay moved to Guam to take over the XXI Bomber Command of the Twentieth Air Force. Although the Twentieth Air Force was in General MacArthur's theater, General Hap Arnold had intentionally headquartered the Twentieth in Washington, D.C., technically outside of the theater. Command protocol would be for the theater commander to have tactical and strategic control of all military units within his theater. By keeping his headquarters in Washington, General Arnold had prevented MacArthur from ordering or controlling operations of the air force in the Pacific. For the first time, the air force could develop and execute strategic missions, rather than be an ancillary force to the ground war that MacArthur was fighting. The air force could become an independent force in the Pacific theater.

LeMay was determined that his air force could win the war in the Pacific, and he was positive that the B-29 was the plane to do it. But the B-29 was having problems. The high-altitude tactics that he had perfected with the B-17, and that had proven so successful against the Germans, were failing miserably against Japan. The overall effect of the B-29 bombing raids of Japan to date had been at best inconclusive. The Superfortresses were experiencing high rates of mechanical failures, forcing a sizable number to abort missions. Bombing accuracy from 30,000 feet was abysmal. During the month of January, most of the targets in Japan bombed by B-29s had suffered little damage. Japanese production of war matériel continued unabated while Japan's industries remained unscathed. Unless Japan's industrial output could be disrupted and the will of its military broken, the Japanese war machine would remain robust and ready to meet the advancing American forces. Such a prospect was chilling to our commanders, who would be sending their troops to fight yet another bloody land battle against forces yet again prepared to fight to the death in defense of their territory—this time the mainland.

LeMay had a solution, which Paul Tibbets had recommended several months earlier. Instead of high-altitude bombing, he would send hundreds of B-29s in at 8,000 feet at night. Each airplane would carry thousands of pounds of incendiary bombs filled with napalm, which would incinerate entire Japanese cities and the war industries located in them. The tactic would take advantage of the mostly wooden structures built in

Japan and the fact that the Japanese had concentrated their major war industries in the hearts of most of their large cities.

LeMay's goal was not to bomb civilians. He wanted to destroy Japan's industrial capacity. The night before a mission his pilots would drop leaflets over target cities warning civilians that the bombing was imminent and they should evacuate. If his plans were to bomb two cities, leaflets would be dropped over four. The Japanese military, however, with the assent of the political leaders, explicitly kept the civilians in harm's way. When Kyoto first appeared on a list of bomber targets, LeMay expressed opposition. He preferred Hiroshima because of its concentration of troops and factories.

Having assembled five wings of B-29s on Guam, Tinian, and Saipan, LeMay commenced the most intense air campaign of the war against Japan starting in February. The firebombings were horrific. City after city was incinerated. The fires, started by the napalm and fueled by the burning wooden structures, consumed all the available oxygen in the area. The lack of oxygen would cause a vacuum that generated high-velocity winds that would implode, further intensifying and spreading the ever-consuming fires. Temperatures exceeded 2,000 degrees Fahrenheit. The napalm itself was an insidious weapon because it could not be extinguished. It splattered and stuck to any surface it struck: a building, a house, a person.

In mid-March the campaign reached its apex. On the night of March 9, 334 B-29s struck Tokyo, blanketing the city with firebombs. Tokyo was reduced to rubble. It was the single most destructive bombing in history—125,000 wounded, 97,000 dead, over a million left homeless. In a ten-day period in March, thirty-two square miles of Tokyo, Nagoya, Osaka, and Kobe were leveled.

The Japanese fought on.

In April it became clear that a final assault on the mainland of Japan would be necessary. The Japanese showed no inclination to surrender. In fact, as American forces drew closer to the mainland, the Japanese military became even more fanatical and suicidal. As brutal as the battle for Iwo Jima had been—leaving 21,000 Americans wounded and over 6,000 marines, soldiers, and sailors dead for an eight-square-mile hunk of rock—Okinawa revealed an even more vivid and chilling window on things to come. Just 325 miles off the coast of Japan's southern island of Kyushu, Okinawa was the site of the last and largest amphibious invasion of the war. Defending it, the Japanese fought for almost three months in a hopeless struggle. Virtually all of the Japanese troops fought to the death—110,000 of them. Taking the island required half a million men. Almost 50,000 of them—marines, airmen, sailors, and soldiers—were wounded or killed.

The Japanese had also introduced another terror to the hell that had become the Pacific: the kamikaze, "the Divine Wind." Young flyers willingly committed suicide by diving their bomb-laden aircraft into our fleet so that they could kill as many Americans as possible in one single effort. By their glorious sacrifice, they were promised eternal life. Their orders were more religious than military: 'The death of a single one of you will be the birth of a million others. . . . Choose a death which brings about a maximum result."

For centuries Japan had been a closed militaristic society. In five hundred years it had never lost a battle. The code of the samurai guided its destiny. During World War II not a single Japanese military unit surrendered. *Bushido,* "the way of the warrior," was not only ingrained in the psyche of every Japanese fighter, it was also codified in the Japanese Field Service Regulations, which made being taken alive a court-martial offense. This was the culture and the mind-set we faced.

In the battles of Leyte Gulf, Iwo Jima, and Okinawa, suicide pilots inflicted massive casualties on the Pacific fleet. At Okinawa, five thousand sailors were killed, 30 ships were sunk, and 368 ships were damaged. These actions foretold a prolonged and bloody killing field for the young Americans who would wade ashore on the Japanese mainland.

The plans for the invasion of Japan were code-named Olympic and Coronet. It would be a two-stage invasion. The southern island of Kyushu would be invaded on November 1, 1945, Operation Olympic, with a force of 800,000 men. In April 1946, Operation Coronet would commence with the invasion of the main island of Honshu, near Tokyo, with a force of over one million men. The wheels of inevitability started to grind forward with a momentum that at some point would be unstoppable—unless another way were found to end the carnage.

In anticipation of the invasion, and having predicted with extraordinary accuracy exactly where the Americans would land, the Japanese began to fortify the cliffs leading up from the beaches of Kyushu. The terrain would provide the perfect slaughterhouse for American G.I.s coming ashore. Those troops who survived the beaches and made it inland would face an intricate network of caves, tunnels, and bunkers. In this lethal battlefield matrix, American forces would be shredded as they fought for each yard of dirt. In addition, thousands of airplanes, as well as submarines, were being stockpiled for kamikaze attacks on the invasion fleet and its landing craft. Two and a half million battle-hardened troops, supported by four million able-bodied civilian military employees, were being massed on Kyushu to meet the invasion force. Thirty-two million civilians—women, children, and the elderly—were being drilled in the art of resistance and guerrilla warfare.

The southern command headquarters for coordination of the defense of Kyushu was located at Hiroshima.

President Truman and the American military planners, with the benefit of having cracked the Japanese military and diplomatic codes early in the war, and thus knowing what awaited our troops, had to confront the magnitude of the casualties our forces could reasonably expect to sustain. If Iwo Jima and Okinawa were any measure, the possibilities were unthinkable.

ELEVEN

BACK AT WENDOVER, we were ready.

After final assembly at the Martin Aircraft Company, our brand-new and redesigned B-29s were delivered during March and April of 1945 via Offut Air Force Field in Omaha, Nebraska. Each airplane was assigned to one crew, although occasionally crews would fly different airplanes if their B-29s were undergoing maintenance. My crew was designated as C-15. Our assigned aircraft as delivered from the factory was Number 89, which was painted in block numbers on the nose of the fuselage. Later the fuselage would be painted with our name, *The Great Artiste*, and our logo, a debonair magician in tails. For the missions, however, all nose art would be removed. Our unit markings would also be changed prior to the missions to confuse the enemy about who we were and where we came from, in case they got to us with fighters.

We spent March and April flying the new airplanes and getting accustomed to them, continuing the never-ending practicing. We rehearsed every detail again and again and again to the point of exasperation. All fifteen crews were at the peak of their readiness to fly the mission.

Although it had never been said, I sensed that Paul Tibbets considered crew C-15 one of the best in the 509th, maybe even the best. One indication of his confidence in our crew was that he had chosen us to fly a critical test for the scientists who were still working to perfect the fusing system for the bomb. Tibbets briefed me on the mission. We would drop a pumpkin from 30,000 feet with a new version of a proximity fuse, intended to detonate at 1,890 feet. He stressed that the scientists were having considerable trouble correcting problems with the system and that this test was crucial to them. Although the pumpkin would be filled with concrete, a pound of high explosives would be attached to the fusing system so that the scientists could tell if the fuse functioned as predicted at the correct altitude with an aerial explosion.

By that time, Kermit Beahan and I had become almost as one on a bomb run. Able to anticipate each other's moves, he called out minor adjustments to me on the approach from the IP to the aiming point for release of the bomb. This coordination between the pilot and his bombardier is more an art than a learned procedure. For this test, we were flying over the test range adjacent to Wendover so that the gathered multitude of scientists, ordnance personnel, and assorted technicians could observe the drop and the fruits of their labors.

Beahan yelled, "Bomb away!" and the airplane jumped up as ten thousand pounds suddenly departed. Instantaneously, I was taking the airplane into a sharp 155-degree diving turn when an explosion ripped upward and slammed into the fuselage. The new improved fuse had just detonated directly below us. The airplane shuddered and I gripped the yoke to maintain control in case any damage had occurred. But the airplane was

okay. I was told after we landed that the explosion had occurred less than one hundred feet beneath us—too close for
comfort.

On the ground, my crew gathered around waiting for my
reaction. I said what all of them were thinking, "I hope they
get it right before we carry a real one." As much as I respected
and trusted the scientists, a voice in the deep recesses of my
mind reminded me that ultimately, it was the weapon we
would carry that was important to the scientists, not our safety.
They wanted the bomb to work. They were seeking the success
of their voyage from theoretical physics to a real-world applica-
tion. Success for them didn't necessarily mean our survival. It
was a dark thought.

The 509th's readiness was another concern. It is hard to
keep a unit at high alert for an extended period of time without
action. The level of proficiency will inevitably begin to deterio-
rate. Our entire organization—from the air crews to the maintenance and engineering staff to the air support personnel—had
been melded into a unified command, and we were firing on
all twelve cylinders, like a fine-tuned Rolls-Royce engine forced
to idle in Park.

The problem manifested itself in the increasing volume of
calls from the Salt Lake City Police Department to our base
each weekend. A string of offenses ranging from traffic violations to property damage to assaults mounted. The men were
bored, restless, and frustrated.

From an operational standpoint, though, the last indispensable piece of the puzzle, the First Ordnance Squadron, had
been officially added in March. The First Ordnance was
manned by the highly skilled technicians, ordnance experts, and
machinists who would actually manufacture many of the
bomb's delicate components and assemble them on Tinian.
They had been working with the Manhattan and Alberta people

for many months perfecting the various components that would have to be assembled in the confines of the bomb casing. These specialists developed many of the techniques necessary to machine the parts that were essential to the close tolerance required by the theoretical scientists who were working to fit the pieces into the package that would be the weapon.

Because of their work and their intimate contact with, and knowledge of, the internal components of what would eventually become a nuclear weapon, they were under even more restrictive security than we were. Cordoned off from the rest of the 509th, they were totally segregated, prohibited from speaking with other 509th personnel about what they were doing. When they traveled off the base, they couldn't mix with anyone, military or civilian. They were always accompanied by security men, and when they were outside their area, even within their own group, they were not allowed to discuss their work for fear an offhand remark might be overheard. Even construction work within their compound was done by them to prevent any possible leak of information, no matter how seemingly unimportant.

The First Ordnance Squadron was at the core of the many-layered levels of secrecy and security, like the concentric rings of an onion, that was Wendover—the 509th, Silverplate, Project Alberta, and the Manhattan Project.

With all the pieces of our organization working like the proverbial well-oiled machine, it seemed that my rather unusual arrangement of commanding the transport squadron while maintaining a bomber at my disposal would remain in place. No one voiced any objection or raised any question. It was working, so don't monkey around with it.

But fate was once again about to step in just a matter days before we were to begin our deployment overseas, setting off a chain reaction that would put me in command of the bomber squadron. Even for an eyewitness to the event, it was hard to believe at the time.

I was down at the flight line when a C-54 transport landed. While the C-54 was parked at its hard stand, the deputy group commander, a lieutenant colonel and technically the number-two guy under Tibbets on the organizational chart of the 509th, stepped out of the airplane. A jeep that had been waiting off to one side pulled up to the transport. Two armed MPs and two security men greeted the deputy group commander and an animated conversation ensued. While the conversation continued, one MP took a duffle bag from the jeep and dumped it on the ground. The conversation was brief. The security men, even from a distance, were emphatic. With little ceremony, one MP took the colonel's arm, the other grabbed the duffle bag, and they escorted him to a waiting transport, which immediately took off.

It struck me as I watched this scene unfold that there was no attempt to make it discreet. It was all played out quite publicly.

Later in the day, Tom Classen, the commander of the 393rd Bomber Squadron, was promoted to serve as the new deputy group commander of the 509th. James Hopkins, his operations officer, was named the 509th's group operations officer, leaving two slots open in the bomber squadron. Colonel Tibbets called me and matter-of-factly informed me, "Chuck, you're the new commander of the 393rd." I requested, and he agreed, to name my old friend and deputy John Casey to command the 320th Transport Squadron. I named George Marquardt my operations officer for the 393rd. It was one hell of a day. I now had the position to go along with my responsibilities at the very moment when we were about to go into action.

As I later learned them in detail, the facts were that the

★ Charles W. Sweeney as
an Air Cadet, 1940

★ *(l. to r.)* Admiral Purnell, General Farrell, Colonel Tibbets, and
Commander Parsons

★ The Hiroshima Mission Briefing. Colonel Tibbets is seated third from the left, holding his pipe. Major Sweeney is two rows back over Tibbets's right shoulder.

★ Tinian.
General Spaatz awarding Colonel Tibbets the Distinguished Service Cross, August 6, 1945, after the *Enola Gay* landed. At the time, the DSC was the second highest award for valor.

★ The crew of the *Bock's Car* immediately after landing on Tinian, after returning from Okinawa on August 9, 1945. *(l. to r., bottom row)* Kuharek, Spitzer, Gallagher, Buckley, Dehart; *(top row)* Sweeney, Albury, Olivi, Beahan, Van Pelt, Beser

★ The *Bock's Car* after the Nagasaki mission

★ The atomic explosion over Nagasaki

★ The destruction
at Nagasaki,
September 1945

★ General Davies awarding Major Sweeney the Air Medal after the Nagasaki mission. Later, he would be awarded the Silver Star for bravery by Lieutenant General Nathan Twining.

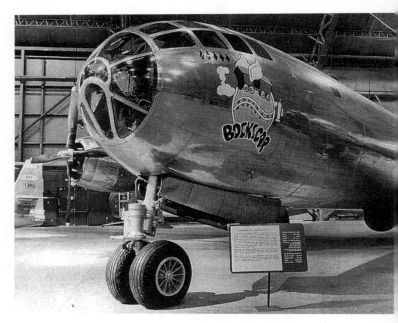

★ The *Bock's Car* on display at the Air Force Museum, Dayton, Ohio

★ Major General Charles W. Sweeney today

extricated lieutenant colonel, who had been a holdover from the existing headquarters staff at Wendover when Paul Tibbets arrived, had seriously breached security by using our code name, Silverplate. The deputy group commander's duties at the beginning required no particular skills related to the mission. But this lieutenant colonel was the kind of guy who had an inflated sense of his own value and, frankly, was pompous. For whatever reason, he had gone to Colorado Springs on an errand. While he was there, a junior officer didn't respond either quickly enough or with the proper respect to something he wanted done. The lieutenant colonel, who did not have clearance to use our code name, invoked "Silverplate" as an important project he was attached to. This caused a flurry of activity. At any use of this highly secret code, our security people would be advised by security personnel at the scene. A serious breach had been committed over something inconsequential.

Since the lieutenant colonel had no special skill necessary to our mission, Tibbets could take decisive action. The incident also presented him with an opportunity to reinforce with every man in the outfit who might stray that regardless of rank or position, no one was above the strict rules of security. We could afford to lose an unessential officer without setting our progress back, unlike the problem Tibbets would have faced if a key pilot or technician had committed the indiscretion. The point was driven home by the immediate and public imposition of the penalty—banishment. Everyone would understand that if the deputy group commander could be dispatched to the frozen tundra of Alaska for the duration of the war, anyone could be similarly dispatched to oblivion. The lieutenant colonel was never spoken of again. Even fifty years later, his name is never mentioned.

We seemed stuck in place at Wendover. Curtis LeMay was mercilessly pounding Japan, city after city, his tactics of low-level, incendiary bombing proving very effective in destroying key Japanese industries. Even though Japan continued to produce significant military matériel and the Japanese will to fight on remained unbowed, we had to wonder if the 509th would be necessary after all. Maybe LeMay had been right. Maybe he *could* bomb the Japanese into submission and win the war.

As for the scientists, their confidence in the weapon seemed to be waning as they got closer to an actual test. They appeared to be mired in the minutia, looking for the perfect weapon. Of course, these observations are from a military man trained to act, not ponder. In all fairness, the scientists certainly had reason to doubt. No one could predict what the final package, assuming it worked at all, would produce. A big bang or a fizzle? And how big was big? Five tons of TNT? Twenty tons? Fifty tons? Global conflagration? Who knew? They couldn't even tell us if we'd survive the blast at eight miles. And, of course, there were the fuses. Even if they worked, there was no certainty they wouldn't detonate the bomb right under the airplane. This posited a good news–bad news scenario: "The bomb worked, but we lost the crew." Unlocking the secrets of the universe is a tricky business.

There was so much we didn't know. Such ignorance can oftentimes calcify into inaction. Sadly, as time passed, more Americans died. Only action on our part to deliver the weapon the scientists had developed—perfect or not—could help end the war. The bomb might have been a theoretical problem to solve, a blizzard of incomprehensible numbers spilling off a chalk-dusted blackboard, but the dead, dying, and crippled in the Pacific were real.

Colonel Tibbets sensed the stalling of momentum and seized the day. He knew that moving our personnel, equipment, and supplies overseas would be a time-consuming process. Some would go by air, but most would move by ship.

Better to be in place and ready to go when the weapon was
ready than to wait and then deploy to the Pacific, losing precious weeks. Invoking his broad authority and circumventing
even the small circle of his superiors in this project, including
General Leslie Groves, the overall commander of the entire
Manhattan Project, Tibbets caused the orders for our deployment to be issued. He called Washington, spoke the magic
words necessary to get the bureaucracy moving, and the wheels
started to move. In spite of the flak I understood he took for
overstepping his bounds, including a tongue-lashing from General Groves, he had gotten us on our way, and no one counter-
manded the orders.

Our destination was appropriately code-named Destination.
What the name lacked in originality, it made up for in
precision.

On May 6, 1945, twelve hundred of our support personnel
boarded the troop ship S.S. *Cape Victory* at Seattle and sailed
west. They would arrive three weeks later at Destination. The
C-54 transports would set down on May 18. Finally, at the
beginning of June, our fifteen B-29s would touch down at
North Field to join our fellow comrades on Tinian Island, in
the Marianas.

During our deployment, on May 8, the Germans surrendered. The elation felt by all Americans was short-lived as they
realized that their soldiers who had survived years of war in
North Africa and Europe were now being moved to staging
areas in the Pacific for the final assault on Imperial Japan. It
was expected that at least two million men would take part in
the elaborate invasion of the Japanese home islands. In the
Pentagon, the grim process of estimating dead and wounded
already had begun.

Our young fighting men sailing across the Atlantic, through

the Panama Canal, and into the deceptively tranquil Pacific, would have ample time to contemplate what lay before them.

Just a few weeks before the Germans surrendered, Franklin Delano Roosevelt died. My generation had never known another leader. He had taken us through two back-to-back cataclysmic disasters unprecedented in American history—the Great Depression and World War II. With my Catholic upbringing, it seemed to me almost biblical that, like Moses, President Roosevelt would not be with his people in their moment of triumph. With the finish hopefully in sight, his death seemed a cruel blow to our nation. On hearing the news, I felt a hollowness, a need to deny that he was gone. Later, my feeling of unease was not lifted when I heard the tinny Midwestern twang of a man the nation and I barely knew. On April 12, 1945, at a little after seven P.M. eastern standard time, Harry S. Truman took the oath of office and became the thirty-third president of the United States.

History records that the first matter brought to the new president moments after he was sworn into office was delivered by Secretary of War Henry Stimson, who informed the president that the United States was in the process of developing a new weapon of "almost unbelievable destructive power."

TWELVE

THE B-29S STARTED their long flights to Tinian Island during the first week of June. My crew and I were among the last to leave the windswept desert of Wendover.

Dorothy had known for over a month that I was shipping out. There was no question she would return to Boston. Wendover had the feel of a ghost town. No one in their right mind would want to stay there, and in any event, there was no telling when I'd be back—a year, two . . . who knew? On June 19, our last morning together, we had breakfast, said our good-byes, kissed and hugged, and spoke of when we'd meet again. My crew and I lifted off for the last time from the hardscrabble place that had been our home for the past several months. I swung around toward our house, circling it at about 100 feet. There was Dorothy, standing alone in the dust bowl we called our front yard, waving. I dipped my wings to let her see me and then waved the wings in a final good-bye as I continued my turn. Banking the airplane up, I swung around back toward the west and on to Sacramento.

During the afternoon of June 21, we landed in Hawaii at the end of the first leg of our journey. After a brief layover that night, we flew on to Kwajalein, where we stayed the second night, and then on to the Marianas and the island of Tinian the next morning. There was an unconcealed excitement among the men. We were going to war.

One year earlier, as marines stormed ashore and eventually took Tinian, hundreds of Japanese soldiers went into hiding in the caves, jungles, and hills around this tiny island. They continued to radio reports of our activities to neighboring islands still held by Japanese forces. We were warned not to venture too far out after dark. Not long after our arrival, in spite of the tight security surrounding our group, Tokyo Rose welcomed the 509th to Tinian and encouraged us to go home to our loved ones before we were killed. In later broadcasts, she assured us that Japanese fighter planes and antiaircraft gunners would take special aim at the mark on the tails of our airplanes, our distinctive arrowhead inside a circle. Although none of us would admit it, her broadcasts were a little unsettling.

Approaching from the air, each of the islands of the Marianas is a green, lush oasis in a vast blue. Up until then, those islands had been only names I had read about or seen in the black-and-white starkness of movietone news clips, or in the more graphic uncensored military combat films. Saipan, Tinian, Guam. It was hard to square the beauty of the Marianas with the human suffering visited upon them so recently. With the exception of our foray into Cuba, this was my first trip ever outside the continental United States.

After getting clearance from the tower, I began my final approach from the west and landed on one of the four parallel 8,500-foot-long runways on North Field that ran east to west across the northern tip of Tinian. Literally overnight, navy construction battalions, the Seabees, had constructed these mammoth airstrips and ancillary facilities. These facilities constituted the largest airfield in the world at the time.

Servicemen overseas like to bring a feeling of home to their bases whenever they can. Some enterprising engineer—I suspect he was from New York City—found a way to bring New York to our new base. Tinian is shaped much like the island of Manhattan—elongated, north to south. The streets on Tinian were laid out and named after the streets in Manhattan. Broadway and Eighth Avenue ran the length of Tinian, with Wall Street, Forty-second Street, 110th, and so on, intersecting. The address for the 509th was the corner of 125th Street and Eighth Avenue, formerly occupied by the Seabees. We lived in "Upper Manhattan." It pleased me to no end that someone had named the road that ringed North Field, Boston Post Road.

Before we arrived, Tinian had been occupied by the 313th Bombardment Wing of the XXI Bomber Command, flying incendiary missions over Japan and dropping mines by parachute into the waters of Japan's harbors to stop the flow of ships supplying Japanese troops. Our group was to be nowhere near the 313th on the island, however. The 509th was totally isolated within its own compound, connected by taxiways to North Field. The compound was enclosed by a high fence with a main gate that was guarded around the clock by armed sentries. The perimeter of the fence was patrolled by heavily armed MPs. Inside the security perimeter were our living quarters and offices, a series of Quonset huts connected by a network of roads. Our working areas were the flight lines, located two miles from our living quarters. This area contained the only windowless, air-conditioned buildings in the Pacific, where the Alberta and Manhattan scientists and technicians and the First Ordnance personnel were laboring. Here the various components of the bombs would be assembled. The actual bombs' casings and electrical circuits were also kept in this area, awaiting the internal workings that would breathe life into the weapons—uranium and plutonium firing mechanisms and cores. Anyone trying to gain access without proper clearance could be shot.

At North Field, our airplanes were under the same degree of security. No one was allowed near our aircraft or the specially dug concrete loading pits. Unauthorized personnel were also subject to being shot.

The accommodations within our compound were the best on the island—and possibly in the entire Pacific. The Seabees, who had built and lived in our quarters, had spared no amenities. Tibbets and I, for example, had private showers. Each day tubs constructed on top of the huts were filled with water by a tanker truck. I would step into a closet enclosure, pull a chain, and down cascaded water warmed by the sun. I would then soap up, pull the chain to rinse off, and I was done. Just like home.

As combat-hardened veterans, the Seabees were the first to go into forward areas, constructing vital airstrips and facilities, many times under enemy fire, as the marines pressed on from island to island. They were leaving for duty on Okinawa as we were arriving on Tinian, and we inherited their quarters. This started an undercurrent of ill will toward the 509th among other units on Tinian, which was intensified by our isolation and apparent special treatment.

After the bleak, dreary endlessness of Wendover, life on Tinian was lush. It was a tropical island, hot and humid. We swam in the warm, crystal-clear ocean during the day and at night sat under a star-encrusted sky.

We attended the 313th Wing ground school to learn the particular operations in this theater, such as weather patterns, air-sea rescue procedures, and flight patterns in and around airfields. We did not, however, fly missions within the command, and our aircraft could not be reassigned to non-509th crews, regardless of the need. Our maintenance operation and vast resources were not subject to the jurisdiction of the wing commander or the island commander. We were untouchable.

The other B-29 crews were flying into the teeth of the enemy every night, carrying maximum loads of bombs, often barely making it into the air to start a journey of thousands of miles round-trip. Many never got airborne. Their airplanes would perhaps lose an engine on takeoff and then crash and explode in the ocean if they were unable to dump their pay-loads quickly enough before impact. Loaded with thousands of pounds of weaponry, the B-29 could be unforgiving in those first few moments as it struggled to gain altitude. Crashed-out hulks of the unsuccessful were not an uncommon sight.

These brave men looked upon us as contributing nothing to the war effort. We had no mission they were aware of. From an objective point of view, I could sympathize with their disdain. We seemed destined to finish out the war training for an illusory mission.

We got the green light to commence practice missions over the neighboring islands of Rota and Guguan, which were still occupied by the Japanese. Our forces had bypassed those islands because they possessed no strategic value and, with their supply routes cut off, posed no danger to our forces in the Marianas. The missions would give our crews an introduction to theater operations without exposing them to enemy antiaircraft fire. The last thing we needed was to lose one of our specially trained crews while it was dropping practice bombs on an irrelevant target.

The airplanes on these missions would drop pumpkins, but unlike the Wendover pumpkins, these would be filled with Torpex, an enhanced explosive with an enormous destructive yield for a conventional bomb. We would release from 30,000 feet and the explosion would allow us to spot where it hit, whereupon the crew would maintain course until it took vertical photos of its own damage.

After a series of runs we were authorized to bomb Truk and Marcus, where the Japanese had such limited antiaircraft batteries to throw up at us that they would have little or no effect. This provided our first combat conditions, even though these runs were still recorded as "practice" missions by the air force.

On July 20 we were finally cleared to fly missions over Japan. The targets were Otso, Taira, Fukashima, Nagaoka, Toyama, and Tokyo. With the exception of Tibbets and a handful of the men he'd brought in at Wendover, most of the members of the 393rd would be flying their first combat missions. Tibbets, Beahan, Ferebee, and Van Pelt had flown missions in Europe. Captain Fred Bock and Lieutenant Colonel Classen had seen tours of duty in the South Pacific. It would be my first combat over enemy territory. At long last, we were in the war.

These missions over Japan would have the same profile as the real one, if it ever happened. Each airplane would carry a single pumpkin filled with Torpex, drop it on a target, and then take vertical photographs of the damage. Although inflicting damage on the enemy would be welcomed, it was a collateral objective. We were dress-rehearsing for the big day. The crews would be navigating long-range over water to a primary city in heavily defended enemy territory and dropping the weapon visually from 30,000 feet on a specific enemy target. The target might be a factory or a military base or a railroad yard. The goals were accuracy and assessment.

Unfortunately, these missions would also confirm that the fuses were still unpredictable. On at least two occasions, fuses detonated *before* the pumpkins reached the point where they were scheduled to explode. The airplanes were far enough away from the explosions at the time not to have taken any damage, but after all the tactics and maneuvers our crews had perfected, we were silently aware that for one piece of the puzzle, all we could do was hope that perfection would be achieved.

Each crew would be briefed on a secondary target and a tertiary target if the primary target could not be bombed because of weather or any other problem. If the secondary and tertiary targets were obscured, the pilot, on his own initiative, could drop on so-called targets of opportunity. The only prohibition in the theater was that under no circumstances were the Imperial Palace in Tokyo, where the emperor resided, and the ancient city of Kyoto, a religious and cultural center for the Japanese, to be bombed. We were not seeking to destroy a culture but to stop an aggressor. And as a practical matter, killing or injuring the emperor or destroying a center of cultural and religious importance might also give the regimented Japanese public another rallying point around which to mobilize in a final suicidal defense of the home islands. Also on the off-limits list were Hiroshima, Kokura, Nagasaki, and Niigata for reasons that were not explained to us by Colonel Tibbets.

The Torpex drops also had the effect of allowing the Japanese to get accustomed to seeing a single B-29, unescorted by fighter aircraft, drop a single bomb from 30,000 feet. Perhaps they would become comfortable with a tactic that inflicted so little damage and choose to concentrate defensive measures against other more destructive air assaults. Some of the men wondered aloud if this was the reason we had been training so hard and in such secrecy—to drop new, huge, powerful iron bombs, one at a time. Could the brass have overestimated the desired effect?

There were two further prohibitions. Colonel Tibbets and I

were never to fly together over Japan, and Tibbets was prohibited from flying any of these combat missions. His capture by the Japanese could jeopardize the entire Manhattan Project. Within the 509th, he was the only one who knew practically everything.

Four days before we began our assault on the Japanese mainland, at Alamogordo, New Mexico, the first nuclear weapon had been successfully detonated. Events were now gaining momentum. On July 26, we heard over Armed Services Radio that the terms of the Postdam Declaration called for the unconditional surrender of all Japanese armed forces.

Japan stalled. The killing went on. Every day hundreds of Americans continued to be killed and wounded in battles throughout the Pacific, in Southeast Asia, and in barbarous prisoner of war camps. The Japanese treatment of our POWs defied humanity. When their army decided to force-march thousands of prisoners from Bataan in the Philippines sixty miles north to Camp O'Donnell—many of the prisoners wounded and some barely alive—they murdered over seven thousand American and other Allied prisoners on the march alone. The men were shot, stabbed, decapitated, or otherwise physically destroyed during that agonizing journey. Their captors withheld food, water, and medical treatment. Those prisoners who were still alive at the end of the march, along with other POWs, were placed in camps that were repositories of unmitigated horrors, camps such as the one at Palawan, where 150 emaciated prisoners were forced into an air raid shelter. The guards poured gasoline into the shelter and then set it ablaze. Those who tried to stagger out were machine-gunned, clubbed, or bayoneted to death.

Years later we could learn of the Nazi-esque medical experiments conducted on prisoners.

Of the 140,000 Americans held by the Japanese, 34 percent—47,000—would die in captivity. The survivors would be remnants of the men they had been.

In words and deeds, Japan also made known its intention to execute every Allied prisoner of war at the start of any planned invasion of the mainland. Everywhere they were held, prisoners were ordered to dig slit trenches to serve as mass graves for the executions. On Formosa, the prison camp commander was directed, in the event of an invasion, to kill all prisoners. On Java, 300,000 Allied prisoners—American, Dutch, British, and Australian; civilian and military—were in jeopardy. At Davao, in the Philippines, machine gun emplacements were constructed to face inward and stores of gasoline were being stockpiled to burn bodies. Earlier, at places like Tarawa, Ballale, and Wake Islands, the Japanese shot or beheaded all of their POWs in anticipation of American invasions.

Thus, the United States had good reasons to take the Japanese threat seriously.

In the context of this reality, on June 18, in a meeting at the White House, Admiral William Leahy advised the president that, based on our experience at Iwo Jima and Okinawa, in the first thirty days of an invasion we could realistically expect casualties in the range of 230,000 to 270,000. For a 120-day campaign to invade and occupy only the island of Kyushu, casualties could reach 395,000.

But President Truman possessed the means to perhaps bring the war to a quick and decisive end.

In the following week the list of targets grew. On July 24 I flew a strike against the marshaling yards at Kobe.

The 509th almost made history of a different kind during these missions, and the legend of Claude Eatherly grew in ways he did not intend. On Eatherly's first flight, his primary and secondary targets were socked in by cloud cover. He had his navigator chart a course to Tokyo. His intended target: the Imperial Palace. This action was in direct violation of American policy, not to mention direct orders from the commanding general of the theater, General LeMay, and Colonel Tibbets. It was a court-martial offense. Aiming at his target, Claude found that Tokyo was also obscured by cloud cover, making a visual drop impossible. Undeterred, he dropped the bomb by radar. Fortunately, the Torpex-filled pumpkin fell wide of its intended target and no damage was done to the emperor or the palace. The bomb did obliterate a railroad station, though. History had not been altered by the act of a single loose cannon.

As events set in motion years earlier approached reality, Tinian, in a sense, became the center of the universe. Two billion dollars of our national treasure; years of tireless work by thousands of scientists, technicians, and mechanics; and the efforts of the best minds of the century were about to be handed over to us. On the morning President Truman announced the terms of the Postdam Declaration, the cruiser *Indianapolis* arrived at Tinian. Its cargo contained the firing mechanism for a bomb, and a machined uranium "bullet" resting in a lead container to prevent radioactive leakage. This cargo was stored in the assembly building to await delivery of the uranium core at which the "bullet" would be fired. Also awaiting delivery was the plutonium core for the second bomb, the real pumpkin. These additional components were en route from Hamilton Air Force Base in California aboard three B-29s, each carrying separate radioactive packages.

A few days after we watched the *Indianapolis* depart from Tinian en route to Leyte, in the Philippines, a Japanese submarine sank her. Although a radio distress message had been transmitted before she slipped to the bottom of the ocean, rescue did not come to the men who baked in the relentless tropic sun, floating helplessly in the tranquil, shark-infested waters, for four days. In the fog of war, by some perverse oversight, military authorities at Leyte didn't notice that the *Indianapolis* was missing. A lone aircraft chancing over the area spotted the remaining survivors. Before surface ships arrived, over eight hundred men had died, many devoured by sharks. It was the last American capital ship sunk in World War II.

THIRTEEN

SHORTLY AFTER NOON on August 1 Colonel Tibbets called me in and told me the mission would be carried out on August 6, weather permitting. He then briefed me on the specifics and my role.

Seven B-29s would take part in the mission. Tibbets had conceived a seamless plan designed to address every possible tactical problem, the first of which would be the weather at the target. Theater weather forecasts were at best less than totally adequate. We would need accurate pinpoint reports as near to the real time of the drop as possible, so that if conditions were not good, we could divert to the secondary or the tertiary target. Three airplanes would fly ahead to the potential targets one hour ahead of the strike force to report on weather at the targets—Claude Eatherly in *Straight Flush* to Hiroshima, John Wilson in *Jabit III* to Kokura, and Ralph Taylor in *Full House* to Nagasaki. The nose art, of course, would not be on their planes.

Tibbets would fly the strike airplane, as yet unnamed, carrying the bomb. After rendezvous over Iwo Jima, I would fly *The Great Artiste* in formation with him to the target and drop the instruments that would measure heat, blast, and radiation. It was unusual in a combat mission for instruments to be dropped. But the scientists had precious little data about effects of a nuclear explosion, and this would provide them with at least some important information. Much of their theoretical projections depended on accurate measurements at the target.

George Marquardt had been assigned to pilot *Necessary Evil,* the photographic airplane, accompanying Tibbets and me to the aiming point to record the explosion and damage on the ground. The scientists, as well as the military, had to have photo information at the moment of explosion to assess the true destructiveness of the weapon.

In the event of a mechanical failure, Colonel Tibbets sent a spare B-29, the *Big Stink,* flown by Charles McKnight, to Iwo Jima. Iwo Jima was the midway point in our flight, and the waiting B-29 would serve as a backup if needed. Tibbets also had had a loading pit dug at Iwo so that the bomb could be offloaded and then transferred to McKnight's airplane, if necessary.

Finally, in addition to being essentially unarmed, we would

also fly unescorted by fighters to and from the target. The plan assured that we would be self-contained and self-reliant.

As we had practiced, our approach to the target and release would be from 30,000 feet. The bomb had to be dropped visually—no radar. The bombardier would have to see the target, even though a radar drop could be almost as accurate and effective.

Colonel Tibbets stressed that the instruments must be dropped simultaneously with the bomb. Parachutes on the three canisters carrying the delicate measuring devices would deploy at 14,000 feet and float above the explosion, which would occur at 1,890 feet. I would have as passengers three scientists who would monitor the signals radioed back from the instruments and relay the data to us. Precision would be critical, as I would be in formation off the colonel's right wing. A thirty-second tone signal would be broadcast from the *Enola Gay,* and when it went silent, the bomb would release. At that moment, Beahan would let the instruments go.

The code name for our mission was Centerboard—or, in the sterile bureaucratic language of the military, our operational orders were officially designated Field Order No. 13, Special Bombing Mission No. 13, Operations Order No. 35 of the 509th Composite Group.

The criteria for target selection had been formulated at the highest levels of the Manhattan Project and the War Department. In order to accurately measure the effect of the bomb it was essential that only cities that had not been previously bombed be considered. This was also important to demonstrate clearly to the Japanese the destructive force of the weapon. If a city that had previously been damaged were chosen, it would be difficult to separate the damage from incendiary bombing from that of the atomic bomb. Given Curtis LeMay's daily pounding of Japanese cities, the choices were being considerably narrowed.

One obvious choice was Kyoto. Untouched by bombs, it had been placed on an early list. But Secretary of War Stimson removed it, not only because Kyoto had no military significance, but mostly because its ancient cultural and religious institutions were a treasure to the Japanese people. It is not in the American character to aim for the destruction of cultural and historic places as a matter of policy, even though the world saw no similar restraint by the Japanese military in China and Manchuria, where their policy of destroying anything in their path while brutalizing the civilian populations defined the concept of total war in the 1930s.

A second criterion for target selection was that the targets have military significance. Hiroshima, Kokura, and Niigata remained from the original list. Nagasaki was added.

Hiroshima was the site of command headquarters for the Second Japanese Army, which would mount the defense against any invasion. It also contained major armaments plants, including Mitsubishi Heavy Industries and a huge army ordnance supply depot. Kokura was Japan's most industrialized city. It was called the Pittsburgh of Japan and was its most heavily defended city. Nagasaki housed the major shipbuilding facility and was home to the great Mitsubishi steel and armaments plant and torpedo works, where the bombs and torpedoes used at Pearl Harbor had been manufactured. Even though war-related industries vital to Japan's ability to stay at war were located in Niigata, it was in the end considered an unlikely target. Geographically, Niiagata was situated much farther north than the other cities and would have required a longer flight to the target and return to Tinian.

I was thrilled that Colonel Tibbets had selected me. I had

hoped to be a part of the mission, but I'd never known for sure
that I would be until that private briefing.

The next day, suddenly and unannounced, Tibbets left Tinian. Shortly after he left, on August 3, Tom Classen called
and asked me to join him in his office at six o'clock. He requested that I keep the meeting confidential. Tom was a good-
natured combat veteran, well respected by the group. I was
sure that something of great importance must have come up.

When I arrived, waiting in Classen's office were Group
Operations Officer Colonel Hopkins, Group Intelligence Officer
Hazen Payette and his assistant Joseph Buscher, and Squadron
Intelligence Officer Jim Hinchey. Hopkins, Payette, and
Buscher were staff officers—military, straight-laced, all busi-
ness. They were serious even when they were having fun. All
of them, except Hopkins, were crackerjack intelligence officers.
Tom motioned me to take a seat.

"We have a potential crisis," he began somberly. The men
around the table remained impassive. Whatever was coming,
it was clear they already knew the details. I began to suspect
that maybe the stone faces staring at me were the reason the
meeting had been called. "Colonel Tibbets is gone, and I'm
uncertain where he is or when he'll return."

I saw nothing unusual about Tibbets's absence. He was
always coming and going, and rarely told anyone where he
was off to or returning from. The nature of the entire project
had required this secrecy of movement. I was puzzled that Tom
would be concerned.

Tom continued, "In the event Paul doesn't return by the
sixth, I'll take the first one and Hoppy will take the second."

What the hell were those guys thinking? I had all I could
do to stifle a laugh, except they weren't kidding. I felt like Alice
being invited to the tea party. Either my grasp of reality had
slipped away or these guys were in Wonderland. The idea that

Paul Tibbets would not return was preposterous. I knew as sure as the sun would rise tomorrow, Tibbets would fly the first mission.

None of the four discussed tactics, number of airplanes, the game plan, nothing. Just that they would take the missions. Tibbets must have briefed Classen about them, but maybe he hadn't filled him in on the details. Or maybe they didn't want to fill me in.

Classen taking the bomb? Maybe. But the prospect that Hopkins would take the second mission was beyond comprehension. He had virtually no experience in the whole gamut of specialized maneuvers required to command such a mission, and at best was an adequate pilot.

I didn't say a word because I couldn't figure out what was going on. Perhaps Classen was just covering any possible eventuality. The meeting seemed to come to a stop, and after an awkward pause, Tom said, "Just thought you should know." I thanked him for keeping me apprised and left.

My life during the previous year had moved at dizzying speed. New and highly consequential, often top secret, tasks had greeted me frequently. In this environment, Tom's meeting added a bizarre twist, a dose of unreality. I looked forward to Colonel Tibbets's return.

Later, in passing, I commented to Tibbets about this incident. He just shook his head and grinned. To this day it is a mystery to me why the meeting was called.

Even before Colonel Tibbets had briefed me, it was obvious that the big day was approaching. Over the previous two weeks the tempo of activity on Tinian had been building to a crescendo. Transports were dropping off new groups of civilians from the Manhattan Project daily. Activity at the assembly building was picking up. Navy Captain "Deak" Parsons, who would be the weaponeer in charge of the bomb itself on Tinian and would watch over it on the first mission, had flown to Los Alamos in mid July for what we later learned was the Trinity test at Alamogordo. He would bring back film of the test to show us and would brief us on the world's first nuclear explosion prior to the mission.

On July 29, the 509th flew its last pumpkin strike against Japan prior to Hiroshima. Koriyama, Osaka, Kobe, Shimoda, Ube, Nagoya, Wakayama, and Hitachi were hit by our single conventional Torpex blockbusters.

The war raged on in Asia and the Pacific with no sign from the Japanese that they would surrender. On July 31, Curtis LeMay launched a thousand B-29s to pulverize Japanese cities. Two days later another eight hundred B-29s hit more cities. Still Japan declared its intention to fight to the death. The Peoples Volunteer Corps pressed into service every able-bodied civilian: man, woman, and child. This mass of thirty-two million would supplement the two and one half million soldiers and four million civilian military employees preparing for the invasion force. All of Japan had become an armed camp, all of its population combatants. Their military leaders were prepared to sacrifice their people to achieve a greater glory.

Tibbets arrived back at Tinian on the morning of August 4. That afternoon he gathered all seven participating crews in the briefing hut. The Quonset hut had been cordoned off by armed MPs. Everyone entering was carefully checked by security. Inside, each crew sat together on rows of straight-backed wooden benches on either side of an aisle leading to the front of the long, narrow hut. Two recent arrivals on Tinian also were present to observe the mission—Winston Churchill's personal representatives, Group Captain Leonard Cheshire, recipient of the Victoria Cross for valor, and British scientist William Penney. At the front, on a slightly elevated podium, were two large blackboards draped with white cloths. The rest of the area resembled any other briefing room, with maps of Japan and adjacent islands covering the walls.

There was a buzz in the room as the crews chatted among themselves. When I arrived, I sat about three rows back with my crew. At three P.M. Paul Tibbets strode in with Intelligence Officers Payette and Buscher in tow and proceeded directly to the podium. Captain Parsons joined them. Tibbets explained that we were going to drop a bomb of unimaginable destructive force. The word *atomic* or *nuclear* was never uttered by him or any of the others who would shortly brief us. He told us this single bomb would be the equivalent of twenty thousand tons of TNT. That got everyone's attention.

He then introduced Captain Parsons, who motioned to a projectionist at the back of the room. The room went dark. In the thirty-five years that I have served in the military, I have never been at one briefing where they didn't screw up the projector. This briefing was no different. The film was not feeding onto the projector's sprockets. A single beam of light divided the darkness in the center aisle. Dust and insects fluttered in the beam. After some fumbling in the dark, the images started to flicker onto the screen before us. An intense flash erupted out of the darkness, and from the desert floor an angry, seething fireball exploded upward, blossoming into a mushroom-shaped cloud. We sat immobile, riveted by what we saw.

The lights flickered on. Parsons explained the Manhattan Project and gave a vivid account of what we had just witnessed. He said the flash at Alamogordo, New Mexico, had been seen over 250 miles away in El Paso, Texas. The sound had been heard 100 miles away. He told of a blind girl who had never had vision seeing the flash.

He then said that no one knew for sure what the bomb would do. We were about to drop this thing—something that had never been done before—from 30,000 feet. We could expect a blinding flash of light, at which point we should be wearing welder's goggles with thick polarized lenses, which were then distributed to us. Parsons stressed that we must wear the goggles and under no circumstances were we to look directly at the explosion. Estimates were that a mushroom cloud would rise from the explosion to at least our altitude and continue past us to 50,000 or 60,000 feet. We were not to fly through or near the cloud. It would contain nuclear debris and be radioactive.

Tibbets resumed the briefing as Payette and Buscher unveiled the blackboards. Displayed were high-resolution reconnaissance photographs of Hiroshima, Kokura, and Nagasaki. These were the targets in order of priority. He explained the assignments for each of the seven aircraft and details on the flight plan. Fly at 8,000 feet to Iwo, where the three strike aircraft would rendezvous and fly for two hours in loose formation toward Japan. Then commence ascent to 30,000 feet to target. There would be strict radio silence throughout the mission. The expected date would be August 6, weather permitting.

The group meteorologist briefed us on the weather. It was iffy. In the area of the targets, weather was not good. He expected a clearing trend, however, and said that the targets should be improved by the sixth.

Payette and Buscher briefed us on the latest intelligence. Hiroshima was ringed by antiaircraft batteries, but they were concentrated to the west and south of the city, making the east our best approach. Kokura was more heavily defended because of the density of the industries in the city. It was uncertain if the Japanese would throw up any Zeros at us at either city.

Air-sea rescue was then detailed. Navy flying boats, affectionately called Dumbos, would maintain constant patrol of our flight path to and from the empire. They would work in conjunction with surface vessels and submarines to pluck us from the water if we were downed. B-29 "Superdumbos" were also prepared to drop survival equipment. It was one of the more elaborate efforts I had ever seen.

Tibbets then closed the briefing by telling us that this bomb would end the war. He reminded us that the mission was still top secret. We were not to talk about it even to each other. No letters home. We shouldn't even hint that there was a possible mission about to take place. He offered that anyone who did not want to take part could leave and there would be no questions asked. No one responded. He concluded by telling us he was honored and proud to serve with men like us.

The briefing was over, leaving each of us to his thoughts.

FOURTEEN

Sᴜɴᴅᴀʏ, Aᴜɢᴜsᴛ 5, I attended morning mass as had been my practice since childhood. The priest from the Eighth Bomber Group conducted the service under a brilliant blue sky, behind him a distinct horizon separating the ocean from the sky, heaven from earth. It was a balmy, tropical morning. A faint wind blew across the rows of worshipers. My faith has always been a source of comfort to me, and that morning I felt peace, a tranquillity borne of belief in a higher power.

The predictable ceremony of the mass, spoken in the mysterious and lyrical cadence of a language long since extinct, allows for reflection. I prayed that the carnage of four years of war would soon be brought to an end. My faith teaches the innate goodness of man. Yet how do we explain the barbarism man inflicts? The answer found in our teachings is that evil also dwells among us. Not as the symbolic serpent in the Garden of Eden, or as some metaphor for bad acts, but as a living force. We are engaged in a constant battle for our souls, a struggle that demands more of us than being just passively good. We must confront and overcome evil.

Never in my lifetime has evil been more clearly defined than in the specters of the Third Reich and the Japanese military of Emperor Hirohito.

I received Communion. During the previous evening's confession, I had taken Colonel Tibbets's prohibition about discussing our impending mission literally, even within the priest-penitent privilege of the confessional. I would silently commune with God and tell Him about our mission.

After breakfast, George Marquardt and I met with Colonel Tibbets to briefly go over some of the details of the mission. All the crews would receive a final briefing later in the evening, a few hours prior to takeoff. We reviewed the basics: take off at approximately 0230 (2:30 A.M.), fly at 8,000 feet to conserve fuel, rendezvous over Iwo at 0600, prior to reaching target climb to 30,000 feet. Strict radio silence would be observed. Our codes and radio frequencies were confirmed. The aiming point at the primary target would be the T-shaped Aioi Bridge across the Ota River in the center of Hiroshima, a geographic feature that would be distinct even at 30,000 feet.

It had also been decided that because of concerns that a crash on takeoff might detonate the bomb, we would take off with the bomb unarmed. Captain "Deak" Parsons would arm Little Boy, the name given to the uranium bomb, en route to Iwo Jima and before we climbed to 30,000 feet. The firing mechanism on the bomb was relatively simple. A uranium bullet was fired down a gun-barrel-like cylinder at a core of uranium in the nose of the barrel to create a "critical mass" that would start a chain reaction. It was feasible to keep the cylinder blocked, preventing the uranium slug from smashing into the uranium core by accident, and arm the bomb in flight. This would be a delicate and laborious task for Captain Parsons in the cramped confines of the bomb bay, but it was a better option than the unthinkable if a crash occurred. The B-29, carrying a full load of fuel, a full complement of men, and a nine-thousand-pound bomb, would far exceed the maximum weight specifications for a safe takeoff.

George and I lingered for a few minutes after the meeting. George was the perfect man to be with us on this first mission. He was a serious guy when it came to flying. Not dour, but intent on getting the details perfect. You knew that if you told George to do X, he would do X perfectly. He absorbed what he was told. For this mission, nothing less would be required.

The news of the day was that there was no news, except for the names of killed and wounded added to the daily list of casualties. The Japanese had given no indication that they were ready to quit. In fact, the official Japanese response to the Potsdam Declaration had been to characterize it as beneath contempt and unworthy of a response.

Even if one didn't get the message in the stultified language of diplomats, the actions of the Japanese military continued to speak clearly. During Curtis LeMay's air campaign, we had dropped leaflets on four potential targets to be firebombed the following night, yet the Japanese leaders refused to evacuate civilians from those cities. The next night two of the cities would be obliterated. It was extraordinary that the Japanese would absorb the crippling devastation of the nightly firebombings and still go on. But they did. It was within their power to end the war at any time by surrendering. We didn't have this option.

As we got closer to the time of takeoff, the anticipation of flying the mission became paramount. My full concentration was on what we were about to do. There was no more time to think about the events unfolding daily across the theater, or about the reports we had received on Tinian detailing the brutal treatment reserved for captured B-29 crews. There was only the mission. It was what I had trained to do, and it was now the single focus of my world.

After lunch I went down to the flight line, where my airplane was parked at its hardstand. The entire runway complex and the interconnecting roads, rampways, and paths were sealed off and under heavy guard. MPs with carbines and Thompson submachine guns were prominently posted everywhere. By that time the breezy warmth of the morning had given way to the blazing heat of the tropic's midday sun beating down on and reflecting off of the black asphalt. The ground crews were dressed in shorts and most were bare-chested, busy getting *The Great Artiste* ready and checking all systems. On the hardstand across the way, about fifty yards from me, I could see similar activity where Paul Tibbets's airplane was parked. The arrowhead in a circle on our tails signifying the 509th had been painted over with a large block letter *R* for another group assigned to the Twentieth Air Force. Every detail, including confusing the enemy as to our identity and point of origination, had been thought of by Tibbets. I spoke with each member of the ground crew, a practice I always followed before any flight.

From three to four in the afternoon, I tried to get a little shut-eye, but I couldn't sleep. The heat, humidity, and anticipation made sleep impossible. Beahan, Albury, Van Pelt, and I ended up sitting around in our hut making conversation, no one mentioning what was really on our minds.

Later that afternoon, while I was resting in my quarters, Armed Forces Radio announced the release of a new feature motion picture starring Fred MacMurray and titled *Captain Eddie*. It was the story of World War I ace Eddie Rickenbacker. That war to me seemed like ancient history.

The day was dragging. I wanted to get going. It has been said from the beginning of time—by everyone from ancient Greek warriors to those huddling in the slit trenches of World War I—the waiting is the hardest. Waiting is the most wearing on the mind. I tried to fill the time, but I was only killing it. After the evening meal at 1800, I again went over to the flight line. I walked around my airplane, looking for nothing in particular, just looking. I knew that the "special," which was how we now referred to the weapon, had already been loaded into the bomb bay of Tibbets's airplane.

Some civilian scientists from Project Alberta were making adjustments to the sensitive measuring devices stored aboard my airplane. On the mission, Drs. Luis Alvarez, Lawrence Johnston, and Harold Agnew would monitor the instruments from positions in the rear compartment. These men were among the most brilliant people in the world. I felt honored to be in their company. In the preceding days I'd had the chance to get to know them and Dr. Norman Ramsey, who headed Project Alberta on Tinian. For all their brilliance, these scientists didn't have their heads in the clouds. They were committed to the project and clearly understood what was at stake.

In one of our secure discussions with Drs. Ramsey and Alvarez and some of the Project Alberta working group, I had asked the question, "What is the potential if this works the way you want it to?" They answered that this bomb would be a "firecracker" compared to what might eventually be developed.

I had nothing to compare their prediction with, even in theory. That is until after Hiroshima and Nagasaki. Only then would the comparison have substance, a reference point from which to glimpse into the future. If what I had witnessed over those cities was only a "firecracker" compared to potential future atomic weapons, then the nature and ultimate stakes of any future war were forever changed. For the scientists whose domain was the expansion of human inquiry, the knowledge they had acquired could not be erased. As Einstein had warned President Roosevelt, the science to build an atomic weapon was known. It was only a question of who would develop it. How would human nature adjust to the greater infernal possibilities knowing that in any future war the ultimate price of aggression could be annihilation?

At 2200 hours (ten P.M.), our final briefing began in the briefing hut. Prior to going over to the brief, all crew members deposited their personal belongings with a designated man in their quarters for safekeeping, as is required before every combat mission. We were to carry only our dog tags. In the event of capture, we would give the enemy no more than was required by the Geneva Convention—name, rank, and serial number. Any information, no matter how inconsequential, could be used by the enemy to break you.

Everything was a go. The weather looked good; it would be a cloudless day over Japan. Intelligence reported no changes in air defenses at the three targets since the fourth. Air-sea rescue would be on station and ready. The Japanese had not surrendered. Recall codes were reviewed in the event we were ordered to return. Our call sign for the mission would be Dimples.

The intelligence officer stepped forward to synchronize our watches. On his instructions, we set our watches at 11:30, with the second hand at 12. He began, "Thirty seconds, twenty-five, fifteen, ten, nine, eight, seven, six, five, four, three, two, one, hack." In unison, we all pushed our winding stems in. The second hands began their sweep.

We then proceeded to the Dogpatch Inn, the name given to the 509th's mess hall, for our preflight meal. If all went well, we would be back at this mess hall in about thirteen hours.

The three weather crews had already finished up and were being trucked to the runway, when, at about midnight, Tibbets came into the mess hall. Our three crews quieted down as he spoke. Again, without using the words *atomic* or *nuclear,* he told us we could end the war by dropping this very powerful bomb. He reminded us to do our jobs, the jobs we had trained so hard to do. He then asked Chaplain Downey to step forward and offer a prayer.

Our heads bowed, the 509th's chaplain's deep, rich voice invoked the Lord's blessing for us and our mission. He beseeched Almighty God to deliver us safely so that we might bring the war to a speedy end.

Each crew boarded a six-by-six lorry that deposited it at the Personal Equipment Supply Hut, where we each drew and signed for a parachute, a flak vest, a flotation device, a combat knife, a survival kit with first-aid package, fish hooks, food rations, a drinking water kit, and a .45-caliber automatic pistol with ammunition.

I gathered up my stuff, dumped it into the back of the truck, and climbed up front with the driver. I strapped on the web belt from which the holstered .45 hung and removed the clip of ammunition and placed it in the leg pocket of my flying overalls. I never carried a loaded weapon, remembering my father's admonition that I should be careful I didn't shoot my foot off.

Boxed lunches and jugs of pineapple juice and water that had been delivered from the commissary earlier were also loaded onto the trucks. As each crew was ready, the three trucks proceeded to North Field and the assigned hardstands. It was now a little after one A.M. The weather airplanes were already conducting their final preflight checks and would be airborne in about half an hour.

FIFTEEN

THE TRUCK CAME to a stop at the last security checkpoint within half a mile of our hardstand. MPs with Thompson submachine guns blocked the front and sides of the truck as a security officer asked for and reviewed every man's entry pass. Sitting in the passenger side, I could see in the distance roving patrols as well as stationed guards. Satisfied that we belonged, the officer waved us through and we drove to the airplane.

As my crew stowed their gear and food and checked their positions in the airplane, I jumped into a jeep and drove over to Paul Tibbets's hardstand. I wanted to wish him luck. The scene I encountered was surrealistic. There had to be two hundred people, in addition to the ground and flight crews, standing in an island of intense light. Mobile generators were powering all forms of illumination: stands of high-intensity shop lights, floods, popping flashbulbs, and klieg lights like those you'd see at a grand opening of a movie or the Academy Awards ceremony. Army photographers and film crews, MPs, technicians, senior officers, and civilians—who, I presumed, were the scientists—milled about. If there was some order to the scene, I didn't see it. I caught sight of Tibbets in conversation within a group. He looked fully engaged, and I decided it was best to let him be. It was then that I saw the foot-high black block letters painted on the fuselage beneath the pilot's window, *Enola Gay*. His would be the only airplane on our mission to have a name painted on the fuselage, and he'd named it after his mother.

Unknown to all of us that morning, the names Tibbets, Hiroshima, and *Enola Gay* were to become a unified icon for a new age—an icon whose meaning would be interpreted by many seeking to prove some theory of the human condition. We who were about to undertake this mission to end the war were to be seen in coming years merely as images frozen in black-and-white photographs, or flickering in grainy military films of the moment—props in the historic drama. But our meaning as we knew it and had lived it to that moment was not the stuff of obtuse philosophical musings. We were ordinary men called upon to execute a dangerous mission whose outcome was far from certain. The only thing that was certain at that point was that the aggressor would not surrender.

On returning to my hardstand, I; Albury; my flight engineer, John Kuharek; and the ground crew chief began our walkaround. In a set, methodical procedure carried out by every pilot of every airplane who has ever flown or ever will fly, we examined every surface of the airplane. From the nosewheel well, to the engine cowlings, to the tail—every surface was inspected one more time. Tire pressures were checked. Any telltale drops of fluid found were brought to the attention of the crew chief for explanation or repair, if minor. I watched as Pappy Dehart, our tail gunner, checked the 20mm cannons, the only guns we'd be carrying. With one thousand rounds of ammunition, they weren't much if we had to use them. A few bursts and we'd be toothless.

Before getting aboard, I assembled the crew for another time-honored procedure, inspecting them and making sure they all had the personal gear required for the mission—parachute, Mae West, and so on. Their helmets and flak vests had already been stored by each man at his assigned position in the airplane. I spent a few extra minutes with Drs. Alvarez, Johnston, and Agnew. I knew they had never flown a combat mission, and I wanted to make sure they had what they needed. I also wanted to answer any questions they might have. For civilians, they were remarkably calm, although I thought I could detect an understated excitement about the fact that we were actually going.

Albury, Beahan, Kuharek, Van Pelt, and I climbed through the hatch in the nosewheel well. The rest of the crew and the civilian scientists entered through the aft hatch. Kuharek ordered the putt-putt, a portable auxiliary gas-fueled generator that supplied electrical power to the airplane before the engines were started, fired up. Once the engines were running, they would turn the generators that powered all electrical systems. With the auxiliary power on, each system was checked by the flight engineer while Albury and I went through our preflight checklist. All systems were go. In sequence, engines number 3, number 2, number 4, and number 1 came to life with a faint whir and then a surge of the propellers, the hum vibrating through the fuselage. The four 2,200-horsepower, thirty-six cylinder, fuel-injection, Wright R-3350 radial engines were running smoothly. It's a sound that is as comforting to a pilot as a lullaby is to a baby.

Everything was perfect.

It was time to go. At exactly 2:30 A.M., I heard the tower

respond to Paul's request for taxi and takeoff instructions: "Dimples, eight-two. Clear to taxi to Runway A for Able. Over." Then, "Cleared into position on runway."

In a few minutes I would receive clearance to taxi and take off from Runway B, and then George Marquardt would be cleared for Runway C. The three weather airplanes had lifted off an hour earlier and were already heading for their respective cities. An hour before we reached our potential targets, they would report back to Tinian on the weather conditions at each location. We could intercept their transmission in our aircraft for decisionmaking.

As I idled on Runway B, I could see over to Runway A. At 2:45 A.M. Colonel Tibbets started his run. I saw him lift off and then lost sight of him in the darkness. We were using no running lights.

Precisely two minutes after Tibbets's takeoff, I lifted off into the clear starry night, and precisely two minutes after me, George Marquardt lifted off. We would be staggered at about ten-mile intervals until we reached our rendezvous over Iwo Jima, the halfway mark on our journey. Once in the air, we turned toward the northwest. At a rate of 500 feet per minute, we began our climb to 8,000 feet, maintaining a cruising speed of 250 miles per hour. We would conserve fuel by flying at this lower altitude, because at higher altitudes, where the air is thinner, the internal combustion engines powering our aircraft would require more fuel to compensate for the diminished volume of air per square foot, just as a car being driven at higher altitudes in the mountains requires an adjustment to its carburetor.

Out ahead of us in the darkness, "Deak" Parsons would be climbing from the forward crew compartment into the forward bomb bay to begin the delicate task of arming Little Boy.

I lit my Cuban Romeo y Julieta and settled back for the

three-hour flight to the rendezvous. There was little chitchat. The crew tried to catch some shut-eye. The atmosphere on board was relaxed. Not loose, but tension-free. Relaxed in the way that any group of professionals is when its members are carrying out a job they're supremely trained to do and confident in their abilities.

It was about 5:45 A.M. when we caught sight of Iwo. Rising prominently above the island was Mount Suribachi. Six months earlier, five marines and a navy medic had raised the American flag on its summit. No other photograph of the war captured the grit, the sacrifice, and the ultimate triumph that defined the marine corps in the Pacific better than that picture, flashed around the world, of those marines raising the flag. Over 6,000 leathernecks, army soldiers and sailors had died taking this killing field. Another 21,000 had been maimed or otherwise wounded. Because of their sacrifices, hundreds of B-29 crews were able to land their crippled aircraft at this strategic spot off the Japanese coast when returning from missions to the mainland, while the Japanese military was denied a key fighter defense base.

George and I slipped in behind Tibbets in formation on each of his wings as he circled Suribachi. The sky was crystal clear. As I looked to the east I saw the sun emerging above the horizon, a huge red ball rising up from the ocean. It was now 6:00 A.M. Tibbets set course to Japan. We were on our final leg. In three hours we would deliver what we hoped was the final blow to the enemy.

Two hours out of Iwo, we began a slow climb to 30,000 feet as we approached the mainland. The weather airplanes were now circling each of the possible targets. The report came in from Claude Eatherly's *Straight Flush*. We deciphered the coded message: "Target Clear." The final coded transmission, "C-1," meant we should bomb the primary target. In fact, all the targets were clear. Eatherly circled around Hiroshima, turned southeast, and headed back to Tinian.

I advised the crew over the intercom that we were headed to our primary, Hiroshima. We crossed over from the ocean to the mainland of Japan at 7:30 A.M. Our ETA to the target at Hiroshima was 8:15 A.M., Japanese time.

At 8:12, with my plane off the *Enola Gay*'s right wing, Colonel Tibbets arrived at the IP about fifteen miles east of the target, from which he would begin the bomb run to the aiming point. Hiroshima lay before us, distinct and bright in the morning sun. I reminded the crew to put their goggles on. No flak was coming up, and there were no indications that enemy fighters had been scrambled to intercept us. Nothing to interfere with our run.

At our cruising speed of three hundred miles an hour, we would be at the aiming point in three minutes. Kermit Beahan readied himself to release the three instrument canisters. Ahead, I could clearly make out the Aioi Bridge. Thirty seconds from the release point, Tom Ferebee, aboard the *Enola Gay*, flipped a switch that sent a high-pitched tone signal out to all the airplanes. When it stopped, Little Boy would fall free, and Beahan, at that precise moment, would release the canisters holding the scientific equipment. I was now about thirty feet off Tibbets's right wing.

The *Enola Gay*'s bomb bay doors snapped open. Then the tone fell silent. I saw the bomb release. Beahan let the canisters go.

It was 8:15. In forty-three seconds the bomb would detonate, or at least that was when it was *supposed* to detonate. As I watched the bomb falling free on its forward arc, a thought flashed through my mind: "It's too late now. There are no strings or cables attached. We can't get it back, whether it works or not. But if it works, it just might end the war."

Further reflection was a luxury I didn't have the time for. My immediate task was to get my airplane and my men the hell out of there—fast. I banked the airplane 60 degrees into a sharp 155-degree diving turn to the right. Tibbets had already executed the same maneuver.

Something was wrong. I had pulled down my goggles right after the bomb fell free, but the polarized glass of the lenses was so dark it was almost opaque. I couldn't see my instruments. In one swift motion I shoved the goggles up onto my forehead. I didn't consider the consequences to my eyesight when the bomb exploded. For the moment I had to see clearly. My future ability to see was not an immediate concern. We would be about twelve miles from the target when the bomb detonated.

The bomb was to my back as we continued to move away from ground zero. Suddenly the sky was bleached a bright white, brighter than the sun. I instinctively squeezed my eyes shut, but the light filled my head.

At that instant my tail gunner, Pappy Dehart, began uttering gibberish over the intercom. In combat, a gunner has to report what he sees precisely, distinctly, and once, and then wait for the pilot's acknowledgment. Pappy, an experienced gunner, was now running over his own words, his alarm garbling what he was saying. I tried to break in. "Pappy, say again."

Just then the airplane was hit with violent force and jounced mightily. Kermit Beahan, a man familiar with taking fire, turned to me with panic on his face and yelled, "Flak!" With that, we were hit again, with less force but still jarring.

I soon realized that Pappy was trying to describe a sight no human being had ever seen. Rushing up toward us were concentric rings of donut-shaped, clear, superheated air that were striking the airplane with unexpected force. But they didn't appear to be causing any damage. The airplane was still handling fine. I continued my turn, rolling out southeasterly to get off the coast and head to Tinian.

Hiroshima now lay to the west, on the right side of my airplane. I looked down and saw a roiling, dirty brown cloud spreading out horizontally over the city. Out of it was emerging a vertical cloud that looked like it contained every color of the rainbow, and more. The colors were vivid—hard to describe— some I had never seen before. I saw a series of fires breaking through the quickly spreading smoke that was covering the city. The vertical cloud was rising rapidly. In what seemed an instant, it had reached 30,000 feet, and it continued rising to over 45,000 feet. As it gained altitude, a huge white mushroom shape formed at the top.

Aboard the *Enola Gay,* Dick Nelson had already radioed a strike report to Tinian advising that the primary target had been bombed visually, results good. A few minutes later Captain Parsons handed Nelson a more detailed coded message to be radioed back to General Farrell on Tinian:

CLEAR CUT. SUCCESSFUL IN ALL RESPECTS. VISIBLE EF-FECTS GREATER THAN ALAMOGORDO. CONDITIONS NORMAL IN AIRPLANE FOLLOWING DELIVERY. PRO-CEEDING TO BASE.

We headed back to Tinian. Mission accomplished. We were nearly two hundred miles away from Hiroshima before Pappy Dehart lost sight of the mushroom cloud. The atmosphere among the crew on the flight back was quiet but buoyant. Surely the Japanese would have to surrender. It was inconceivable that they would not, after what we had just witnessed.

On the return flight I stayed in a loose formation trailing the *Enola Gay.* George Marquardt was farther behind, having stayed at Hiroshima a bit longer to complete the photographic mission. As I approached Tinian, I eased off some power, reducing my airspeed. This was Paul Tibbets's day, and I wanted to be sure his would be the first airplane to touch down at North Field.

It had been a picture-perfect mission from beginning to end.

SIXTEEN

IT WOULD BE several days before the magnitude of the destruction was understood. Reconnaissance airplanes from LeMay's XXI Bomber Command flew hourly missions in the area near and over Hiroshima, but the fires and smoke would continue to obscure the ground for the next couple of days, making damage assessments speculative. Yet we who had flown the mission knew the city of Hiroshima was gone.

While we made our final approach to North Field, Colonel Tibbets had already landed and was taxiing in. As I touched down on Runway B, I saw a throng of people who had massed on the area near Tibbets's hardstand. The hundreds of cheering men was a sight to behold. As we rolled down the taxiway past Tibbets's airplane, it was clear that a full-scale celebration was under way. All of the men of the 509th, the other units on Tinian, and soon the world, would know what was so special about the 509th. At about the moment we taxied by the *Enola Gay,* General Carl "Tooey" Spaatz, commander of all air forces in the Pacific, was pinning the Distinguished Service Cross, the second-highest medal for valor, on Colonel Paul Tibbets's sweaty, wrinkled flying coveralls, right there on the macadam, while generals, admirals, and other officers and enlisted men looked on. The assembled mass had crowded around the *Enola Gay,* engulfing it and the men who had flown her. Even if I had wanted to get to Tibbets after deplaning, it would have been impossible. He and his crew would soon be whisked off to an intelligence debriefing presided over personally by Spaatz, General Farrell, and Admiral Parnell together with senior intelligence officers.

We were met by our ground crew and a waiting truck. My crew and I climbed aboard and were taken to the medical tent. Standard procedure after every combat mission was that the medics checked you over, making sure you had all your fingers and toes. Then you'd be given two shots of 100-proof whiskey for medicinal purposes. For those who declined the libation, there was always someone ready, willing, and able to step forward and help out. No sense leaving perfectly good whiskey in the medical tent.

This time we were also checked over by two doctors, one of whom was a radiologist. They were anxious to determine if we had been exposed to radiation. A methodical pass of a Geiger counter put to rest any concern that we had been irradiated. It also put to rest any lingering worry among the crew that exposure to radiation would have caused sterility. Not much was known about the effects of massive dosages of radiation. I was told later that an air burst of the bomb at 1,890 feet had been favored over a ground burst to maximize the blast effect and reduce the radiation on the ground.

Toes, fingers, and our reproductive systems intact, we were driven to an intelligence hut for debriefing. All crews returning from any combat mission had to be debriefed—it was standard operating procedure. It was in the manual. A team of intelligence officers questioned us together as a crew. They read from the usual script used after every mission: "What did you see?" "Any flak?" "How much? Light . . . medium . . . heavy?" "Any fighters?" "How many?" "From which direction?" "Anything else unusual?"

Anything else unusual? Why, yes. We'd just destroyed an entire city with a single bomb.

Of course, the main act was in another Quonset hut, where Tibbets and his crew were providing their own details to the assembled brass. And this was fine with my crew and me. We were just glad to be back in one piece, and we hoped to be on our way home soon.

Walking out of the briefing hut into a bright sunny day, I was stopped by someone who said a marine lieutenant by the name of Paul Burns was looking for me. As if the day hadn't already been strange in ways both big and small, there, on Tinian, on that day, my future brother-in-law had come to pay me a visit. I was in the most secure facility in the world, under the most impenetrable cloak of secrecy of any unit in the military. And Paul Burns was waiting to see me. How the hell had he found me? Well, why not? This was a day on which all things seemed possible.

"Are you sure it's Paul Burns?" I asked.

"Yeah. Big strapping guy. Kind of brash. He's down with the crowd at North Field, a beer in each hand."

Yup. It was Paul Burns.

I made my way down to the baseball field. The flight line had been sealed off and the celebration was in full swing. On receiving news of the mission's success, plans for a party to welcome us back had been hastily put together that morning. A flatbed truck loaded with cases of free beer was parked on the baseball field. Thousands of sandwiches, salads, and hot dogs were prepared and ready to be served. The mood was jubilant. The talk was that the war was over, we'd all be going home soon. The party would go on all day and well into the night.

I had no trouble finding Paul Burns. At six foot two, he literally stood out among the crowd. He was dressed sharply in his marine khakis. We hugged and slapped each other on the back and expressed our joy at seeing each other. Paul was engaged to my sister Marylyn. They'd met while he was a student at Boston College and Marylyn was attending Emmanuel College. He told me he had hitched a ride over on a transport from Guam, where his unit was stationed, taking an educated guess that I might be on Tinian. He knew I wasn't with the organization in Guam, and he didn't think I was among the first arrivals in Saipan. He connected the dots and found me on that extraordinary day.

We shared a beer. By talking to people in the crowd, Paul had picked up the broad outline of what had happened. He had heard the term "atomic bomb." With the need for absolute secrecy now gone, I told him I had been on the mission and that indeed we had dropped the first atomic bomb. It had destroyed an entire city. Sensing he still didn't comprehend the magnitude of it, I explained that this one bomb had the explosive equivalent of twenty thousand tons of TNT—of thousands of conventional bombs. He nodded. What he did understand was that he and tens of thousands of other young American men would be spared further death and suffering.

I brought my future brother-in-law over to my quarters and introduced him around to Beahan, Albury, and Van Pelt. There was plenty of room in our hut to accommodate ten comfortably, so I told him he could stay with us while he was on

Tinian. After a quick shower, we headed over to the officers' club.

It was close to six P.M. when we walked in. The club was a large Quonset hut, elevated on stilts, with a small plywood bar at one end and tables and chairs scattered about. A wild celebration was under way. The walls were bulging. Although the club typically served only beer, bottles of hard liquor had appeared from unspecified sources. I suspected that maybe someone had commandeered the stash of whiskey stored in the medical department. Wherever it had come from and however it had gotten there, no one was asking any questions. All work on the island had stopped, and it is accurate to say now that the order of the day was to get drunk.

I was just about out of gas. It was then around seven in the evening, and I was exhausted. What I craved most was sleep. I bid Paul Burns a good night and had just started out when I saw Paul Tibbets. I hadn't noticed him come in. He motioned for me to join him off to one side.

As the party raged around us, he said, "Chuck, if it becomes necessary, the second one will be dropped on the ninth. Primary target will be Kokura. The secondary target will be Nagasaki." He paused, then added, "You're going to command the mission."

He went on to explain that if the Japanese still did not surrender, it was vital that they believed we had an unlimited supply of atomic bombs and that we would continue to use them. Of course, the truth was that we had only one more bomb on Tinian. Delivery of a third bomb was several weeks away. But if we were to sustain the psychological impact necessary to force a surrender, there could be no prolonged delay in the second mission. Long-range forecasts predicted that the weather would worsen over the next several days. We couldn't wait for a perfect day. The last possible acceptable date would be August 9. After that, the weather would force a delay of at least another week, maybe longer.

Even as we spoke, Tokyo Radio was minimizing the true impact and devastation at Hiroshima, reporting that some damage had been caused at Hiroshima after B-29s dropped incendiary bombs. The Japanese military was arguing that the weapon must be so complicated it was unlikely that we had more. They were wrong by only one. Having sustained the worst we could inflict, they could certainly fight on.

My head was in a spin. I had assumed that if a second strike were ever needed, Tibbets would be in command again. But he was entrusting me to deliver the knockout punch with my first combat mission command. "Yes, sir," I answered.

"You'll use the same tactics," he went on.

I wondered about that. Three unescorted B-29s, preceded by a single weather aircraft and coming in at 30,000 feet, was now a distinctive signature. The Japanese might figure it out and throw everything they had up at us. "The same tactics?" I repeated.

"The same," he replied.

"Yes, sir."

Even though I had some reservations, I didn't raise them. But my response was more than just a reflexive reaction to an order. I trusted Tibbets's judgment and experience. If he believed that was the right way to carry out a second mission, then it was the right way.

"We're going to have to do one more fuse test in the next couple of days, when the scientists are ready," Tibbets continued. He explained that the second bomb would be a plutonium bomb and that it was much more complex than Little Boy.

As I left the club I was elated that Colonel Tibbets had chosen me. This was a supreme compliment from a man I admired and respected.

When I arrived at my quarters, Beahan, Albury, and Van Pelt were there, still awake. I told them the news. Nonplussed, they responded that we could do it, no problem. None of us was in a reflective mood, given the day we had had. The next morning I would assemble the remainder of my crew on the flight line and fill them in. But just then, I hit the sack and drifted off into a deep sleep.

While I slept, the Japanese had to come to grips with the reality that the prospect of "total destruction" as promised in the Potsdam Declaration was now upon them. From Washington, President Truman's formal statement was released to the world:

> Sixteen hours ago an American airplane dropped one bomb on Hiroshima. It is an atomic bomb. It is a harnessing of the basic power of the universe. We are now prepared to obliterate more rapidly and completely every productive enterprise the Japanese have above ground in any city. We shall destroy their docks, their factories, and their communications. Let there be no mistake; we shall completely destroy Japan's power to make war. If they do not now accept our terms they may expect a rain of ruin from the air, the likes of which has never been seen on this earth.

Armed Forces Radio immediately began transmitting to the Japanese mainland the fact that the atomic bomb had destroyed Hiroshima and that more would follow. Millions of leaflets were dropped over Japanese cities:

> To the Japanese people: America asks that you take immediate heed of what we say on this leaflet.
>   We are in possession of the most destructive explosive ever devised by man. A single one of our newly developed atomic bombs is actually the equivalent in explosive power to what 2,000 of our

giant B-29s can carry on a single mission. This awful fact is one for
you to ponder and we solemnly assure you that it is grimly accurate.

We have just begun to use this weapon against your homeland.
If you still have any doubt, make inquiry as to what happened to
Hiroshima when just one atomic bomb fell on that city.

Before using this bomb to destroy every resource of the military
by which they are prolonging this useless war, we ask that you now
petition the Emperor to end the war. Our President has outlined for
you the thirteen consequences of an honorable surrender. We urge
that you accept these consequences and begin work on building a
new, better and peaceloving Japan.

You should take these steps now to cease military resistance.
Otherwise, we shall resolutely employ this bomb and all our other
superior weapons to promptly and forcefully end the war.

Evacuate your cities now!

To the president's message, and to the millions of leaflets
dropped, there was no response.

On August 7, Curtis LeMay would launch 152 B-29s to
inflict more conventional destruction upon Japan.

There would still be no response.

On August 8, 375 B-29s would pound Japanese cities, including 224 B-29s that would firebomb the industrial city of
Yawata, an event that would have grave consequences for me
and my crew the next day. Fifty years later, a revisionist historian on CNN's program *Crossfire*, in an attempt to characterize
the Japanese in 1945 as the victims of American aggression,
would tell me face-to-face that General LeMay had stopped
firebombing Japan in late July. I believe he read it somewhere.
Thus, his story went, because Japan had been militarily defeated before either atomic bomb was dropped, the missions
were unnecessary.

Still there would be no response from the Japanese.

In spite of military and diplomatic efforts to convince, coerce, and otherwise force the Japanese to stop fighting, the samurai mentality of their militaristic society made the notion of accepting unconditional surrender inconceivable. And as hundreds of thousands of American troops anxiously waited at staging areas in the Pacific, dreading the possibility of an imminent invasion, the jubilation America was feeling at this moment was now tempered for me by the growing realization that the Japanese were going to continue the war.

With barely enough time to digest and reflect upon the historic event my crew and I had participated in on August 6, we had already begun preparing to do it again.

August 7 dawned brightly over our Pacific home with what I thought might develop into an international incident, with me at the center of the storm. I should have sensed that something was amiss when Paul Burns casually mentioned at breakfast that he had gotten into a little beef the night before and hoped it wouldn't embarrass me. A few punches had been thrown; no one had been hurt. In fact, I did dismiss it. Unlike the other services, the air force was much looser and more casual about rank and protocol among its officer corps. Rank was never a barrier, particularly when we partied. I remember one incident at Grand Island when a renowned general and a major, both pickled, got into a no-holds-barred fistfight over a comely blond at one of the officers' club's Saturday night dances. The next day, no hard feelings, no court-martial, just business as usual. In any other branch of the military, the incident would have ruined one, if not both, careers.

So, given the celebration of the night before, how much everyone had been drinking, the general aura of goodwill, and the fact that Paul Burns wasn't in the stockade, I reasoned, how bad could it be? But gradually Paul gave me at least the vague details of what he could remember, and others began to fill me in as the day progressed.

Paul, being Boston Irish, had an antipathy toward the British. It was ingrained in his psyche. Half in the bag, he managed to find his way into the company of the only two Englishmen on Tinian, Group Captain Leonard Cheshire and British scientist William Penney, Winston Churchill's personal representatives. He'd decided to provide them with a little entertainment in the form of a particularly satiric rendition of a song calling into question the manhood of the British in the war effort:

> *I don't want to be a soldier,*
> *I don't want to go to war.*
> *I'd just rather hang around*
> *Piccadilly Underground*
> *Living off the earnings of some 'ighborn lady . . .*

I was told by observers that this musical interlude had been punctuated by increasingly vitriolic argument, mostly emanating from Paul, who by then was pickled beyond reason. Finally, either Paul or Cheshire invited the other to settle the matter like gentlemen. So my future brother-in-law, a six-foot-two marine first lieutenant combat veteran, and Churchill's personal representative and holder of the Victoria Cross, the equivalent of our Medal of Honor, stepped outside.

At this point the story gets unclear. According to Paul, he taught the Englishman a lesson. According to other witnesses, the fight ended inconclusively after a few ineffective punches were thrown. In any event, Paul didn't look the worse for wear.

To this day I don't know if Leonard Cheshire, who was a gentleman in every sense of the word, knew that Paul was with me. After the war, I would maintain a warm friendship with Leonard and his wife, who was a member of the House of

Lords. But on August 7, 1945, I expected the boom to drop on my head. Thankfully, it didn't. In fact, when I saw Group Captain Cheshire the next day, he was pleasant, conversational, and fine. Obviously the incident hadn't caused him any concern and was soon forgotten.

A crisis with Great Britain averted, I still had a mission to prepare for. I attended to the details that any commander must see to prior to a mission.

I went over to the intelligence hut. Reconnaissance photographs were providing a better view of the destruction on the ground as some of the smoke cleared. Sixty percent of Hiroshima had been laid waste. Preliminary casualty estimates were 80,000 killed or seriously wounded. It was still uncertain exactly what effect the radiation might have. The city's industrial base had been crippled, if not destroyed. Its activities as an urban center had ceased.

This had to be the end. No nation could ignore the breadth of destruction there and continue to offer up its own people.

I caught up with Paul Burns at lunch. So far his visit had provided a certain relief, a soothing feeling of a connection with home, from all else that was swirling around me. Plus, I liked his company. He was a good and loyal friend. Our relationship was built on a mutual respect that allowed for continuous good-natured razzing and kidding. At lunch we went back and forth about who was responsible for winning the war, the marines or the air force. Our positions were pretty evident.

He knew I was going again on the ninth, if necessary. In response to some barb, I mockingly said, "I'd take you on this mission, Paul, but you don't have the nerve."

Paul shot back, "I'll go anywhere you go."

We each upped the ante, progressively calling each other's

bluff. Finally, I threw the ultimate trump card on the table, "I'll take you, you son of a bitch."

And I really intended to take him. I had been given a lot of flexibility and could include on my crew just about anyone I wanted within certain limits. This one would be really close to the limit, though—a marine lieutenant without orders on an air force secret mission. I decided I had better run it by Paul Tibbets.

Tibbets puffed on his pipe and said, "I have no objection." I thought I had it made. "But," he added, "I think we'd better clear it with Parsons."

Captain Parsons had no formal command, but he was the military liaison with the Manhattan Project, and we always wanted to make sure everything was done with his concurrence—to make sure Manhattan, Alberta, and Silverplate all marched to a single drummer.

I asked Captain Parsons. Like Tibbets, he had a relaxed, confident way about him. And, as could Tibbets, he could simply mandate that something happen or not. But it was not his style to mandate unilaterally, which made him a well-liked and respected officer.

He heard me out and then rationally offered, "Well, I don't really have any objection. But on the other hand, if anything went wrong, it would look strange."

I felt this was his way of telling me the idea was not a good one. "That's the better part of wisdom, Captain," I responded.

Paul Burns had come within a whisker of going on the second atomic mission.

Of course, I didn't let him get away that easy. I later accused him of getting to Parsons before I spoke with him to make sure Parsons wouldn't approve.

The last time before the mission that I would see Paul Burns would be at dinner the next night. We would both know what was ahead for both of us. But we wouldn't talk of the mission or the war. We would talk about the good times in the past and those to come. Paul would take me in a big bear hug, and say, "See you when you get back."

"Tell the medics to be ready with that hundred-proof Old Crow," I'd reply.

It wouldn't be macho bravado. It was a way men in a war deal with the moment.

SEVENTEEN

AFTER MEETING WITH Captain Parsons, I walked back to my quarters alone, turning over in my mind the details of the mission and the work to be done the next day in preparation for the flight. A nagging need to talk through my beliefs intruded on my thoughts. My faith and belief in God were the core of who I was. Since I was a child I had found guidance in the teachings of Jesus and the Church. Jesus taught us to love. He turned the other cheek. Where would He draw the line?

I borrowed a jeep and drove over to one of the other groups of the 313th Bombardment Wing, our neighbors on Tinian. Although I could have met with Captain Downey, a Lutheran minister assigned to the 509th, I wanted to speak with a priest. I took Riverside Drive along the ocean instead of the more direct route down Eighth Avenue. To my right, the last yellow light of day cast a broad beam stretching from the horizon across the smooth, blue, glassy surface of the Pacific.

After a number of inquiries I found the priest. We walked

over to the open-air theater where Sunday services were held. He couldn't have been much older than I was, but he had that way about him, common to most clerics, of seeming older than his years. We found two straight-back metal chairs off to one side and sat facing each other.

I'm sure he recognized that I was from the 509th, and by now he knew what the 509th's mission had been the day before. But he made no comment about that and neither did I. He began by asking me what I would like to talk about.

Now that I sat there looking at him, I wasn't quite sure what he could do for me or what I wanted from him. He offered in a quiet tone, "Do you feel the need to confess?"

The question helped focus me. No, I didn't feel the need to confess. I felt a need to talk about the teachings of my church and the world in which I found myself that evening. In time of war there is precious little opportunity to reflect upon or even entertain deep philosophical or theological questions. But that night I needed to understand the Church's position on the war. I needed to pursue the meaning behind its teachings that under certain circumstances war may be "justified."

I posed the question, "Is it a sin to wage war, Father?"

To my slight relief the young priest said, "This is a question I have spent considerable time thinking about myself. For here I am, a cleric, in uniform, in a war."

"But you're not a combatant, Father. You simply tend to the spiritual needs of those called to fight," I pointed out to him.

"That is true. But I bless the men and their airplanes that fly off to kill and be killed. I condone their actions by my blessings. So it is not that simple. Fortunately, our faith recognizes that man is a thinking being endowed with intellect. God wants us to think, to reason about the consequences of our actions and inactions. For me, then, whether this is a just war

is not an academic exercise. I have to consider the circumstances and measure them against the moral teachings of the
Church and then reach a personal conclusion, as must you and
every Christian." He paused for a moment. "Someone far more
saintly than you or I, Thomas Aquinas, struggled with this
same question."

I recalled some of Thomas Aquinas's teachings from my
earlier religious readings. Thomas Aquinas had recognized the
unity of intellect and faith. He'd brought his intellect to bear
upon real-world dilemmas that plague the human condition,
like the anomaly of war. He had concluded that in the real
world there were situations that render a war "just."

"Thomas believed that under certain circumstances war is
justified," Father continued. "First, he said, the cause must be
just. Secondly, the intention must be to advance the common
good—to secure peace and punish evil. And, finally, a just war
must be declared by the lawful sovereign in defense of the
common good. The absence of any one of these elements
would make the act of war a sin."

The priest and I talked at length about these conditions.
How had we gotten into the war? What was our objective?
What was our intent?

I believed that the last thing the overwhelming majority of
our generation had wanted was a war. America is not a nation
of warriors. Americans don't subscribe to the code of the samurai or believe they are a master race.

While the United States was struggling through the Great
Depression, Japan was embarking on the conquest of its neighbors. Imperial Japan saw itself as a nation destined to rule all
of Asia, enslaving its people into service, possessing its natural
resources, and occupying its lands. It called the undertaking the
Greater East Asia Co-Prosperity Sphere, an innocuous name to
cover hideous intentions. Co-prosperity was to be achieved by

first waging total war against China and Manchuria. Without
a shred of moral conscience or the slightest hesitation, the Japanese army had proceeded to slaughter innocent men, women,
and children. In the infamous Rape of Nanking, Japanese soldiers had butchered up to 300,000 unarmed civilians.

In the plan to fulfill its divine destiny in Asia, Japan had
determined that the only real impediment was the United
States. It had launched a carefully conceived sneak attack on
our Pacific Fleet at Pearl Harbor. Timed for a Sunday morning,
the attack had been intended to inflict the maximum loss of
ships and human lives, dealing a blow to the American fleet from
which it could not soon recover. As the priest and I sat together
in the dying light of dusk talking about the start of the war,
hundreds of sailors were still entombed in the hull of the USS
Arizona, sitting on the bottom of Pearl Harbor. Thus, the war
had been thrust upon us.

During the years following Pearl Harbor, the actions of the
Japanese military had done nothing to disabuse the world of
their intentions—and of the means they would use to achieve
them. Always, they would fight to the death. They would use
any means, even if it meant their own deaths. By war's end
the Japanese forces would have killed twenty million of their
Asian neighbors and over one hundred thirty thousand Allied
troops.

What, then, was our cause? Our intention?

Our intention in the Pacific was to stop the Japanese aggression, to eradicate the evil that festered in Japan, and to restore
peace—just as in Europe we had to stop the Nazis. To stand
by and allow the slaughter to continue would have been a
repudiation of the sanctity of life.

I did not mention Hiroshima or the mission scheduled for
August 9. But I asked, "What about weapons of mass destruction? Are they justified?"

The priest considered this for what seemed a long time before answering. "War as we know it today *is* mass destruction. The weapons may become more fearsome, but the moral issues are the same. The death of a single person is no less a tragedy than the death of ten thousand. Will greater weapons bring a quicker end to the war? I don't know. But you must be certain of your cause and your intentions, because the nature of modern weapons makes the stakes much higher."

Neither of us had noticed that we were sitting in almost complete darkness, the only light coming from the window of an adjoining hut. He blessed me, wished me well, and said he hoped he had helped. I assured him he had.

I was at peace with myself.

EIGHTEEN

■N THE AIR-CONDITIONED hut we called "the shed," assembly of the third and last atomic weapon in the United States arsenal, the Mark III combat unit F31, Model Y 1561, had been proceeding over the past few days; its fraternal twin had exploded to life three weeks earlier on a hundred-foot tower at Alamogordo. The Fat Man, named because of its rotund shape, was more complicated than the primitive Little Boy—and more powerful: twenty-three kilotons, 46 million pounds, of TNT. Instead of having the gun-barrel design of Little Boy, Fat Man was an implosion device. A solid core of precision-machined plutonium was surrounded by finely shaped lenses of high explosives placed in a precise configuration around the core to ensure an instantaneous symmetrical implosion. Plutonium, which emits alpha particles, is warm to the touch, as if it is a living thing. The implosion would compress the plutonium sphere in a nanosecond to a critical mass that would then start a chain reaction and nuclear explosion. All of the explosive lenses had to detonate simultaneously. An infinitesimal delay in any lens would result in a big bang, but no nuclear explosion. The numerous and interconnected mechanical and electrical systems necessary to accomplish this result had to be painstakingly set into the confines of the bomb casing, together with the multiple and redundant fuses and switches required to detonate the explosive charges.

To make the bomb live, four sets of fuses would be installed: barometric, timing, radar, and impact. The four different kinds of fuses would be used for redundancy. There would be two fuses of each kind—again, for redundancy. Only the impact fuses would detonate when the bomb hit the ground. The last resort. Ideally, all six of the other fuses would activate at 1,890 feet: the barometric fuses were set to detonate when the bomb reached 1,890 feet; the timing fuses would detonate forty-three seconds after release, at which point the bomb would have reached 1,890 feet; the radar fuses would receive echoes from the ground at 1,890 feet and detonate. The scientists had toiled over the fuse function for so long, they nearly ended up throwing in the kitchen sink for insurance.

After the fuses were installed, the two half spheres of the bomb casing would be bolted together and the 550-pound tail section would be attached to the casing.

Because the entire assembly was so complicated, the plutonium bomb would have to be armed and live when it was loaded onto the airplane. There would be no way to arm it in flight, as Captain Parsons had armed Little Boy on the Hiroshima mission. Thus, my crew and I would be rolling down the runway with a live, 10,300-pound plutonium bomb, and because of its weight, there would be just barely enough runway to gain the proper airspeed. If we crashed on takeoff, we could obliterate the island.

Even before the technicians made Fat Man live, it was an

extremely dangerous unit to be around. The quantity of high explosives laid in around the plutonium core made the unit the largest conventional bomb in our inventory. Inside, over 5,000 pounds of two types of high-grade explosives, Baratol and Composition B, surrounded the nickel- and gold-coated orange-size eleven-pound sphere of plutonium, whose density was nine ounces per cubic inch. At its center was a pea-size ball of polonium and beryllium, the initiator that would commence the chain reaction by releasing neutrons when the compressing sphere of plutonium crushed in on it.

A single spark, or even heat generated by friction, could set off the explosives inside the bomb and wipe away the assembly hut and most of what surrounded it. To reduce friction, baby powder was dusted onto some parts that might rub against other components during assembly. In addition to having air-conditioning, the entire shed had a specially rubberized floor grounded by a copper wire grid system to prevent an accidental explosion from a spark or any other source of heat. All personnel had to wear rubberized shoes in the shed and move about carefully and deliberately. This slowed the progress of the work and added to the tension.

Hours before the bomb was to be transported to the loading area, the assembly crew encountered a snag that would have been comical except for the circumstances. It was discovered that holes on the bomb casing and the tail section had been improperly drilled, making it impossible to align the two components and bolt them together. Many a father had confronted similar problems on Christmas Eve when trying to assemble cheaply made toys for his children. However, this was no toy, and it had cost two billion dollars. Cool prevailed, and without missing a beat, a technician with a metal file labored to scrape away enough of the aluminum plating on the fins to enlarge the holes so that the sections could be joined by the bolts.

*   *   *

I had already decided that because all the delicate measuring instruments we had carried on the Hiroshima mission were still installed in my airplane, *The Great Artiste,* it made no sense to have the ground crews and technicians work through the day to remove the instruments, reinstall them in another B-29, and then recalibrate them. Instead, I would take Fat Man in Fred Bock's airplane, the *Bock's Car,* with my crew, and he would fly *The Great Artiste,* with his crew.

However, on August 8, I would fly *The Great Artiste* one more time before the mission. The scientists were finally ready with a new improved fuse. The last fusing test at Wendover had resulted in a premature detonation right below the belly of my airplane. Similar problems had occurred when we flew practice drops there at Tinian. My feeling was that I trusted the brilliance of these scientists. I had confidence in them. If they wanted to use a round fuse today and a square one tomorrow, then that was fine with me.

I was to take a concrete-filled pumpkin to 30,000 feet and release it over the ocean off shore of Tinian. Alberta staff, including Luis Alvarez and Norman Ramsey, lined the shore to observe the pumpkin and the fuse, which was set to detonate at 1,890 feet. A small charge would explode with a visible puff of smoke.

At mid-morning I arrived at the initial point to commence the bomb run. Beahan activated the thirty-second tone signal. Just as we would do the next day when the tone stopped, Kermit yelled, "Bomb away," and I took the airplane into a sharp 155-degree turn. The bomb raced in its forward arc toward the designated altitude of 1,890 feet. A puff of smoke plumed into the sun-drenched tropical sky. The fuse had detonated. The inert pumpkin plopped harmlessly into the ocean.

The test, we later learned from the scientists, had been successful. I guess that was good news, considering that in less than twenty-four hours we would be taking the actual bomb—fuses and all—on board with us to Japan.

I had tasks to attend to as the command pilot for Special Bombing Mission Number 16, the military designation for our mission. After lunch, I drove over to the hardstand to chat with the crew chief and his men, who were busily checking and rechecking all systems on the *Bock's Car*. Basically, I kicked the tires, just wanting to make my presence felt. Those guys were the best, and I knew they would have the airplane in tiptop shape well before takeoff.

At two P.M., Beahan, Albury, Van Kirk, and I attended a briefing to study the maps and reconnaissance photographics of the two possible targets for our mission, Kokura and Nagasaki. For the last week we had studied those very same maps and photos, which, until August 5, had included Hiroshima. We knew these cities as well as we knew our own hometowns, perhaps better. Every inch of them—streets, buildings, bridges, factories, rivers, lakes—was committed to our memories. We walked through every sequence of the bomb runs at each city. The intelligence officers in attendance reviewed the latest information about antiaircraft emplacements, intensity of fire, and potential fighter intercepts at each target.

We could expect significant antiaircraft fire at Kokura, where heavy industries were concentrated. The target would be the Kokura army arsenal, the primary source supplying the Japanese army. It sat smack in the heart of the city. The Japanese war effort depended on keeping factories like this operating. Ringing the city were concentrated and well-placed antiaircraft batteries that could throw up a withering hail of flak. Kokura also had fighter protection to intercept incoming bombers.

Nagasaki was another industrial base, home to two massive Mitsubishi armament plants. It was defended, but with far less concentration. I looked at the Nagasaki field orders: FIELD ORDERS, NUMBER 17, 8 AUGUST 1945—(2) Secondary Target: 90.36 Nagasaki Urban Area.

I located the coordinates on the aviation chart of Japan in front of me. Pressing my finger to the chart at Nagasaki, I saw that the city sat in two valleys split in the middle by a low range of hills. Although residential and commercial districts lay in the flat land surrounding the large harbor where Nagasaki's shipbuilding and torpedo factories were located, maximum blast effect could be achieved only by dropping over this flat area below the range of hills.

My first reaction to the aiming point was that the casualties could be even greater than at Hiroshima. My second reaction was that I hoped the target would be Kokura. Updated weather reports predicted fairly clear conditions at both targets for the next day. The meteorologists confirmed that after the ninth conditions would worsen. A weather front was moving over Japan that would cause unsettled weather for at least five days.

None of us had slept well over the past two days, and as the afternoon briefing dragged on, the tedium and tension grew. We finally finished up, and I returned to our hut to try to grab a little nap. The heat and anticipation again made sleep impossible. I went over to the Dogpatch Inn, where I saw Paul Burns and we had supper. After eating, I took a walk alone up the hill overlooking the runways. I lit up a cigar and began contemplating the mission. A steady flow of B-29s from the 313th were taking off in the darkness on the strips below. I saw an airplane struggling to lift off with its full load of fuel and bombs. It didn't make it. The burning aviation fuel and exploding napalm-filled bombs sent plumes of flame and smoke billowing up into the sky. Sounds of explosions punctuated the night. I didn't know it then, but 224 of those B-29s were going to bomb the industrial city of Yawata, the neighboring city of Kokura.

Our scheduled arrival at target was still at least fifteen hours away. Maybe this firebombing strike would compel the Japanese to surrender. It was possible. We were given a recall code to abort the mission if hostilities ended. But as the Mother Goose childhood rhyme reminds, "If wishes were horses, beggars would ride." Wishing, I knew, wouldn't be productive at this late hour. The Japanese had to be shaken from their self-delusion that they could grasp victory with some final, cataclysmic spasm of violence. Historians after a war may hypothesize about the what-ifs, ponder the maybes, and reflect upon what rational men of goodwill should have done, but in war it is the harsh reality of the present that controls events. Lives are not "theoretically" at stake. Death and maiming are absolutes. As Robert E. Lee observed, "It is good that war is so horrible, or we might grow to like it."

No beggars would ride that evening.

All of the crews gathered in the briefing hut at nine P.M. sharp. We were joined by the British observers Penney and Cheshire. The mood was quiet. The men knew what was coming, whereas on the first mission no one had known what to expect. My crew specifically understood what was before them. No one expressed any concern, but you could feel it in the air. There was a sense of hastening toward a destination that you hoped someone would tell you you didn't have to reach. But the men maintained their professionalism. We had a job to do and we were going to do it.

Paul Tibbets opened with a few remarks. He explained in broad terms that Fat Man was a much more powerful bomb and quite different from the one he had dropped on Hiroshima.

Because of our bomb, the Little Boy was now obsolete, and the brass in Washington were following our mission very closely. He knew we would do a good job and wished us well.

An intelligence officer started laying out the mission: "Major Sweeney will take the bomb, Captain Bock the instruments, and Colonel Hopkins the photographic equipment."

In discussing the mission earlier with Paul Tibbets, I had asked for Fred Bock because of his experience and expertise as a pilot. Fred was a steady and reliable man to have on your wing. I knew that, in a crunch, I could depend on him and trust his judgment. But I was somewhat surprised when Tibbets told me he'd assigned the photographic airplane to Hopkins. Hopkins had had limited experience with the B-29 since he joined the headquarters staff of the 509th as group operations officer. In fact, if I were ranking the fifteen pilots in the 393rd available to fly the mission, he would not have been even among the group I would have considered the most proficient. Other than Hopkins's own belief that he could fly the mission, as demonstrated in the meeting I'd had with Tom Classen when Tibbets wasn't around, I was at a loss as to what recommended him for this flight.

But I dismissed the thought. Tibbets had chosen him and that was fine with me. I wasn't going to second-guess him. I never had. Anyway, all Hopkins had to do was trail behind us and take pictures. No fancy maneuvers at the drop, just a straight-in flight. Simple. My major concern was to reach my target, release the bomb with Fred Bock close in beside me, and then get our tails out of there as fast as possible.

The operations officer went over air-sea rescue plans. Again, a network of submarines, surface ships, and specially equipped aircraft would line our flight path to and from the empire.

We then reviewed the details of the mission. The intelligence officers conceded in their most circumspect manner that yes, because of the Hiroshima mission, it would be difficult to predict with any certainty exactly what kind of opposition we might encounter if the Japanese discovered three unescorted B-29s crossing over to the mainland. In other words, they just might be waiting for us and throw every damn thing in the air at us they could. Or maybe not.

We were reminded in no uncertain terms to drop only visually, which was a natural introduction to the weather report. A typhoon was gathering momentum off Iwo Jima, and that required a change in the rendezvous point. A small island directly off the southern coast of Kyushu, the southern island of mainland Japan, was selected as the new rendezvous—Yakoshima. Because of the bad weather at lower altitudes and our proximity to the Japanese mainland, the rendezvous would be at 30,000 feet instead of at 8,000, as on the Hiroshima mission. This meant we would be flying through some turbulent weather for about five hours in complete radio silence. Then all three of us had to arrive at a tiny spot in the ocean within one minute of each other. At dawn on a gray, overcast day, it can be pretty tricky seeing another airplane at any distance.

After the briefing was finished, I asked Hopkins to wait up. I wanted to have a private word with him.

When the hut emptied, I said, "You know, Hoppy, it's difficult to rendezvous up there at thirty thousand feet on a bad day. If we circle Yakoshima, we won't know exactly how close we are to the shore. I could be a mile off, you could be three . . . you simply can't tell. We'd never see each other. So I've picked a point on the southwest corner of the island— here." I pointed to the map tacked to the wall. "From this point, we'll run on a compass bearing a hundred and eighty degrees for two minutes and then back at three hundred and sixty degrees for two minutes and continue making this oval to and from that corner until we hook up."

Hopkins and I had never been close. Our contacts had been businesslike and formal in a military way. He wanted to be regular army, everything by the book. His ambition to make the military his career and rise to the rank of a general officer were well-known. I certainly wasn't one of his buddies, but I didn't expect the response I got from him.

"Look, Major, I know all about that. I know how to make a rendezvous. You don't have to tell me how to make a rendezvous," Hopkins said with pronounced emphasis, his voice conveying aggravation at the intrusion.

Without another word, he turned and walked away.

To this day I don't know if his reaction was because of his senior rank—he was a lieutenant colonel and I was only a major—or because he thought I was talking down to him. Or some belief that he should have commanded the mission. I don't know. What I do know is that a few minutes later I had the same conversation with Fred Bock, a very experienced pilot, and he listened attentively and nodded in agreement.

Our final briefing would be at midnight. With time on my hands, I headed down to the flight line to look things over one more time. Portable lights illuminated the hardstand of number 77, Fred Bock's airplane. For this mission, like the first, our aircraft would not have any nose art painted on the fuselage, just the black block tactical numbers assigned to each B-29. Nearby I could see my airplane, number 89. And on the other adjoining hardstand I saw the airplane Hopkins would pilot, Captain Herman Zahn's B-29, number 90, named by its crew the *Big Stink*. As I surveyed the flight line I had no idea exactly how prophetic and fitting it was that Hopkins would be piloting the *Big Stink*.

I walked around number 77 slowly, visually checking every surface of the aircraft, looking for any telltale signs of fluid on the tarmac below. The ground crew was still performing various procedures and systems checks. My formal walk-around with my flight engineer and ground crew chief would take place later, during our preflight check. The bomb bay doors were open, so I hunched down and took a look.

There it was. Secure in the bomb bay, the Fat Man waited. Ten feet eight inches long, five feet across, painted with high-gloss yellow enamel and black tail fins. It weighed 10,300 pounds, at least 1,000 pounds heavier than Little Boy. It resembled a grossly oversized decorative squash. I could see that many people had signed the bomb or left poems and messages with varying degrees of vitriol.

Backing out from beneath the fuselage, I came face-to-face with an admiral whom I had never seen before. By his questions, he seemed to know who I was.

"Son, do you know how much that bomb cost?"

"No, sir," I answered. I had things to do other than ponder the cost of military matériel, and I wanted to get a move on.

He paused a moment, I presume for effect, and then stated, "Two billion dollars."

"That's a lot of money, Admiral," I answered with a slight whistle.

Before I could respond further he went on, "Do you know how much your airplane costs?"

Bingo. In fact, I did know the answer to that one almost to the penny. "Slightly over half a million dollars, sir."

"I'd suggest you keep those relative values in mind for this mission," the anonymous admiral said.

I related the story of this encounter to Paul Tibbets shortly before takeoff. My crew and I instinctively understood that the bomb was more important than our airplane. We didn't need to be reminded of it.

The final briefing commenced at midnight. Our weather airplanes would precede us by an hour to the two possible targets. Charlie McKnight would fly number 95 to Nagasaki, and George Marquardt would fly number 88 to Kokura. Weather forecasts remained the same, clear at each target.

Added to my crew for this mission were three more officers, specialists in their fields: Lieutenant Jake Beser, who had been aboard the *Enola Gay* and would be responsible for monitoring radar frequencies in the event the Japanese tried to jam our radar and possibly detonate the radar fuse on Fat Man; Navy Commander Fred Ashworth, the weaponeer in charge of the bomb itself; and Lieutenant Philip Barnes, who would assist Commander Ashworth in monitoring a device connected to the bomb's fuses. This monitoring device, connected to the bomb by an inch-thick cable, would alert Ashworth and Barnes if anything went wrong with the complicated electrical circuits wired to the four sets of fuses.

Chaplain Downey offered a prayer beseeching the Lord to see us safely through the mission. The words I remember well were, "Above all else, our Father, bring peace to thy world. . . ." After this, we headed over to the mess hall, and at about one A.M. the trucks delivered us to our hardstands.

Paul Tibbets had come down to the flight line to see us off. There were no throngs of cameras and lights and bigwigs. The atmosphere was reserved, everyone busy doing his job. The men spoke among themselves, anticipating the mission but talking about everything but. The mood was expectant. A couple of army photographers and one cameraman were on hand. A single newsman, Bill Laurence, the science and technology writer for the *New York Times,* who had been given unprecedented access by the War Department to chronicle the development of atomic weapons and our missions, wandered about. His reporting would earn him a Pulitzer Prize for journalism. He expressed disappointment at not being allowed to accompany Tibbets to Hiroshima but was excited about being aboard for this mission. He would fly with Fred Bock.

Not knowing that Fred and I had switched airplanes, he thought I was flying my own, *The Great Artiste,* and so in his eyewitness account identified it as the strike aircraft, an error that would persist for many years after the war.

On the adjoining hardstand stood our British observers, who were to fly with Hopkins.

I started my walk-around with Kuharek, Albury, and the ground crew chief. The airplane looked in pristine condition, not a drop of fluid on the ground, tire pressures perfect, surfaces clean and clear, everything in tiptop condition.

The crew assembled along the side of the aircraft for their preflight inspection. I decided that as the mission commander it was incumbent upon me to say a few words of encouragement to my men about so pivotal a mission. I respected and liked these men. They were all highly skilled professionals who knew their jobs and would do their duty. They didn't need a pep talk or a lecture on how important the mission was. They were extremely intelligent; they knew. I just felt I owed them a statement.

"You were all with me the other day at Hiroshima. It was a perfect mission flown by Colonel Tibbets. Perfectly executed, perfectly flown, and dropped on the button. I want our mission to be exactly the same—for Colonel Tibbets. He has chosen us, and we owe him and our country the same. We will execute this mission perfectly and get the bomb to the target. I don't care if I have to dive the airplane into the target, we're going to deliver it."

I had no intention of taking them into the target. I would have tried to bail them out and Beahan and I could have handled the rest, if it came to that. But I wanted to make a point.

I looked down the line of men, into each one's eyes. What I saw was determination and resoluteness. If they had doubts, they didn't show it in their eyes. We had trained for this day, which could bring the horrible war in the Pacific to a rapid end. It could be the day we began our journey back home to our friends and loved ones. It could be the day we started our return to our lives, which had been so suddenly and completely interrupted by the bombs that had fallen on our comrades at Pearl Harbor. Whatever happened, it would be a day of historic proportions.

As the crew climbed aboard and settled into their positions, I went over the maps one more time with our navigator, Jim Van Pelt, and Kermit Beahan. Satisfied that all was well, I bid Paul Tibbets farewell and climbed aboard.

I settled down into the leather seat, strapped myself in, and began my checklist with my copilot, Don Albury. Behind us, Sergeant Kuharek went through his systems check, and across from him, Van Pelt reviewed his navigational material and Ed Buckley checked his radar equipment.

We were at the point of "Start engines." I prepared to give Kuharek, the flight engineer, the command when he leaned around toward me and said, "Major, we have a problem. The fuel in our reserve tank in the rear bomb bay bladder isn't pumping. We've got six hundred gallons of fuel trapped back there."

"Any idea what the problem is?" Could it be the instruments?" I asked.

"My guess is it's a solenoid. It would have to be replaced," he replied evenly.

"How long to fix it?" I asked.

"With all the special precautions, several hours," he responded.

I unstrapped my harness, lifted myself out of the seat, and climbed down the nosewheel well ladder. Tibbets was standing off to one side as I emerged from under the wing.

"The auxiliary transfer fuel pump in the rear bomb bay bladder is malfunctioning, boss. We've got six hundred gallons trapped," I advised him crisply.

Tibbets puffed calmly on his pipe as we discussed the options. Of our 1,000 gallons of reserve fuel, 600 gallons were trapped. This left me with 6,400 gallons total for the flight instead of 7,000. Replacing the pump could take hours. Transferring the bomb to another airplane would be equally time-consuming and was risky because it was live. Our window of opportunity was rapidly closing on us. If we didn't take off soon, the mission would be scrubbed. The entire psychological impact of a one-two punch would be lost, and with it any real prospect of a quick end to the war.

I considered the consequences of going. We would have to carry the extra weight of 600 gallons of fuel for the entire flight without deriving any benefit from it. This extra weight would cause us to consume more fuel. En route to the rendezvous, I would have to fly at 17,000 feet to get above the storm, which would consume more fuel than if we flew at 8,000 feet. My payload was heavier than the Little Boy, requiring more fuel than had been needed on the first mission.

Tibbets, as was his style when he gave a man a job, said, "It's your call, Chuck."

Rolling all the factors around in my mind, I determined that I had more than enough fuel to make it to target. The problem was, if I encountered any delays, the likelihood of making it back to Tinian was zero, and getting back to any

American-held base would be problematic at best. I would have to ditch in the ocean and get picked up by a rescue vessel. The anonymous admiral's admonition had been prophetic. Losing the airplane was a small price to pay if we delivered the weapon. I had total confidence in my men, my machine, and myself.

I looked at Colonel Tibbets and said, "The hell with it, I want to go. We're going."

I climbed aboard, advised the crew we were taking off, and gave the order to start engines. With all engines turning, we rolled to the taxiway and proceeded to Runway A. It was about 2:45 A.M., slightly behind schedule. But we were on our way.

NINETEEN

AT THE EASTERN end of Runway A, I stared out into the darkness. Before me stretched 8,500 feet of macadam. The spotlight that illuminated the end of the runway at the water's edge had been turned off for reasons not explained to me, although it struck me as odd. Somewhere ahead of me lay the ocean, restless. Off toward the horizon, lightning pierced the black, overcast sky.

I thought back to my first instructions at flight school in an open-cockpit biplane. Just point the airplane in the right direction, and when it reaches flying speed, it'll take off on its own. That evening, reaching flying speed would be the problem. I had to get over seventy-seven and a half tons—the combined weight of the B-29, its crew of ten, three additional passengers, 7,000 gallons of aviation fuel, and, oh yes, a 10,300-pound "hot" nuclear bomb that might detonate if I didn't make it into the air—airborne. I knew that I'd have to hold her back until the very last moment to gain as much speed as I could before

I let her rise off the ground. I also knew that, three days earlier, the *Enola Gay,* with a lighter load, had used virtually every inch of the runway at takeoff.

I ran the engines up one at a time. I advanced the throttle, moving it slowly. The tachometer needle rose to 2,000 rpm and then dropped back to 1,800 rpm. I pushed the throttle to full open. The needle rose promptly to its limit, 2,600 rpm. Each engine surged in sequence, sending a rhythmic vibration through the airplane.

I held her in place, with "brakes on" full. A slight shudder shook the aircraft. For this mission there would be total radio silence, which meant that even in preparation for takeoff I would not communicate with the tower and the tower would give me no instructions or clearance. We didn't know if the Japanese had figured out the point of origin of the first mission. I was on my own.

Don Albury lowered the flaps 25 degrees. I advised Kuharek, "Ready for takeoff."

"Stand by for takeoff," I instructed the crew over the interphone. It was 2:56 A.M.

I opened the throttle gradually and released the brakes. We rolled forward, gathering speed—95 mph, 125 mph. I could feel her want to make the effort to rise, but I held the yoke tight, keeping her down—140 mph. Even without the spotlight at the ocean's edge, I knew instinctively that we were running out of runway. Taking quick glances at the air speed indicator, I held her until our speed reached 155 mph. At that instant I knew we had no more ground underneath us.

We launched off over the water, rising to about 50 feet. The *Bock's Car* was straining. I kept her level, giving her time to increase lift. Then I eased her up ever so slightly, and we began our lumbering turn toward the north, climbing to 7,000 feet.

On Runway B, two minutes behind me, Fred Bock lifted off. On Runway C, however, a little subdrama had been unfolding that, because of the radio silence, was happening unbeknownst to me and to everyone else on Tinian. Dr. Robert Serber, the Alberta Project photographic expert, had been assigned to fly with Colonel Hopkins aboard the *Big Stink* to operate the highly delicate and sophisticated photographic equipment. Dr. Serber's expertise was vital to recording the blast. As Hopkins was taxiing out to Runway C, he discovered that the doctor had forgotten his parachute. Air force regulations required that every crew member and passenger aboard any military aircraft have a parachute. Hopkins—by the book— wasn't about to allow such a flagrant violation of military regulations by this civilian. Never mind that Dr. Serber was the only person competent to operate the high-speed camera. No parachute, no ride. He ordered the doctor off his airplane right there, leaving the stunned scientist standing on the taxiway in the pitch dark.

After making the long walk back from the taxiway in the dark, Dr. Serber arrived at the communications center an hour later and reported what had happened to General Farrell. I can only surmise what General Farrell's thoughts must have been at that moment.

This incident, however, would prove to be the least of our problems on a mission that had already experienced its share of snafus and oddities.

Because of the turbulent weather, I took the *Bock's Car* up to 17,000 feet, where we'd cruise above the worst turbulence and then climb to 30,000 feet for the rendezvous over Yakoshima. At that altitude we were using fuel at a faster rate than if we'd stayed at 7,000 feet, but I didn't want to risk a turbulent ride with the sensitive cargo sitting just a few feet behind me in the forward bomb bay. But even at 17,000 feet the ride had its dips and jumps.

The atmosphere in the airplane was subdued. Each man was alone with his thoughts. Behind me, Commander Ashworth and Lieutenant Barnes crouched over the "black box," the fuse-monitoring device connected to the bomb.

About an hour into the flight, we were skating along the edge of the storm front and the ride had smoothed out. Don Albury commented that the trapped fuel could become a problem. "Let's not cross that bridge until we have to," I responded matter-of-factly. "Right now we're on course and we can at least make it to the target."

I decided to let Don take the wheel for a few minutes so I could stretch out a bit and loosen the stiffness in my neck and shoulders. Turning around in my seat, I surveyed the compartment. Ashworth and Barnes sat intently watching the black box. Kuharek had his eyes fixed on the flight engineer's instrument panel. His job was to keep tabs on the rate of fuel consumption as well as on all other aircraft systems. Lieutenant Fred Olivi, our third pilot for this mission, was asleep in the rear corner, as was Kermit Beahan. Directly behind was Jim Van Pelt, whom I couldn't see clearly but who I was sure was busily checking and rechecking our course to the rendezvous.

All seemed right in our pressurized, air-conditioned, encapsulated universe.

It was seven A.M. We had been in flight for a little over four hours. I started our climb to 30,000 feet as the dull gray light of the overcast morning filtered into the forward compartment. From behind me, I heard Barnes say something. I didn't quite make it out, but his tone had an urgency to it. Ashworth's reply sounded equally disturbed. The red warning light on the bomb's fuse monitor had suddenly started flashing! That meant the firing circuits were closed and some or all of the fuses had been activated. Ashworth reported the situation to me in a clipped fashion. My mind hurried. I knew it couldn't be the contact fuse or we would never have known what hit us. If the barometric or radar fuses had malfunctioned, we would be all right unless the airplane dropped below 1,890 feet. But if the timing fuse had been activated, we had less than forty-three seconds to find the problem and fix it.

Options: jettison the bomb and hope to escape the blast. Rely on the weaponeers to correct the problem. Pray that it was the barometric or radar fuses. There was no way I was going to jettison the bomb. I would rely on the weaponeers.

Behind me, staying calm, Phil Barnes opened the monitor and started examining the device as he had been trained to do in case of an emergency. Methodically, he inspected the labyrinth of wires and switches in front of him, searching for any abnormality in the circuitry. After a few moments he found the problem: someone on the ground had placed two rotary switches in the wrong positions, causing a malfunction in the monitor's circuits. The firing circuits had not closed. The fuses had not activated. Barnes quickly and gingerly flipped the switches back to their proper positions and resumed his monitoring.

Ashworth moved forward and reported that all was well. I thought, "To have come this far and end in a vaporizing flash." My only response was to whisper, "Oh, Lord."

At 30,000 feet, we arrived at the rendezvous at 7:45 A.M. on the button. Yakoshima was visible through breaks in the clouds. We had been flying for almost five hours through bad weather in complete radio silence. Within moments, Fred Bock appeared on my right wing. A few minute passed, but there was no sign of Hopkins. We circled the southwest corner of the island as briefed. By coded messages, our weather planes at Kokura and Nagasaki reported morning haze at both targets, but that clear skies were soon expected at Kokura and that less than two-tenths clouds would be covering Nagasaki. In nonmeteorological terms, the conditions were fairly good at both cities. Good news for a change.

But my sense of well-being was evaporating rapidly. After ten minutes, fifteen minutes, no Hopkins. My orders were to wait fifteen minutes and then leave for the target, but the mission brief also called for three airplanes to proceed to target. The photographic airplane was vital to fulfill the mission plan. I decided to give Hopkins a little more time. Maybe he had been delayed getting through the en route weather. Twenty minutes . . . thirty minutes. There was still no sign of the photographic airplane. With radio silence, there was nothing I could do to contact him. Turning to Don Albury, I hollered rhetorically, "Where the hell is he?"

We were using up valuable fuel. Kuharek gave a status report. At 30,000 feet, our rate of consumption was high—500 gallons per hour. Jim Van Pelt rechecked his charts to confirm the direct route to our primary, the IP for Kokura. In anticipation and as a precaution, he charted the direct route from Kokura to Nagasaki.

We scanned the empty sky. Hopkins was nowhere to be seen. I had spent forty minutes at the rendezvous point. "That's it," I barked to Albury. "The hell with it. We can't wait any longer."

I wiggled my wings, signaling Bock that we were departing the rendezvous point and proceeding to the target. The mission might not have a photographic airplane, but I fully intended to deliver the bomb to the target.

After the mission, I picked up bits and pieces about what had happened and heard that Hopkins had insisted he was at the rendezvous. I would learn the complete story of his absence several years later from an eyewitness, Group Captain Leonard Cheshire, who had been aboard Hopkins's airplane.

Cheshire was invited by Hopkins to move forward from the rear compartment of the airplane into the cockpit. Because he had to climb through the connecting tunnel, which was about two feet in diameter, Cheshire removed his parachute and left it behind. When Cheshire arrived in the cockpit, Hopkins noticed that he had left this parachute behind. He began to lecture Cheshire about his breach of and disregard for standard operating procedures. Hopkins finally dropped the matter, and Cheshire settled back.

According to Cheshire, Hopkins climbed to 39,000 feet approaching Yakoshima and stayed at that altitude, which was 9,000 feet higher than where he should have been. He commenced making fifty-mile doglegs in the area of Yakoshima, instead of circling the southwest corner of the island. An experienced combat pilot, Cheshire could see the altimeter reading 39,000 feet, and because he had attended the mission briefings, he knew what Hopkins should have been doing. But as a guest in Hopkins's airplane, and in the cockpit by Hopkins's invitation, Cheshire believed it was inappropriate for him to comment on Hopkins's flying.

Also unknown to me until after my return to Tinian was that when Hopkins failed to make the rendezvous and couldn't find us, for some inexplicable reason he broke radio silence and radioed back to Tinian: "Has Sweeney aborted?" The message got garbled in transmission and was received on Tinian as "Sweeney aborted." This inexcusable break in procedure not only could have given away our position to the Japanese, it also panicked the command on Tinian about the status of the mission.

General Farrell, his staff, and the assembled Alberta personnel thought we had scrubbed the mission. They had no idea what had happened. Were we coming back? Would we ditch the bomb in the ocean? Would we bring it back to Tinian? Had there been an accident? Somewhere out there was a ten-thousand-pound nuclear weapon, and they had no idea what I had done with it.

A consequence of Hopkins's transmission was that the air-sea rescue operation intended to pluck us out of the ocean if necessary was canceled. If we had to ditch in the ocean, no one would be there to pick us up.

Kokura lay ahead. Jim Van Pelt had picked it up on his radar screen a few minutes earlier. It was 9:45 A.M. The skies were still hazy, as reported earlier, but they were now mixed with broken clouds.

As we arrived at the IP, some landmarks were reasonably visible—the river, buildings, even streets and parks—so we thought here was a good chance to sight the target, the Kokura arsenal.

I started our bomb run when Beahan suddenly yelled, "I can't see it! I can't see it! There's smoke obscuring the target."

The fires resulting from the bombing of Yawata the night before were still burning out of control, and heavy smoke was being lifted across Kokura by winds that had shifted direction since George Marquardt had radioed his weather report.

As we bore in on the aiming point, Beahan repeated, "I can't see it!" The great Kokura arsenal was safely hidden by the smoke and haze.

I yelled into my intercom, "No drop. Repeat, no drop."

I banked the airplane sharply to the left and swung around to the south to begin a return approach to the IP. Flak bursts started all around us—to the left, ahead, to the right, and behind us.

A moment later tail gunner Pappy Dehart yelled, "Flak! Wide but altitude is perfect." Everyone saw it.

"Roger that, Pappy," I replied. They were crawling the flak up toward us as they tried to zero in on our airplane. I was now doing something a bomber pilot rarely, if ever, does— making a second run on a target. Second runs gave antiaircraft guns second chances.

I changed my altitude to 31,000 feet to try to confuse the enemy flak fusing. As I proceeded toward the aiming point, Pappy broke in again. "This damn flak is right on our tail and getting closer." His voice now sounded a note of panic.

"Forget it, Pappy. We're on a bomb run," I said evenly, trying to keep my attention on the approach to the aiming point.

I waited for Beahan's signal that he could see the target. I hoped he had picked it up through a break in the smoke and haze. I hoped we could catch a break on this mission.

"I can't see it!" he yelled again.

I wheeled into another steep turn as I barked, "No drop. Repeat, no drop."

Ed Buckley, our radar operator, reported, "Major, Jap Zeros coming up. Looks like about ten."

I decided to take us up another 1,000 feet to try to throw the antiaircraft gunners off again, and then approach from a different angle. Maybe from a different angle we might have a chance of finding a hole in the cover.

Beahan and Van Pelt were frantically calculating the run approach data.

The bursts of flak were breaking very close to the airplane, causing it to jump.

The third run was no more successful than the first two. The aiming point was still obscured. Kuharek reported that our fuel situation was very critical. We had enough to get to our secondary target, Nagasaki, and make one run. But we wouldn't make it back to Okinawa, the closest American base. We would fall short by about fifty miles.

Ed Buckley broke in over the intercom, "Fighters below and climbing to meet us."

Jake Beser, who was monitoring Japanese radio frequencies, confirmed increased activity on the Japanese fighter-director bands.

I wasn't as concerned about the Zeros as I was about the flak. Like horseshoes and grenades, close might be good enough if a burst caught us just right. If we hung around any longer, it would only be a matter of time.

Our gunner, Ray Gallagher, muttered into his intercom, "Let's get the hell out of here." Abe Spitzer, our radio operator, kept saying, "What about Nagasaki? What about Nagasaki?"

"Cut the chatter," I ordered sharply.

I again banked sharply to set us on a southerly direction toward our secondary target. The quick maneuver caught Fred Bock by surprise. By the time I'd completed my turn, he was on my left wing. Not seeing *The Great Artiste* on my right, I asked, "Where's Bock?" Unknown to me, my elbow had hit the selector button, changing the intercom function to the transmit command function, sending my words spilling out over the empire. To my disbelief, Hopkins, somewhere out there, replied excitedly, "Chuck? Is that you, Chuck? Where the hell are you?"

I don't know whether I was more upset by my carelessness or at hearing from the long-lost Colonel Hopkins. What did he want me to do, broadcast my position? I flipped the selector back to intercom, bit my lip, regained my composure, and calmly directed our navigator, "Jim, give me the heading for Nagasaki."

For the second time in three days the city of Kokura had been spared.

"Roger." Van Pelt, who had already completed the calculations, responded quickly, giving me the heading. "Of course," he added, "this route will take us right over the Kyushu fighter fields."

I couldn't afford the extra fuel we'd consume if I swung out over the water, away from the bases. A direct line was the only way we could go. For anyone monitoring our progress from the ground, our direction and flight path would not be that difficult to figure out. In the back of my mind I remembered Dr. Workman's reassuring calculations that at best a Zero would have less than one second to fire on us at 30,000 feet. With everything else that had been hampering us, maybe this would be some Zero's lucky day.

"I can't avoid it, Jim," I said as I made the adjustments to put us on a precise heading. I was now an hour and a half behind schedule. The Fat Man was still resting in the bomb bay. I would have one shot to get this done when we arrived at Nagasaki. God only knew what awaited us there. Turning to Don Albury, I said, "Can any other goddamned thing go wrong?"

I couldn't believe my eyes. Nagasaki was obscured by 80 to 90 percent cumulus clouds at 6,000 to 8,000 feet. A visual drop was improbable. We were approaching from the northwest and would arrive at the initial point in a few minutes. Kuharek confirmed again—we had enough fuel for a single bomb run.

I called Commander Ashworth forward and laid out the situation. He was in charge of the bomb; I was in command of the aircraft. If we didn't drop, we were out of options. We had about 300 gallons of fuel. If we stayed too long at Nagasaki by making a second bomb run, we might be forced to crash-land on the ground in Japan or in the ocean. If we didn't get a visual on our first run and then depart, we'd have to dump the bomb into the ocean.

I summed up quickly, "We haven't got the time or the fuel for more than one run. Let's drop it by radar. I'll guarantee we come within five hundred feet of the target." This was a commitment whose execution would be up to Ed Buckley, Kermit Beahan, and Jim Van Pelt. I didn't have time to consult with them, but I had supreme confidence in my radar man, bombardier, and navigator.

"I don't know, Chuck," Ashworth said.

"It's better than dropping it into the ocean," I answered.

"Are you sure of the accuracy?" Ashworth pressed.

"I'll take full responsibility for this," I assured him.

Ashworth could see that my mind was made up. He perhaps didn't realize that my only reason for any consultation was an interest in interservice harmony.

From the IP, Van Pelt and Buckley started to coordinate the approach to the aiming point. The outline of the city appeared on the scopes in front of Van Pelt and Buckley. Buckley called out headings and precise closure rates to Beahan, who fed the data into the bombsight, all the while hoping for a break in the clouds.

I reminded the crew to put on their goggles. I decided to leave mine off so I could see what I was doing.

We were thirty seconds from the bomb's release. The tone signal was activated and the bomb bay doors snapped open. Twenty-five seconds. Then Beahan yelled, "I've got it! I've got it!"

I answered, "You own it."

Beahan had spotted a hole midway between the two great Mitsubishi armaments plants in the industrial valley. It was two miles north of the assigned aiming point and away from the residential area, now shielded by the low hills beyond the coastal plain. He locked onto a racetrack reference point and made his adjustments, which were fed into the course direction indicator on my panel, from which I adjusted the flight path as required. I was still flying the airplane manually to the release point. Earlier in the run, Beahan had caught a momentary glimpse of the assigned aiming point, but it would have disrupted the radar run if he took over. He reconsidered, hoping for a better view, which proved to be fortuitous for us and the city below.

"Bombs away," Beahan shouted, and then quickly corrected himself. "Bomb away."

At the moment of release the airplane lurched upward, suddenly ten thousand pounds lighter. It was 11:01 A.M. The bomb bay doors snapped shut. I took us into a steep, diving, 155-degree turn to the left, in a northeasterly direction, to get away from the blast.

Time seemed suspended. As the seconds ticked by, I began to wonder if we had dropped a dud.

Then suddenly the entire horizon burst into a superbrilliant white with an intense flash—more intense than Hiroshima. The light was blinding. A moment later, the first wave of superheated air began hitting us with unexpected force. The shock waves were more severe than those at Hiroshima. But the airplane was still handling fine. Having been buffeted after the first atomic explosion, we knew it was not flak coming up from the ground. At Hiroshima there had been four or five shock waves of diminishing force, but these kept coming one after another with equal impact, maybe five in all.

As I completed my turn, I could see a brownish horizontal cloud enveloping the city below. The bomb had detonated at 1,890 feet, and in a millionth of a second compressed its core into a critical mass, releasing forces that were still incomprehensible. From the center of the brownish bile sprung a vertical column, boiling and bubbling up in those rainbow hues—purples, oranges, reds—colors whose brilliance I had seen only once before and would never see again. The cloud was rising faster than at Hiroshima. It seemed more intense, more angry. It was a mesmerizing sight, at once breathtaking and ominous.

Although we were twelve miles away, it appeared to some crew members that the cloud was heading straight for us. At about 25,000 feet, an expanding mushroom cloud broke off, white and puffy, and continued to burst upward at accelerating speed, passing us at 30,000 feet and shooting up to at least 45,000 feet.

I continued to bank around to allow Beahan to write his strike report. The blast damage seemed to be concentrated in the industrial Urakami Valley, where all we could see was a blanket of thick, dirty, brownish smoke with fires breaking through sporadically. The center of the downtown south of the ridge of hills separating the Urakami Valley from the coastal plain appeared untouched. The ridge of low-lying hills had shielded the residential area. Fires had broken out along the slopes of the hills. There was no question in my mind that the two Mitsubishi arms plants at Ohashi, and the Morimachi and Mitsubishi steelworks plants sitting in that valley, were no more. The bomb had exploded almost dead center among the three industrial giants. In a single stroke, they were gone.

The mushroom cloud towered above us. The vertical cloud continued to rise with unbelievable rapidity, its colors continuously changing. Satisfied that we could make a preliminary strike report to Tinian, I told Abe Spitzer to transmit Beahan's report, "Nagasaki bombed. Results good." When the transmission was received at Tinian, it was both a surprise and a relief. The military commanders at Tinian and Guam and in Washington had spent the previous two and a half hours unsure about where we were or what we were doing.

I then told Spitzer to call for air-sea rescue. John Kuharek reported that we had barely 300 gallons of usable fuel left. Not enough to make it to Okinawa, almost 350 miles away. I had already done the math in my head when Kuharek confirmed, "Even if we slow down our rate of consumption, the best we can do is get within seventy-five, maybe fifty, miles of Okinawa."

Jim Van Pelt had charted a direct line to Okinawa. He and Kuharek confirmed their calculations. We were going into the ocean. It was only a matter of when, not if. This prospect didn't disturb me that much. We'd get a little wet, wait for a Flying Dumbo or a friendly destroyer to pick us up, and we'd be home free. I didn't like the idea of losing my airplane, but at least I'd get the crew home safely.

Spitzer reported, "Major, I'm getting no response."

None of us, of course, knew that after Hopkins's transmission to Tinian, the brass had thought the mission had been aborted. Everyone in the air-sea rescue system resumed normal posture. If we dropped into the ocean, there was no guarantee that anyone would be there to get us.

As we departed Nagasaki, I told Abe to transmit a message of the results and our situation:

> Bombed Nagasaki 090158Z visually. No opposition. Results techni-
> cally successful. Visible effects about equal to Hiroshima. Proceeding
> to Okinawa. Fuel problem.

The details would best be dealt with when we returned.

With Fred Bock planted on my right wing, I knew we were not alone. It was noteworthy to me that, given our precarious personal situation aboard the aircraft, the mood among the crew was upbeat. With everything that had gone awry, they were relieved to have survived. The attitude was congratulatory. Maybe the war was really going to end and they could all go home.

My thoughts were somewhat less buoyant. The survival of these brave men was now my paramount concern. Setting this magnificent airplane down onto the water was tricky but not impossible. But in the absence of special air-sea rescue forces, the odds were somewhat skewed against us. Sitting in the water for any length of time is not an optimum situation.

We would hit the road for Okinawa, the first and closest petrol station in the neighborhood.

TWENTY

PAUL TIBBETS HAD taught me a technique that caused a lot of controversy among pilots, some vehemently denying it existed and others vocal apostles that a skilled pilot could do it. It was called "flying on the step." In theory, it was very simple. If you kept the power settings steady and took the aircraft into a gradual descent, the airplane would pick up a fraction more airspeed without using more power and fuel. The pilot would then level off. To retain that increased airspeed and perhaps even supplement it a bit more, you would start down another step and then another step, and so on.

You could milk only a little bit more speed and fly a little farther without consuming more fuel, but that was all I needed—a little bit more. I had the advantage of being at 30,000 feet, so I started my way down the staircase.

I also decided to add some insurance and save a little more fuel by throttling back the propellers to 1,800 rpm from the recommended cruising setting of 2,000 rpm. Turning the numbers over in my mind, I knew this wasn't going to be enough. So I throttled back to 1,600 rpm, well below the engine specifications for any circumstance. This could damage the engines, but balancing the risks against the benefits, I concluded that I'd rather replace four engines and get my crew safely tucked away for the evening than be bobbing in the Pacific aboard a life raft hoping we'd be picked up.

At the new settings we were consuming 300 gallons of fuel an hour. Flight time to Okinawa was about seventy-five minutes. Theoretically, the airspeed we gained as we came down each step might be just enough to get us to Yontan Field on Okinawa. Of course, we presumed that these procedures could buy us another fifty miles of flight and that the engines would continue to purr at 1,600 rpm.

I'm not sure that I could have found a Las Vegas oddsmaker willing to take book that we'd make it.

We were about fifteen minutes from Okinawa. I called the tower at Yontan. No response. I tried a few more times. "Yontan tower. Yontan tower. This is Dimples 77. . . . Yontan. Yontan. This is Dimples 77. Mayday! Mayday! Over." Silence.

I radioed the neighboring island of Ie Shima. They heard me, and I heard them. My transmitter and receiver were working. At that time, however, there was no direct-communications land link between the Ie Shima tower and the Okinawa tower. And because they were so close, they operated on different radio frequencies. There was no chance that they could raise Yontan for me in time.

I talked to Fred Bock, and he responded. But Fred had to keep his frequency open. If he tried to contact the tower, it might close out my transmissions—or worse, confuse the situation as we continued on a straight line toward the field. It was as if the entire world around us was spinning along and we were somehow suspended just beyond it, cut off from it.

*   *   *

No one was more amazed than I when *Bock's Car* caught sight of Okinawa. Ahead of me I could see heavy air traffic coming and going from the field. As the closest American base to Japan, Okinawa was the busiest airfield in the Pacific theater. Missions were being flown around the clock. A continuous stream of P-38s, B-24s, B-25s, and P-51s was taking off and landing.

Kuharek broke in, "Major, all gauges read empty."

At that moment our right outboard engine quit.

"Increase power to number-three engine," I yelled to Albury.

We were down to fumes. The power to number three steadied us, but the situation was clear. I couldn't afford a long, low approach or to be waved off to go around for another try. If the remaining engines went out on us, I'd be making a deadstick landing—no power, just basically gliding in with a sixty-five-ton airplane. I'd have to come in hot and high, aiming at a point halfway down the runway and maintaining my airspeed well above the usual 110 mph landing speed. It wouldn't be pretty, but it would get us on the ground, hopefully in one piece. I still had 600 gallons of high-test aviation fuel trapped in the belly of the airplane. If we crashed on landing, it very well could explode. We would have one shot to do this.

I told Olivi and Van Pelt to fire the flares of the day. The flare gun was positioned through a porthole in the skin of the fuselage. Red and green flares were fired out in an arc, bursting away from the airplane.

No answer from the field. The air traffic continued to come and go. They were either ignoring us completely or plain didn't see us, which was remarkable, as this massive silver B-29 lumbered toward them.

"Mayday! Mayday! Yontan. Dimples 77," I yelled. I could

hear the tower talking to other airplanes. But not to me. Again I transmitted, "Mayday! Mayday!" Nothing.

My biggest concern was that if the field was not cleared of incoming and outgoing traffic, I might hit an airplane taking off or be hit by one coming in for landing. Either way, it would be a disaster.

"I want any goddamn tower on Okinawa!" I bellowed into the mike.

I yelled back toward Olivi and Van Pelt. "Fire every goddamn flare we have on board!"

"Which ones?" Olivi asked.

"Every goddamn flare we have! Do it now!" I barked over my shoulder.

The flares arced gracefully above the airplane and then exploded into reds, blues, oranges, purples, greens—twenty flares of all colors. We must have looked like the Fourth of July. But it sure as hell got their attention. The multiple flares signaled not only "aircraft out of fuel" but "prepare for crash," "heavy damage," "dead and wounded on board," and "aircraft on fire." It was a potpourri of disaster warnings. On reflection, any one or all could have been true, depending on what happened next. The smell of gunpowder from the Very pistol that fired the flares filled the forward compartment.

I could see traffic being cleared ahead. Airplanes quickly banked away from the field while fire trucks and ambulances sped toward the runway.

I was now barreling in straight ahead, like a runaway freight train. In a few seconds we'd be on the ground, one way or the other. I prayed we didn't lose another engine at that moment. I needed just a few more seconds of power.

I was above the concrete runway. I descended quickly, hitting the pavement midway down the strip at about 140 mph. The *Bock's Car* bounced right back up into the air about twenty-five feet and then slammed back down to earth. When the wheels again met the pavement, the port outboard engine quit. The sixty-five-ton aircraft veered violently to the left toward a line of B-24s parked wingtip to wingtip along the edge of the runway.

I flipped on the reversible props and hit the emergency brakes, barely getting the B-29 straightened out and keeping it on the concrete runway. I thanked God that Paul Tibbets had had the foresight to equip our fifteen airplanes with reversible propellers. Of the 1,056 B-29s in service, only the ones made for the 509th were equipped with reversible props.

I depressed the brakes as far as they would go. The end of the runway was dead ahead. I grabbed the yoke and, using it as leverage, I put my entire weight and strength onto the brakes. The new Curtis reversible propellers added enough reverse thrust, together with the brakes, to finally slow us down to a roll. We came under positive control just short of the end of the runway.

I was so mentally and physically exhausted at that point that I just let the airplane roll to the side of the runway and onto a taxiway. Another engine quit. Instead of taxiing to a hardstand, I slumped back into my seat and decided to wait for the tow vehicles to come and get us. I cut the engines, and a total silence fell over the compartment. No one made a sound. Then the distant wail of sirens broke the stillness. Within seconds, emergency vehicles pulled alongside. We opened the nosewheel door. A head poked in. "Where's the dead and wounded?"

I realized how drained I was. I answered, "Back there," and I pointed to the north, toward Nagasaki.

The crew slowly dropped out of the airplane. Without a word, we drew together. I told them to get something to eat but to say nothing to anyone—not where we'd been or where we were going. The men climbed aboard a waiting truck. I dropped into the passenger seat of a jeep and told the driver to take me to the senior ranking unit commander. I needed to make a more comprehensive report to Tinian and advise them of my location and condition.

The jeep pulled up to the operations center. I told the lieutenant on duty that I needed access to his communications facilities, explaining my mission vaguely and the need to contact Tinian. In a few moments he returned, and to my surprise, I was ushered over to General Jimmy Doolittle's headquarters. Doolittle was the commander of the Eighth Air Force. Just a couple of weeks earlier he had deployed his headquarters from England to Okinawa, where he soon commanded the "Mighty Eighth."

The irony struck me immediately. I was about to meet the man who had flown the first American air strike against Japan by bombing Tokyo in 1942. His mission had inflicted very little damage. It had been symbolic, intended to show the Japanese people they were not invulnerable from attack as their military had claimed. And I had just flown what might be the last mission of the war—a mission that had demonstrated to the Japanese people that they could be on the verge of annihilation in spite of what their military and civilian leaders were telling them. The general gave me full access to his communications facilities, and I arranged for a detailed report to be transmitted to Tinian. When I finished, I had a brief and formal interview with General Doolittle.

Doolittle was no-nonsense, a legend in his own time. But I was surprised or maybe disappointed that he received the news of Nagasaki with no sign of emotion. He just wanted the facts.

"What was the extent of the damage?" he asked.

"I can't be sure, General. Smoke obscured the target," I answered.

"But you hit the target?" he pressed, stone-faced.

"Yes. Definitely, sir."

Doolittle was silent, unsmiling. He sat reflectively. Maybe he, too, was thinking about the irony of the moment. Or about the long struggle that had stretched over the previous three and a half years since he and a brave band of pilots and their crews flew their B-25s off the heaving decks of the USS *Hornet,* barely making it into the air. "It's been a long time coming," he finally offered.

"Yes, sir. I hope it means the end," I replied quietly.

Sensing that the interview had come to an end, I snapped a salute and turned to go. As I reached the door, Doolittle called me back.

"Sweeney?"

"Yes, sir?"

"I can only tell you what they said to me," he began, a smile creasing the corners of his mouth and then spreading across his broad face. "Well done!"

I joined my crew in the mess hall. There was a buzz of excitement as I walked through the line getting some chow. The talk around me was that a second atomic bomb had been dropped. In the military, scuttlebutt moves fast. How they knew about the second drop was amazing to me. Of course, no one paid any attention to me or knew who my crew and I were or where we had come from. The speculation was fantastic. One guy ladling out mashed potatoes was telling his buddy that he had heard it was a P-38 that flew in with a bomb no bigger than a baseball.

What I was interested in was whether the Japanese had made any announcement about surrender. They had not.

We stayed at Okinawa for about two hours while we ate and the *Bock's Car* was refueled. John Kuharek told me that he had measured the fuel, and that we'd had seven gallons left when we touched down—less than one minute of flight time. We still had a five-hour flight back to Tinian. After takeoff, the mood aboard the airplane was relaxed but very quiet, almost somber. We turned on Armed Forces Radio, hoping to hear news of the Japanese surrender. Instead, the lead story was that our allies, the Soviet Union, had that day declared war on Japan and were massing troops for a push into Manchuria. "How convenient," I thought. To the victor goes the spoils, and I was certain that Stalin didn't want to lose out on the loot he could cart off from Japan.

As the hours ticked by and we plowed through the moonlit sky, no word of Japanese surrender or even about our mission came over the airwaves. The music of Tommy Dorsey and Glenn Miller drifted softly through the airplane. I'm not sure what was going through my crew's minds, but I began to think ahead to the realization that if the Japanese didn't surrender, we would be flying more of these missions. The thought left me cold. I was the only one aboard who knew that we were several weeks away from having more bombs. This interlude would give the Japanese more than enough time to recover, regain their balance, and stiffen their resolve. Having lived through and overcome the devastation of the two atomic bombings, as they had survived the firebombings, they might actually convince themselves, using some perverse inversion of logic, that they could fight through the new horror, too. The samurai code of death with honor might engulf the entire population in a spasm of self-sacrifice.

At 10:30 P.M. I set the *Bock's Car* down on Runway A at Tinian. It had been twenty hours since we had last set foot there. There were no brass bands or cheering multitudes to greet us. No klieg lights or phalanxes of cameras or microphones or film crews. We were met by our ground crew and one photographer, a welcome sight to me and the men of the *Bock's Car.*

We were home. We were alive. We had completed our mission.

From the cockpit, I could see two solitary figures standing off to the left in the dim light. One was Paul Tibbets and the other was Admiral Purnell, the highest ranking naval officer on Tinian. I was the last of the crew to climb out. I was beyond being tired. I felt like I had passed a point of exhaustion and that I couldn't sleep if I'd wanted to. I couldn't have mustered another ounce of energy if my life had depended on it.

A voice greeted me. "Pretty rough, Chuck?"

It was Tibbets. I echoed, "Pretty rough, boss."

I don't remember extending a salute in the presence of a flag officer, and if I didn't, no one seemed to mind. Admiral Purnell extended his hand to shake mine. "You know, Major, those hours before you dropped the bomb, we'd just about given up on you."

The admiral then filled me in on what had happened. He told me that when General Farrell had first read the Hopkins transmission, he'd become violently sick to his stomach. "But although we were worried," the admiral continued, "Tibbets here said if anyone could get it done, you could. I see he was right."

That statement of confidence from the man I most admired washed away the travails we had gone through. Forget the brass bands and the crowds. This moment meant much more to me.

"It was close," I offered. "What the hell are we so gloomy about? Mission accomplished. Now what about some beer?"

Tibbets laughed. "Chuck, I'm afraid I have some bad news.

The beer ran out. But maybe the medics have some medicinal whiskey left," he added with a wink.

"What are we waiting for?"

The trucks dropped us off at the medical detachment, where the medics pronounced us fit. We were told that our rations of medicinal "relaxants" were awaiting us at the officers' club. We were then taken to the intelligence hut. General Farrell, Admiral Purnell, Dr. Ramsey, Colonel Tibbets, and the formal interrogators were in attendance but said little as they listened intently to each of us recite the events as we'd seen them.

When we arrived at the officers' club, a bar had been set up with a full selection of sour mash bourbon, Scotch, and 120-proof grain alcohol. Up to that point the mood among the crew had been subdued. But after almost forty-eight hours without sleep and a couple of drinks, we began to loosen up, relax, and allow ourselves the luxury of drinking ourselves into blissful oblivion.

Some of the crew from the *Enola Gay* joined us, and we partied into the morning light as gradually, one at a time, men wandered off to their quarters.

Paul Tibbets also joined us. He was always with his men. He and I sat off to one side for a bit and informally ran through the whole mission. Not in the stale rote of the intelligence debriefing but in the style of two professionals, two friends, who had the common experience of being the only two pilots to have carried out such a mission.

General Farrell had made a brief appearance to congratulate us. After reading the intelligence debriefing report, he went to the communications hut and sent the following cable to Washington:

CENTERBOARD—To Groves Personal From Farrell APCOM 5479
TOP SECRET

Strike and accompanying airplanes have returned to Tinian. Ashworth message No. 44 from Okinawa is confirmed by all observers.
Cloud cover was bad at strike and strike plane had barely enough
fuel to reach Okinawa. After listening to the accounts, one gets the
impression of a supremely tough job carried out with determination,
sound judgment and great skill. It is fortunate for the success of the
mission that its leaders, Sweeney and Ashworth, were men of stam-
ina and stout heart. Weaker men could not have done this job.
Ashworth feels confident that the bomb was satisfactorily placed
and that it did its job well.

At about five A.M., being well potted, I began to navigate
my way back to my Quonset hut, more by instinct than intellect. I had left Tom Ferebee and Jim Van Pelt at the bar drinking. While I was still trying to find my way home, they got
there first. They'd apparently come up with the great idea of
borrowing General Farrell's jeep and taking a ride around the
compound. Their excursion came to an abrupt and unexpected
end when they drove the jeep into my quarters, where Kermit
Beahan and Don Albury had retired earlier and were sound
asleep. I laid down among the wreckage and drifted into a
deep sleep.

The Japanese were assessing the damage at Nagasaki, and
the Soviets had invaded Manchuria. After Hiroshima, the Japanese military had argued that the United States had only one
bomb, that we had used it, and that we had done the worst
we could do. The military generals' staffs believed the bombing
at Hiroshima could be a rallying point in mobilizing the popu-
lace to rise up against an invading army and inflict massive
casualties upon American troops, forcing a negotiated peace on
terms acceptable to them.

Nagasaki changed the dynamic between the war faction and

the peace faction within the Japanese inner cabinet, the Supreme Council for the Direction of the War. The six members of the council, up to that point evenly split on the direction the war should take, were about to meet to decide the fate of their nation. Without question, the army and navy general staffs still wielded the actual power in Japan and were committed to fight on. Talk of surrender could result in summary execution for any of these council members. General Korechika Anami, a member of the council and Japan's minister of war, had waxed poetically about the last great battle on Japanese soil: "Would it not be wondrous for this whole nation to be destroyed like a beautiful flower?" But the second atomic bomb presented a unique opportunity for the inner cabinet to consider the unthinkable—unconditional surrender.

The inner cabinet convened a formal meeting in the eighteen-by-thirty-foot air raid shelter below the Imperial Palace. They were to be joined in the muggy, unventilated space by Emperor Hirohito. His presence was both unusual and encouraging to those assembled. The lives of millions of his people and of millions of Allied troops depended on what transpired at that extraordinary gathering.

Several hours later I would awake to the news that there was no news. It had been over twenty-four hours since the drop, and still the Japanese were silent. The prospect that these missions might become a matter of routine suddenly seemed all too real and disturbing.

TWENTY-ONE

THE DAYS IMMEDIATELY following our mission were mixed with hopeful anticipation and nagging dread. The hope was that the war was about to end. The dread was that we might have to go into combat one more time and maybe get our ticket punched. Having survived three and a half years of the war, maybe one of us would have the bad luck of being the last one to die in it.

On the morning of August 10, Paul Tibbets, General Farrell, Captain Parsons, Commander Ashworth, Tom Ferebee, Dutch Van Kirk, Kermit Beahan, and I were interviewed, photographed, and filmed by the official photographic unit of the 509th to preserve our thoughts and observations. We eight stood in front of the *Enola Gay* as the film crews prepared to shoot their film, measuring the light, asking us to relax and act natural. But like family members caught in a home movie, we stood stiffly and awkwardly in an effort to affect a posture of being at ease. Each of us in turn was asked to describe the

events of the two missions. And in proper military jargon we
recited the facts: what, when, and where.

Later in the day, at a press conference, the world learned
more details of the two atomic missions. My mother learned
that I had been involved. She would later tell me how shocked
she was to hear my voice on the radio. A war correspondent
who had attended the press conference had announced that the
next voice she would hear would be that of a Major Charles
W. Sweeney of North Quincy, Massachusetts. He asked me to
describe my mission over Nagasaki.

> To start off with we had a little operational difficulty in the matter
> of weather. Secondly, we had to make three runs on one target
> without being able to release because we had instructions to drop
> by visual methods only. We spent fifty minutes in the target area,
> all the time consuming more fuel. We had six hundred gallons of
> fuel in the rear bomb bay that were trapped because of a mechanical
> difficulty. We finally turned to our secondary target at Nagasaki,
> upon which we made a good run and knocked out some of the
> establishments in that city . . . From this point we really had to
> start saving fuel because we had to make an emergency landing at
> Okinawa with very little fuel left . . .

My mother made the sign of the cross. My fleeting voice
from the other side of the world had been almost too much for
her to absorb.

The Japanese stalled and the killing continued. The sight
of a Western Union courier at the front door of hundreds of
American households still brought terror to some young man's
wife, sister, mother, or father: "The Secretary of War regrets
to inform you . . ." During the three short months since Harry
S. Truman had been president, the United States had sustained
almost half of all Americans killed or wounded in the Pacific
since Pearl Harbor. On paper, Japan might have been headed

for defeat, but that didn't alter the basic arithmetic: the closer we got to victory over Japan, the higher the price we paid in American lives.

While we waited, events in Japan were playing out like a Shakespearean tragedy: intrigues, assassinations, suicides, an attempted coup d'etat, and an extraordinary address by the Son of God to his people. Chaos, treachery, and rebellion were in the air.

At two A.M. on August 10, less than twenty-four hours after the destruction of Nagasaki, Emperor Hirohito, the 124th emperor of Imperial Japan, having listened intently for hours to the passionate arguments of his ministers and advisers of the inner cabinet, pronounced, "We must bear the unbearable . . . I cannot but swallow my tears and sanction the proposal to accept the Allied Proclamation on the basis outlined by the foreign minister."

The decisive factor in the emperor's concession was the inescapable conclusion that further armed struggle would lead to the annihilation of his people. The Nagasaki bomb had demonstrated the hollowness of the military's optimistic assessment that by fighting on they could sap the Allies' will to sustain staggering casualties and thereby negotiate a peace settlement on favorable terms.

Incredibly, even after the second atomic bombing of Japan, the war faction within the inner cabinet advocated continuing the war. General Anami vehemently argued, "There is enough determination left in the armed forces to wage a decisive battle in the homeland." General Yoshijiro Umezi, Anami's chief of staff, insisted, "We have a new plan and hope for good results. Regarding the atomic bomb, it might be checked if proper anti-aircraft measures are taken against the planes." And Field Marshal Hata, whose headquarters had been destroyed at Hiroshima, concluded that because the bomb was exploded in the air, underground facilities would be unscathed. In fact, General Anami urged the field marshal to report to the emperor. ". . . the bomb is not so deadly."

The unprecedented personal intervention of the emperor, however, had broken the stalemate between the war faction and the peace faction. The bombing of Nagasaki proved that Hiroshima had not been an isolated event. The prospect that the United States could destroy one Japanese city after another had become a fact to the emperor's inner cabinet. To speak of surrender now was not an act of treason but a rational response to the reality imposed on the Japanese mind by Hiroshima and Nagasaki.

There was one monumental "but."

On Friday morning, August 10, President Truman received from the Japanese their "conditional" acceptance of the Potsdam Declaration. Japan was ready to surrender, but the emperor must remain as "a sovereign ruler."

Before Hiroshima, the Japanese response to the Potsdam Declaration had been *mokusatsu*—meaning "to treat with silent contempt." After Hiroshima, the inner cabinet had split evenly on offering a counterproposal to President Truman that would have allowed the military and civilian leaders who had plunged the Pacific into the hell it had become to remain in power. The major points the Japanese military insisted upon were:

1. Japan would try its own war criminals.
2. Japan would retain control of its troops in the field and disarm those troops itself.
3. The Allies could not occupy the home islands of Japan.
4. Emperor Hirohito would remain as the sovereign ruler of Japan.

Not only the United States, but the Soviet Union, Great Britain, China, and Australia, the latter two of which had suffered cruelly at the hands of the Japanese, would not accept any preconditions. And for very good reason—the same reason the Allies could accept no preconditions from Germany to end the war in Europe.

In 1944 or 1945, had we dropped the atomic bomb over Germany, the actions of the Nazi regime would have been no less evil. The Germans could not have rallied history to claim that they were the victims of the war because they had been bombed. Nor could there have been any suggestion that the Allies should have negotiated a peace with Nazi Germany. The idea would have been so outrageous that no rational person would have considered it. To negotiate with such evil would be to allow it, even in defeat, a measure of legitimacy.

So, too, with the empire of Japan. Their crimes were against humanity. The Allies were not involved in a philosophical debate with them. It was essential that the military elite, who gave life to the forces of evil as a matter of national policy, be clearly and irrevocably defeated. Their demise had to be unequivocal. The Japanese leadership, particularly its military leaders, had forfeited any expectation of diplomatic conciliations.

After the second atomic mission, the Japanese government, over the rabid objection of the military, which insisted that all four conditions be met before hostilities would cease, sought only retention of the emperor as the ruler of Japan. President Truman, wishing to avoid, if possible, further nuclear attacks or an invasion of the mainland, took a middle course to move Japan to surrender within the framework of the Potsdam Declaration, over the strenuous objection of the Soviet Union. Rather than give a flat-out no to Japan, Truman offered that the emperor could stay, but under the direct authority of the supreme commander of the Allied powers. Truman understood that we might need the emperor as a figurehead to assure a peaceful occupation of the home islands and a transition to a democratic form of government.

Because the Japanese had offered their first serious response to the Potsdam Declaration, the United States decided to temporarily ratchet down its offensive against Japan to give it time to surrender. B-29 raids were halted. President Truman suspended his earlier order authorizing the use of atomic weapons: no atomic bombs were to be dropped unless he specifically reauthorized their use. General Leslie Groves, head of the Manhattan Project, independently ordered that no further deliveries of plutonium be made without his consent. In spite of the Japanese intransigence, neither our political nor our military leaders were intent on inflicting additional punishment upon the Japanese people, conventional or otherwise, while waiting for their leaders' response. Instead of bombs, the Twentieth Air Force began dropping millions of leaflets exhorting Japanese civilians and soldiers to surrender in the face of certain destruction.

But the Japanese military leaders were not quite finished. To counter rumors of surrender circulating throughout the civilian and military populations, Japanese soldiers in the field were told by their leaders to fight on, to crush the enemy.

August 11 came and went. As did August 12. August 13 brought no response from the Japanese to President Truman's offer. All American forces in the Pacific during those three days had been cautioned to avoid, where possible, engaging Japanese forces. Finally, President Truman reluctantly directed General George Marshall to authorize resumption of air raids against Japan.

On August 14, General Spaatz ordered into the air just about every aircraft in the theater—bombers, fighters, B-29s, B-24s, B-25s, B-26s, P-38s, you name it, anything that could fly and carry ordnance, strafe a target, or fire a rocket—for one massive show of force to push the Japanese to surrender.

Curtis LeMay ordered his B-29s of the XXI Bomber Command to take part in what was once again hoped to be a final blow that would push the Japanese to give up any belief that they could hold out any longer.

Eight of our airplanes would take part in this final assault. The *Enola Gay,* the *Bock's Car, The Great Artiste,* and five other of the 509th's airplanes would sit this one out—the *Enola Gay* and the *Bock's Car* for obvious reasons, and *The Great Artiste* because all the scientific instruments were still aboard and we didn't know if they would be needed for further atomic missions. *Spook* and *Jabett III* were en route to the United States to take delivery of components for more Fat Man bombs, should the decision be made to proceed with the atomic bombing.

Although I could have stayed at our home base, I decided that as squadron commander this was a mission I must go on. It was my job to set an example. The undercurrent of dread had bubbled to the surface with the news that we were going back to Japan for one more mission. The old bad luck syndrome, that ethereal sense of mortality that some men feel, believing their last mission might be the one that kills them, was in full bloom among the crews. No one wanted to be the Private George Price of World War II. (Private Price was killed by a sniper's bullet at 10:58 A.M., November 11, 1918, two minutes before the start of the armistice ending World War I.)

My crew and I, aboard the *Straight Flush,* headed for the empire. As we cruised at about 8,000 feet on a sunny day, the ocean below glistened. We were carrying a single pumpkin loaded with several thousand pounds of the high explosive Torpex. Our target was the Toyoda Auto Works at Koromo. Once we were in the air, the atmosphere aboard was relaxed. It was as though we were on a milk run. In our bomb bay sat an exact replica of the Fat Man which we had carried five days earlier. This new bomb was a deadly package of high explosives that would devastate its intended target but, unlike the Fat Man, it contained neither the secrets nor the horrors of the universe. It seemed to us oddly benign in comparison.

As we drew nearer to Japan, below us, stretched out as far as the eye could see, was a massive armada of Allied ships—aircraft carriers, battleships, heavy and light cruisers, destroyers, and supply ships of every size and description. They were all neatly grouped in formations of a hundred ships, five across and twenty deep. You could have almost walked to Japan from ship to ship. It looked like a gray carpet rimmed by stripes of deep blue. It was the most awesome display of sea power I—or perhaps anybody—had ever seen.

By the time we reached the empire, airplanes that had already struck their targets in Japan were heading back to base. Wave after wave of airplanes passed us going home, and behind us an endless string of aircraft followed. We were like trains coming and going in New York's Grand Central Station. Before the day was through, over two thousand airplanes would participate in this unprecedented air assault.

Our drop on the Toyoda Auto Works was right on target, and the mission was thoroughly uneventful. It was reported later that our pumpkin actually might have been the very last bomb dropped on mainland Japan in World War II.

With the American reply to Japan's offer of conditional surrender now known, the army of Japan saw a last opportunity to prevail. The opposing factions of the inner cabinet were going back and forth at each other. Outside this tiny group of six men who held the fate of their nation in their hands, a coup began to take shape among younger army officers intent on derailing the emperor's expressed desire to end the war under the conditions imposed by the Allies. Senior officers did not discourage these fledgling insurgents.

By the morning of August 14, the inner cabinet was again in a deadlock that only the emperor could break. A meeting of the supreme council was convened at 10:30 A.M. in the air raid shelter beneath the Imperial Palace. Again the war and peace factions argued point, counterpoint. The emperor reiterated his previous desire to end the war and accept the terms as set forth by the Allies. "I cannot endure the thought of letting my people suffer any longer," he told them.

The emperor then advised the assembled ministers that he would record a message to be broadcast to the people. For the first time ever, the Japanese population would hear the voice of their emperor, bringing them news that was, for most, unimaginable.

After the emperor departed from the meeting, General Anami made one last attempt to convince members of the council to authorize a strike at American forces by attacking a convoy believed to be off the coast of Honshu. He argued that this action might make the Americans rethink their demands.

Such was the atmosphere within, and the mind-set of, the Japanese military.

Later in the day, General Anami would commit suicide. In the traditional way, he committed *seppuku* by kneeling, slitting his stomach open with his ceremonial knife, and then plunging a dagger into his neck. Before the passage of another twenty-four hours, several more high-ranking officers would choose death over surrender.

As August 14 dissolved into August 15, the leaders of the coup were having no luck in gaining overt support from senior army officers, who now doubted that the coup could succeed. When General Takeshi Mori, commander of the Imperial

Guard, refused to join the plot, he was summarily executed and his aide was decapitated. The Imperial Palace was then occupied in the early morning hours by the rebels, and a frantic search ensued to locate and destroy the phonograph disk the emperor had recorded for broadcast later that day. In other parts of Tokyo, other rebel bands searched for Prime Minister Suzuki, high-ranking ministers, and members of the royal household staff, all marked for assassination. The emperor was to be, in effect, placed under house arrest.

Not having the support of the generals, unable to locate and destroy the emperor's recorded message, and thwarted in seizing Tokyo radio stations, the insurgents' revolt petered out as the sun dawned on August 15. Many of the conspirators wandered off to commit suicide.

At noontime the Japanese national anthem rang out from radios all over the home islands. Then the emperor spoke: "[W]e have resolved to pave the way for a grand peace for all generations to come by enduring the unendurable and suffering what is insufferable."

He cast the Japanese defeat as the result of international forces conspiring to destroy Japan, which had acted reasonably and out of the best of motives. "Indeed," he said, "we declared war on America and Great Britain out of our sincere desire to ensure Japan's self-preservation and the stabilization of Southeast Asia, it being far from our thought either to infringe upon the sovereignty of other nations or to embark upon territorial aggrandizement."

I'm sure this was news to China, Manchuria, the Philippines, New Guinea, Java, Indochina, Thailand, Burma, Sumatra, the Solomon Islands . . .

"We cannot but express the deepest sense of regret to our Allied nations of East Asia, who have consistently cooperated with the empire toward the emancipation of East Asia," the emperor continued.

The emancipation of twenty million dead in East Asia?

And, in a final stroke of exoneration, the emperor converted the Japanese from the aggressor in the war to the victim. "[T]he enemy," he said, "has begun to employ a new and most cruel bomb, the power of which to do damage is indeed incalculable, taking the toll of many innocent lives. Should we continue to fight, it would not only result in an ultimate collapse and obliteration of the Japanese nation, but would also lead to the total extinction of human civilization."

Not a word of remorse for the inhumanity inflicted during their conquest and occupation of most of Asia. Not a word of apology for the misery and suffering the emperor's military forces had spread across the Pacific and Asia. Not a mention of the navy men lying in a metal tomb on the bottom of Pearl Harbor. The emperor had stopped the fighting to save civilization. Even as he spoke, prisoners of war were being tormented and executed by units of the Japanese armed forces.

This failure to take responsibility as a nation for the horrors the Japanese military had inflicted on their fellow man has persisted for fifty years. Unlike Germany, which acknowledged its guilt, Japan holds steadfast to the fiction that it did nothing wrong, that it was trapped by circumstances—the theme struck by Hirohito on August 15, 1945, and, unfortunately, perpetuated by some historians in 1995.

Hirohito did much more than fail to acknowledge the motives and deeds of Japan during those desperate years. In his speech, the emperor set in motion an untruth that was to flourish for many years after the war was over: the myth that the Japanese were the victims of the war. Pointing to the devastation brought upon Hiroshima and Nagasaki by President Truman's decision to use all of the weapons at his disposal to end the bloodshed, Japan succeeded in many quarters in diverting its responsibility for the war to President Truman's use of atomic weapons to end it. To this day, history is denied within Japan. Most, if not all, of Japan's aggression prior to and during World War II is left unspoken to its population.

But on August 15, 1945, cloaked in whatever garment the emperor chose to wear, the Japanese surrendered unconditionally.

To the east, across the international dateline, it was still Tuesday, August 14. At seven o'clock in the evening the president of the United States made the following announcement:

> I have just received a note from the Japanese government in reply to the message forwarded to that government by the secretary of state on August 11. I deem this reply a full acceptance of the Potsdam Declaration, which specifies the unconditional surrender of Japan.

The war was over.

TWENTY-TWO

THE NEWS OF the surrender was greeted with unrestrained happiness and celebrating. We were going home. We had survived the war. We were alive, and the probability was that tomorrow we'd still be alive. The mood was buoyant and expectant. A return to our families, friends, and careers awaited us. For the first time in years, the world was at peace. The exact measure of the Nazi and Imperial Japan's decade of murderous excesses was still being uncovered and tallied. The exact nature of the evil loosed upon mankind by the Axis powers would soon tax the comprehension of most human beings.

But for those of us who had fought, the single focus of our lives was that the fighting was over. While Washington finalized the details of the formal surrender and the judicial mechanisms for war crimes tribunals were set in motion, we drank in the blissful monotony of our tropical paradise—swimming in the crystal-clear, coral-blue water, sunning on the sandy beaches, sleeping late into the morning. We drifted from one day to the next. Occasionally I took an airplane up to stay in practice and to do what I loved most, fly. We were missionless and free as birds.

Paul Tibbets told me that I had been awarded the Silver Star for the Nagasaki mission. On August 25, General Nathan Twining flew in from Guam to personally make the presentation to me and to award the Air Medal to each member of my crew. Having a three-star come to Tinian to award these decorations was quite an honor. General Twining was Curtis LeMay's boss in the theater and reported only to General Spaatz, who commanded all army air forces in the Pacific.

On the appointed day we drove over to the wing command at the 313th Headquarters decked out in our starched and pressed class A uniforms. General Twining reviewed us in military formation and then read each citation individually and pinned the medals to the chest of each recipient.

"How would you like to go up to Japan tomorrow?" Paul Tibbets asked. In Tokyo Bay, General MacArthur was, at that very hour on September 2, accepting the formal surrender of Japan aboard the USS *Missouri*.

It took me all of one second to answer, "I'd love it. Let's go."

"Get a couple jeeps and trailers and fill them with ten-in-one rations," he said.

I had my old buddy, John Casey, the commander of the transport squadron, fuel up a C-54 and load it with two jeeps and two trailers. The trailers were filled with ten-in-one rations. Next morning, with Tibbets in the pilot's seat and me as co-pilot, our party of about twenty, including Tom Ferebee, Don Albury, Kermit Beahan, Dutch Van Kirk, and Jim Van Pelt, was on its way to Tokyo.

We landed at Atsugi Air Field in Tokyo. The field had been secured just the day before by advance elements of the First Cavalry Division. Their job was to secure all communications facilities, government offices, and military posts in the area. No one could be certain what reception the American forces might encounter and these guys, in complete combat gear, were ready for anything.

The airlift of the First Cav was in full swing. We were part of a never-ending stream of transports that were landing every one to two minutes without stop. The place was a beehive of activity. Unlike the other olive drab transports, we parked our beautiful, gleaming silver C-54 right in front of the operations office to off-load our jeeps and trailers.

The base operations office was an octagonal, wood-shingled building with an open wooden tower propped on the roof. For a major airfield it was primitive compared to the facilities we were used to. Paul proceeded to the operations office, leaving me with the airplane to oversee the off-loading.

No sooner had Paul disappeared into the building than a young colonel came up to me and demanded, "Whose airplane is this?"

"Sir, this is Colonel Tibbets's airplane," I replied.

"Get it out of here," he ordered.

It struck me that this guy was awful young to be a colonel. My guess was that he was younger than I. He had that serious demeanor of a man who had a job to do and would do it to the letter. He didn't know who we were, and I wasn't about to tell him. It occurred to me that three weeks earlier, with our top secret priority, I could have parked our Green Hornet inside of the operations office and no one would have raised an eyebrow. But I thought maybe I could reason with him. We were, after all, on the same side. "We're only going to be here a couple of days. I can leave the air—"

He cut me off. "I'll give you thirty minutes, then I'll bull-doze it off the ramp." And off he walked.

I told Colonel Tibbets, but added that I had a plan. The map showed a small grass field, Chofu Field, just outside the city. I'd take the C-54 up to that field, hitch a ride into Tokyo, and meet him and the guys at the Dai Ichi Hotel. That would allow us to avoid having to butt heads with the young colonel. I had learned long ago that in the military you choose your spots, and this wasn't worth a fight.

I took a crew chief with me and landed at Chofu Field about ten minutes later. The concrete touchdown pad ran out after about a thousand feet, so I let the airplane roll off onto the grass. Nothing much was happening at this field. A group of P-38s had come in to Chofu to provide air cover for our forces if hostilities erupted. All was quiet, and the fighters sat at the ready. A major pulled up in a jeep alongside the Green Hornet. He introduced himself as the duty officer. I asked for transport into Tokyo, but he told me that only the group com-mander could authorize that request.

Another colonel approached who looked like he was barely out of flying school. "Can't help you, Major. Times are tough. We don't have enough of anything, including gas. Everything's being diverted to Atsugi Field in Tokyo," he offered politely.

I hadn't come all this way to strand Paul Tibbets in Tokyo. But at least this colonel wasn't threatening to plow my airplane into the ground with a bulldozer. I decided to spend a little time commiserating with him. We talked about flying school, what class he'd been in, how young he was to be a colonel, the responsibilities—and then ever so politely I asked again if maybe he could just get me into town. I mentioned that my colonel would be expecting me. He finally relented. An hour later I was standing in front of the Dai Ichi Hotel.

The Dai Ichi Hotel and the Imperial Hotel, which had been designed by Frank Lloyd Wright, were among the few structures left standing in Tokyo. They were situated close to the Imperial Palace, which had remained untouched by our bombers. Standing near the palace, I wondered if the Japanese would have shown such restraint if they had had the opportunity to bomb the White House.

We all decided to take a swing around the city. Someone had the idea that we should find a translator to accompany us while we were in Tokyo. A hotel employee directed us to the major newspaper office in Tokyo, where we found an affable English-speaking reporter who had graduated from Harvard in the 1930s.

Downtown Tokyo stretched out in front of us, barren. Nothing was standing. The only recognizable objects were the burned hulks of safes and vaults among the charred remains of what must once have been banks and insurance companies. The Tokyo fire department and other emergency agencies had fought a losing battle to save Tokyo's downtown in the course of repeated bombings over several months. Driving through the rubble of what had been a great city, I saw the strangest of sights. Children, most of them four or five years old, lined the streets waving tiny American flags as we passed, offering salutes to us with their little hands. Not the adults, just the children. I couldn't understand where they had gotten the flags or why they were doing this. The adults were at best neutral, or perhaps dour, accepting of our presence, but the kids were cheerful.

Our interpreter told us that the Japanese are an orderly people. Since they had surrendered, it was their duty to cooperate with the occupying forces, to accept the shame of their defeat. It struck me that he hadn't mentioned the shame for what they had done. But for the children, it was a time of hope with the war over.

Nowhere in Tokyo did we encounter any hostility toward us.

Our accommodations at the Dai Ichi were neat, clean, and undersized. Everything—the rooms, the beds, the bathtub—was about 60 percent of what similar accommodations would be in the States. For a guy with my dimensions, it was a tight squeeze.

Although the military issued scrip for us to use as currency, we didn't need it. The army had taken over the hotel and the dining facilities. The menu was a delightful array of C rations, which veterans to this day fondly recall as corned beef hash. We could order anything on the menu. So we had hash in the morning, in the afternoon, and at night. We had fried hash, cold hash, hot hash, hash rolled into a ball, hash flattened into a patty, and mashed hash. What saved the day was an endless supply of sake, which we consumed with abandon.

The next morning I took a jeep and one of the trailers filled with our rations and set out for a day of sightseeing. Maybe we could do a little trading with our rations. We came upon Sophia University, which was a Catholic school.

At the university we found a priest who was German but spoke perfect English with a most proper British accent. He told us how bad conditions had become. Much of the population was near starvation. Everything was scarce—fuel, electricity, housing, clothes, medical supplies. Children had been pressed into factory work as the shortage of men had worsened. Yet the government had continued an endless barrage of encouragement promising that victory was theirs.

The priest gave us a tour of the campus and the main chapel. Not surprisingly, the religious icons in the chapel had

Japanese features. A service was under way, and a class of little schoolgirls with white square handkerchiefs on their heads stood in line to receive Communion. In the oriental fashion, they bowed instead of genuflecting. It was all so familiar, comforting, and reassuring.

Food was scarce in Tokyo but we had plenty. And when we ran out, there would be more when we returned to Tinian. In good conscience, I couldn't keep the rations we had stashed in the trailer. I thought that if I gave the rations to the priest he would know how to properly distribute the food to the children of his parish. All of the guys were in agreement. So we pulled the trailer around and unloaded the cases of food.

The priest was elated. Our ten-in-one rations were a cornucopia, not like the C rations. They were crammed with tins of tuna, chocolate bars, crackers, chewing gum, and sundry other delights. To him, it was like a gift basket.

We wanted to go to Hiroshima, but there was no adequate landing facility to accommodate our C-54. There was, however, a field about fifteen miles outside of Nagasaki. It was called Omura, and it was on a naval base where we could land.

What we didn't know was that the Omura naval base and its airfield were still under the control of the Japanese military. As our C-54 set down, we were the first Americans to arrive in the area of Nagasaki. We were met on the ground by Japanese soldiers and their officers. Although I carried a sidearm during the war, I never loaded it. For the first time since I'd joined the military, I took the clip of ammunition from the pouch on my web belt and inserted it into the handle grip of my Colt .45 automatic. I decided against chambering a round, remembering my father's admonition.

The scene was awkward, but not threatening, as we deplaned. The Japanese seemed to be waiting for someone to tell them what to do next. All that was left of the airplane hangars were the charred steel superstructures standing like the skeletons of some long-dead beast. Two Mitsubishi Zero-Sen fighters, known to us as "Zekes," in perfect condition, were parked beside the burned-out hangars. None of the assembled soldiers spoke English, so we communicated in pantomime. We moved our hands as if turning an imaginary steering wheel, driving. We tried to make English words sound Japanese: "Need trucky to drivy Nagasaki." It's amazing how universal the belief is that if you speak loudly, slowly, and, in the case of English speakers, add vowels to the end of words, this will pass as a foreign language.

Our problem was that we had traded our jeeps and trailers to a squad of marines in Tokyo for what we thought were thirty handmade silk kimonos. We didn't care about the jeeps. Like everything else, we had hundreds, maybe thousands, of jeeps back on Tinian, many still in shipping crates. But on closer examination it turned out that the kimonos were made of something, but it sure as hell wasn't silk. We had been hoodwinked, but what the hell. The marines had a practical use for the jeeps. What we were going to do with the kimonos had yet to be decided. In the world of barter, which Japan then was, it seemed like a good idea to have silk kimonos.

The Japanese soldiers finally understood what we were asking for and delivered three trucks to us. These vehicles were a sorry sight—a single headlight in the middle of a dented and leaky radiator grill, rickety suspension, fenders rusted through. They were a far cry from the equipment we were used to operating. I don't know what they ran on for fuel, but they sputtered and shook worse than a diesel engine on a cold morning. I expected them to break down before we drove off the field. Some of the guys jumped into the back of one of the trucks and I sat on the roof of the cab. The rest followed in the other two trucks.

The road to Nagasaki wound up and over hills and down into valleys dotted with small homes along the sides of the road. The hillsides were green and leafy. A summer breeze whispered through the tall grass and shrubs and stands of trees. Here and there, Japanese families toiled in fields and gardens, paying us no attention. Occasionally a single, unarmed Japanese soldier—never a group of soldiers, always one at a time— would be walking along the road, showing no response to us, as if our presence was as normal and expected as any other everyday occurrence in this beautiful countryside. Two weeks earlier, he and the families along the road probably would have killed us on sight.

On the outskirts of Nagasaki, we came upon a small resort inn nestled among ancient trees. It was a charming place, two stories high, with double red-tile pagoda-styled roofs, the second-story roof overhanging a lower roof rimming the first story. We decided to spend the night there before pressing on to Nagasaki. Inside on the reception desk lay the register. I wasn't sure if the Japanese knew the names of the crew who had bombed their city. It crossed my mind that perhaps the better part of valor would be to avoid signing in. We were the only Americans on Japanese soil within three hundred miles of this spot. I watched as Paul walked up to the desk, swiveled the register around toward him, and in a clear hand wrote, "Colonel Paul W. Tibbets USAAF." I stepped right up after him and signed "Major Charles W. Sweeney USAAF," and in turn each of our party registered.

An elderly couple were the innkeepers. They were courteous and attentive, and they spoke English. Before the war, Nagasaki had been a favorite tourist destination for American and English travelers. That night we sat around the inn relaxing and drinking sake. I still wasn't quite at ease, though, and I did something I had never done before or since: I hung the holster with my loaded weapon on the headrest of my bed, within easy reach.

The next morning we proceeded to Nagasaki. The trucks coughed and gagged up the last set of hills. Over the next ridge was the Urakami Valley. At the crest we could survey the length of the valley where a month before the Mitsubishi war plants had been operating at full capacity producing small arms, torpedoes, and various other munitions for the Japanese armed forces.

The valley floor was a stretch of rubble dotted by grotesquely twisted lumps of steel beams and columns. A brick chimney rose here and there amid the wreckage where the munitions plants had once stood. From a distance, the destroyed armaments plants looked like erector sets a child had twisted and bent and carelessly tossed away. We had driven through the verdant hills to a wasteland. As we descended into the valley, we were the first Americans to set foot in Nagasaki and survey the damage. United States naval personnel were waiting on board vessels anchored in the harbor until scientific survey teams were sent in first to test for radioactivity. We weren't even supposed to be in the area, not to mention driving through the valley.

The trucks came to a stop midway in the valley. I walked alone along a brick sidewalk to a point I estimated was where ground zero would have been on August 9. In the distance ahead of me I could see a solitary Japanese soldier walking away along the same sidewalk, unaware or uncaring that we were here. There were very few people around as I surveyed the surroundings.

I looked straight up into the blue sky where at 1,890 feet the Fat Man had exploded. In an instant on that August day, which oddly seemed so long ago, everything around me that morning had been vaporized in a burst of blistering heat and blast.

I walked to what must have been an intersection of main streets. On one corner I peered down into the cellar of what had been a fire station. It was then that I was struck by the significance of our weapon. In the cellar was a fire truck that had been crushed flat, as if a giant had stepped on it. In fact, the entire infrastructure of the city was flat—no water, no emergency facilities, no firefighters. Everything was gone.

This had not been the conventional slow, incremental destruction of a target, as we had destroyed other Japanese cities. This had been instantaneous obliteration. There had been no time for the people to grow accustomed to the bombing, as other Japanese had done in Kobe, Nagoya, and Osaka. There had been no time to allow the mind to rationalize that you could survive. More Japanese had died during a single firebombing of Tokyo on March 9 than at Hiroshima or Nagasaki—97,000 killed, 125,000 wounded, 1,200,000 homeless. For its victims, the firestorms in Tokyo were every bit as horrifying as the nuclear blast. Intense napalm fires incinerated everything. Tornadolike winds whipped through the city as the fires consumed all the oxygen, creating a vacuum that itself suffocated people. Yet the Japanese had fought on. But they could not fight on after the second atomic strike.

Nuclear weapons had changed the human response to warfare. No longer would war be seen as simply an extension of national policies by other means, a condition of the human spirit that occasionally broke out of the bounds of civilized conduct. The Japanese military leaders might wish to fight to the death, but it would be their nation that would die.

The casualty figures at Nagasaki were still a matter of some speculation. It would finally be estimated that in the first instant

40,000 people were killed, and that another 30,000 to 35,000 died of their injuries within a few days. Seventy-five thousand more were wounded. As I looked around, I saw no bodies among the rubble, nor would I see any in other parts of the city. Apparently, and with the efficiency for which the Japanese are noted, the survivors had almost immediately started to clean up and care for the wounded.

Standing amid the rubble, I felt a sadness that so many had died on both sides, not only there but in all the horrible places where the war had been fought. We would learn that over fifty million people had perished because of Japanese and German aggression—the majority of them unarmed men, women, and children—in Asia, the Pacific, Europe, Africa, the Middle East, and a thousand other places. And millions of soldiers, sailors, marines, and airmen, the best and brightest of an entire generation, would never realize their tomorrows.

I thanked God that it was we who had this weapon and not the Japanese or the Germans. I hoped there would never be another atomic mission.

I took no pride or pleasure then, nor do I take any now, in the brutality of war, whether suffered by my people or those of another nation. Every life is precious. But I felt no remorse or guilt that I had bombed the city where I stood. The suffering evidenced by the destruction around me had been born of the cruelty of the Japanese militaristic culture and a tradition that glorified the conquest of "inferior" races and saw Japan as destined to rule Asia. The true vessel of remorse and guilt belonged to the Japanese nation, which could and should call to account the warlords who so willingly offered up their own people to achieve their visions of greatness.

My crew and I had flown to Nagasaki to end the war, not to inflict suffering. There was no sense of joy among us as we walked the streets there. We were relieved it was over, for us and for them.

Although the industrial valley and the shipbuilding facilities along the Urakami River had been totally destroyed, the residential and business districts of Nagasaki had been spared. The life of Nagasaki was going on as usual there. Kermit Beahan, Don Albury, and I walked around the city. Businesses were open; the people went about their daily routine. Children lined up in their uniforms to attend school. The mood was different from the mood in Tokyo. There was an air of sullenness, but not of despair. The people on the street were polite to us. Of course, they didn't know who we were, but they didn't seem fazed at the sight of three American servicemen strolling through their city.

The rebuilding was already under way. Unlike the Russians, who had immediately carted off the spoils of victory from Manchuria, dismantling factories, railroad trains, and rolling stock and literally taking every nut, bolt, and brick, the United States, even in the early days of the Occupation, began to assist in feeding, clothing, and housing its former enemy. Soon money and material would flood into Japan to rebuild the economy its leaders had so recklessly destroyed.

TWENTY-THREE

On November 14, I lifted off from the runway at Tinian for the last time. The entire 509th was being rotated back to the United States lock, stock, and barrel. Our new base would be at Roswell, New Mexico. I brought *The Great Artiste* around for one last look and then headed to Kwajalein, on to Hawaii and then to Sacramento on our three-day hopscotching route back to the West Coast.

It was about nine P.M. when I set down at Mather Field in Sacramento. We had crossed over the bright lights of San Francisco, a sight that had been denied Americans for over three and half years because the city had been kept in darkness in case of an air or sea attack by the Japanese. During the early stages of the war, some parts of the West Coast had been shelled from submarines. In 1944, over two hundred balloons carrying bombs had been floated over the western United States. Some started fires in the heavily forested Pacific coast of Washington State and Oregon. One explosion killed six people in Oregon, another killed a woman in Montana. The more ambitious plan to float balloons over our cities with canisters of deadly biological agents to spread epidemics of virulent diseases in our cities or destroy our livestock industry never came to fruition, although the testing of biological agents on prisoners of war had netted the Japanese valuable data. But all that was behind us on this starry California night.

We were almost home. All that remained was to be officially processed back into the United States. Each airman and airplane was checked in and much of our equipment was taken back into inventory. Emergency rafts from the airplanes, sidearms, and some weapons issued to the crews were logged in and returned to the supply depot. For most of the fifteen hundred men of the 509th, Roswell would be a brief stopover to civilian life.

Dorothy had moved down to Roswell, and we would settle there for the time being. Since all returning combat veterans were given forty-five days of rest and recreation, all expenses paid, we decided to go home.

We took a train from Albuquerque that was packed with servicemen. The good old days of having my own airplane were gone forever. But I must admit that what the train lacked in speed it made up for with a continuous rolling party. The celebrating aboard our club cars had its peaks and valleys, but it never stopped. The first leg was thirty-six hours to Kansas City, then on to Chicago for a four-hour wait to board the Twentieth-Century Limited to New York's Grand Central Station. In New York, we picked up a small commuter train to White Plains, where we stayed a couple of days with my old friend Bill Kelley.

The nation and the military were on an emotional high. Everything seemed possible; the future was bright and unobstructed. When we arrived home there were hugs, kisses, handshakes, and solemn thank-yous from my neighbors. I was invited to speak to local civic groups and, because I was in uniform, paying for a meal or a drink proved to be a battle I always lost.

For my family, there was relief that I had made it through. I hadn't really considered exactly how comforting it would be to be home with the war over. For the past five years, my first years of adulthood, the military and the war had been the core of my life. I had grown up, physically and emotionally, within the military in time of war. No matter what I had done for those five years, it all came back to my duties as a pilot in wartime. And, as any serviceman will attest, you never think you're going to be the one who's going to die. It's always going to be the other guy. Yet there's always a part of your subconscious that says maybe you won't see your family again. In my mother's kitchen once more, I could soak in the warmth of home and family for the first time in years, knowing I would see them again tomorrow. And in our future, Dorothy and I would have ten beautiful children, who would, at last count, give us twenty-one grandchildren.

The press started to call shortly after my return. "What was it like?" "Was there a big bang?" "Did the airplane rock?" "Were you frightened?" "What were you thinking?" The reporters were polite, attentive, and anxious to hear my pearls of wisdom. I didn't view myself as a celebrity or even much of a hero. I had come home in one piece. I explained that I had done my job, like millions of other veterans, to end the war. Because in 1945 the events of the war were seared into the consciousness of the nation and the world, I wasn't asked any questions about whether it had been necessary to drop the atomic bombs.

Overnight the 509th became the hottest unit in the military. Every officer wanted assignment to our group. It was the place to be if you were on a military career fast track. In the short month and a half I had been gone, the entire group had been restaffed to operational levels. Everywhere I looked at Roswell I saw strangers. Paul Tibbets had been moved over as "technical adviser" to the commanding general, Roger Ramey. The new group commander was Colonel Butch Blanchard, Curtis LeMay's operations officer in the Pacific. Blanchard was a West Pointer, as were most of the other officers filling in the new organizational chart. These were all career push guys. With the war over, the professional officer corps wanted their military back, and, in particular, they wanted this elite unit back in normal channels.

I was not a regular army career guy. My path to the military had been set because of my love of flying. And my service during the war had been a call to duty, as it had been for fifteen million other Americans.

Although we were training the new crews, the few of us remaining from the original 509th became the proverbial fifth wheel. Most of us were not integrated into the operations of the group at any level.

Toward the end of January 1946, Paul Tibbets and I were extended an invitation by Curtiss-Wright, the manufacturer of the B-29 Cyclone engines, to be its guests in New York City for a week. The brass liked the idea of us doing a little public relations for the new air force and sent us on our way east.

The company put us up at the Waldorf Astoria, the most exclusive hotel in Manhattan. We were wined and dined in the lap of luxury. Each night we attended private parties with the elite of New York's society and its arts community. At the very posh Stork Club, we were routinely ushered into the ultra-private Cub Room, where we mingled with the likes of Walter Winchell; Sy Bartlett, a scriptwriter and producer for Twentieth Century Fox; and the upper crust of society like the Rothschild

family. Actually, I had known Sy from Grand Island, where
he served on General Frank Armstrong's staff. He would im-
mortalize General Armstrong with his screenplay *Twelve
O'Clock High.*

Months later, when I was in California as a technical adviser on an MGM film about the Manhattan Project, Sy Bartlett
invited me to attend a party with him at the home of Norma
Shearer. Howard Hughes, Gary Cooper, Alice Faye, Phil Har-
ris, Fred Astaire, Hume Cronyn, Brian Donlevy, and Dana
Andrews were some of the stars there. I was partying with the
very same movie stars I had idolized as a teenager. Sy introduced me around as the pilot who had dropped the atomic
bomb. I was congratulated on the success of the mission and
thanked for helping end the war.

Orders were cut for me to report to Fort Dix, New Jersey,
to be processed for discharge the first week of June 1946. The
air force promoted me to the rank of lieutenant colonel as I
moved from active service into the Reserve Officers Corps.

The rest of my life lay ahead of me, and I was anxious to
get started.

EPILOGUE

THE CROWDS WERE gone and the dimly lit, cavernous display hangar was silent. Like any public place after hours, the Air Force Museum in Dayton, Ohio, had an oddly empty feeling, alive only when people were there to view the displays and exhibits and the chatter of adults and the tiny voices of children filled the space. I walked slowly past the meticulously restored aircraft of my youth: there a B-17, here a B-24, off to the side a P-47. They were all on display, every aircraft I had ever flown. Each one elicited a memory.

I walked the length of the hangar and there it was, as shiny as the day it rolled off of the assembly line on March 19, 1945—almost fifty years ago to the day. A simple plaque placed on a stand in front of its nose explained what the *Bock's Car* was and its historic significance. In the background, a display described the development of the atomic bomb, offered a brief video presentation of the battles in the Pacific, including the kamikaze attacks, and exhibited replicas of Little Boy and Fat

Man. A few seats were arranged about the space for those who wished to sit a moment and reflect upon the display. Unlike the *Bock's Car*'s sister airplane, the *Enola Gay,* which had been left rusting and disassembled for decades in a warehouse in suburban Maryland under the care of the Smithsonian Institution, this magnificent airplane had sat in Dayton for thirty-five years, fully restored. During that time, no hint of public controversy or apology about the plane or its mission was sought from or given by the museum's curators. The exhibit was there to speak for itself through the artifacts on display.

I was not there as a tourist, however, on that cool March evening in 1995. I had come on a mission of a different sort. Jim Webb, the former secretary of the navy under President Ronald Reagan, had interviewed me earlier in the year for a story that was to appear in *Parade* magazine. The editor of *Parade* had asked me to go to the museum to be photographed standing alongside the *Bock's Car* by their special correspondent and staff photographer, Eddie Adams, for the cover of the magazine. The museum had graciously allowed us into the exhibit after hours and opened up the *Bock's Car* itself.

The scene reminded me of my brief stay in Hollywood back in 1946 after the war. Eddie and his lighting assistant rushed around positioning lighting stands and cameras, making what seemed to me to be imperceptible adjustments to get the perfect photograph. After a series of shots of me standing beside the *Bock's Car,* Eddie asked if I felt up to getting inside the cockpit. I did.

Climbing up through the nosewheel hatch, I crouched forward toward the flight deck and eased myself carefully into the pilot's seat. It seemed familiar and distant—the yoke, the instrument panel, the throttles. My hands moved about the array in front of me. The interior of the cabin had an ethereal glow caused by the exterior illumination of the high-intensity camera lights positioned around the *Bock's Car.* I looked over to my left and, through the haze of the lights, I could see a restored Japanese Zero, a bright red ball on a field of white emblazoned on its green fuselage, sitting harmlessly within a cordoned-off display area. Time and place. That sight fifty years before would have caused quite a different emotion than the benign nostalgia I felt.

It struck me at that moment that the last time I'd sat in this seat was August 9, 1945.

My thoughts drifted back, not to the atomic missions but to the wonderful men I had served with and the memories of the times, happy and sorrowful, we had shared together. The relentless march of time continued to thin out our ranks more effectively than had our former enemies. In this time and place I sought to help preserve the memory of those men and of the events we had lived through. For today, we veterans of World War II find ourselves confronted by a persistent and ideologically driven attempt to erode the truth of the war—to distort America's motives, its role in the war, and the nature of the enemy we faced—not unlike the erosion of the *Enola Gay,* sitting stored away and forgotten for all those years.

Just as modern-day leaders in Japan still refuse to accept responsibility for what the Imperial Army did fifty years ago—and, more important, for the consequences of its actions—some American revisionist historians downplay or ignore those actions. And because they oppose President Truman's decision to use the atomic bombs to end the war, they sift through thousands of pages of official records, diaries, books, and magazines, searching for a number or a statement upon which they can base their argument that America's motives in using the weapons were contemptible.

During the commemoration of the fiftieth anniversary of the end of World War II, the mayors of Hiroshima and Nagasaki reached new levels of perverse logic to perpetuate the pose of Japan as victim. They declared the atomic missions to be the equivalent of the Holocaust. The Holocaust—where ten million innocent men, women, and children, six million of them Jewish, were methodically rounded up and herded away in trains like cattle to warehouses of torture and death. Where perhaps the more fortunate of them were merely shot to death or forced to labor in tasks perpetuating the villainous scheme. All for reasons of their birth. The enormity of it is almost incomprehensible.

The people of Hiroshima and Nagasaki were the victims of their own warlords, whose savagery and recalcitrance made their citizens the vortex of the final effort to force the Japanese leaders to surrender. President Truman warned of the impending destruction. The Japanese leaders chose to let their people stay—and die.

If ever a comparison is to be made, I would say in response to the mayors of Hiroshima and Nagasaki, it is that fascism flourished not only in the European theater, but in the Pacific theater as well. The similarity of behaviors, of actions, of evil intent of the Axis powers cannot be tempered or whitewashed by relying on the world's fear of nuclear power. And just as it was critical for Germany to face up to and apologize for its actions, it is no less important for Japan to do the same. Only then can the world have some hope that history will not repeat itself.

Some people in Japan have tried to address the truth, understanding what is at stake. Kenzaburo Oe, Japan's Nobel Prize-winning novelist, has written that for Japan to be a true partner in Asia, it must apologize for its aggression. "In the history of our modernization in general but, in particular, in the war of aggression that was its peak, we lost the right to be part of Asia and have continued to live without recovering that right," Mr.

Oe said. "Without that rehabilitation we shall never be able to eradicate the ambivalence in our attitude toward our neighbors, the feeling that our relationships aren't real."

Yukio Shinozuka was the chief of the germ-cultivation office for the infamous Unit 731, the Imperial Japanese Army's human experimentation and biological warfare group, which conducted ghastly medical experiments on prisoners of war during World War II. After serving over ten years in a Chinese prison for his crimes, Mr. Shinozuka returned to Japan to speak out publicly against what his unit had done during the war. "But Japanese at that time would not listen to my kind of talk," he said. "They only wanted to listen to people who talked about being victims, about how they suffered." And perhaps most chillingly, Mr. Shinozuka observed of the present generation, "I've come across many medical students who have the theory that Unit 731 did a good thing." He states that if there had been "sincere, thoughtful reflection, this kind of youthful revisionist thinking would not happen."

For myself, I remember the words of Sumio Shimodio, a prominent Japanese businessman I met at the 1980 reunion of the 509th and with whom I began a long friendship. One evening he told me that he had been twelve years old and in a bomb shelter in Hiroshima the day we dropped the atomic bomb. He said he had just come out and looked into the sky when he saw one of the three parachutes carrying our instruments. He ducked down just as the bomb went off and miraculously was not injured. He said to me, "I love you Americans—you wanted to end the war but that goddamned Tojo wanted to keep it going."

My friend expressed what many revisionist historians seem intent on ignoring—that the bomb was an essential cause of Japan's surrender. Prime Minister Suzuki stated immediately after the war that the atomic bomb had "enabled his military colleagues to surrender honorably." Emperor Hirohito himself, on September 27, 1945, pronounced that "[t]he peace party did not prevail until the bombing of Hiroshima created a situation that could be dramatized." Both Suzuki and Hirohito understood that only the shock of Hiroshima and Nagasaki blocked the military's well-documented intention to fight to the death.

There remains one question for Americans: Why did President Truman order the dropping of the atomic bombs? David McCullough, whose biography of Harry S. Truman provides exhaustive detail of the events surrounding President Truman's decision, offers the most direct and authoritative answer: "If you want an explanation as to why Truman dropped the bomb: 'Okinawa.' It was done to stop the killing."

Revisionists may now claim, without a shred of persuasive evidence, that President Truman used the atomic bombs to impress Joseph Stalin. Or to prove his manhood. Or because he was under the Svengali influence of Secretary of State Jimmy Burns, who controlled a weak and vacillating Harry Truman. Any hook—except the fact that an invasion of mainland Japan would have meant hundreds of thousands of American dead and wounded.

In the summer of 1945, as the historian Stephen Ambrose succinctly observed, Truman confronted death or more death in the Pacific. As commander-in-chief, he, like his predecessor, President Roosevelt, faced the bleak reality that war is an endless series of dreadful choices. It is by definition an immoral condition of the human body and spirit. But once it is thrust upon you, the ultimate goal of victory is achieved only by disrupting, disorganizing, and destroying the enemy.

The only facts and numbers that are relevant to a discussion of Truman's decision, therefore, are those facts and numbers the president had in front of him in July 1945. The staggering casualties at Iwo Jima and Okinawa were not projections, they were memorialized by rows of white crosses and hospital wards filled with broken bodies. In each case, Japanese military forces fought to the death, as they had done everywhere else. The casualty ratio as the United States drew closer to Japan was one to two.

Based upon these realities, Truman's military advisers, in a White House meeting on June 18, 1945, predicted that 30 to 35 percent of the 770,000-man invasion force could reasonably be expected to be killed or wounded during just the first thirty days of the invasion of Kyushu. Translation: 231,000 to 269,000 dead or wounded Americans in the first thirty days of combat. It was estimated that it would take a hundred and twenty days to secure and occupy the entire island. By the end of that four-month period, American casualties could realistically reach around 395,000. And over one million of our troops still awaited the second prong of the invasion. In March 1946 they would wade ashore near Tokyo to take Honshu.

These estimates assumed, of course, that all would go according to plan. Yet Okinawa had been expected to fall in two weeks; instead the battle had dragged into eighty-two days, and even then it took several more weeks after that to secure the island.

As to the Japanese willingness to surrender, Truman was also faced with the reality that America's relentless pounding of Japanese cities with thousands of tons of incendiary bombs, reducing those cities to burned-out rubble, had not broken the will of the Japanese to fight on. Also, it had been clear from our intercepts of their secret military and diplomatic codes that a negotiated peace was acceptable to the Japanese only if it would have left their military in place and allowed them to keep the territory they continued to occupy. They were playing for time. Time that meant another 900 Americans were killed or wounded each day.

This is what President Truman knew. Based upon that knowledge, his decision was not only justified by the circumstances at the time but was a moral imperative that precluded any other option. The president was honor-bound to use every weapon at his disposal to stop the carnage.

The goal of preventing the use of nuclear weapons, however noble, does not justify pseudohistory. Recognizing why—in that time and in that place—the atomic bombs were dropped on Hiroshima and Nagasaki is a critical first step to understanding the important lessons of the history of the war. By examining what happened honestly, we can learn the principles that guide human nature in the painstaking process of making choices that define our conduct. It is from this process that true moral authority is to be found.

Traveling down that road of painstaking process, I found myself sitting in room 106 of the Dirksen Senate Office Building, about to testify before the Committee on Rules and Administration on Thursday, May 11, 1995. The hearings were titled "The Smithsonian Institution: Management Guidelines for the Future."

The chairman, Senator Ted Stevens, opened the proceedings:

We are here today because the Smithsonian decided to present an interpretation of the history of the *Enola Gay*'s historic flight. The veterans in this country reacted strongly, for good reason, to the scripts that emerged from the Smithsonian. In the fifty years since World War II ended, and recently, there has been a constant erosion of the truth of what really happened during that war. This type of erosion is one of the reasons that the Holocaust Museum, that was built with private funds, is so important. It is to ensure that the atrocities committed against Jews and others in the Nazi death camps will never be forgotten.

*   *   *

Our first witness is General Charles Sweeney . . . Let me state that we have asked witnesses to limit their oral presentations to ten minutes . . . We are going to waive the time limit, however, for General Sweeney. We feel that his role is so historic in this matter, and both Senator Ford and I have read the statement . . . I would wish that the public at large could hear every word of what he has written. . . .

APPENDIX

Testimony of Major General Charles W. Sweeney, U.S.A.F. (Ret.) delivered before the United States Senate Committee on Rules and Administration—hearings on the Smithsonian Institution: Management Guidelines for the Future, May 11, 1995.

I am Major General Charles W. Sweeney, United States Air Force, Retired. I am the only pilot to have flown on both atomic missions. I flew the instrument plane on the right wing of General Paul Tibbets on the Hiroshima mission and three days later, on August 9, 1945, commanded the second atomic mission over Nagasaki. Six days after Nagasaki the Japanese military surrendered and the second world war came to an end.

The soul of a nation—its essence—is its history. It is that collective memory which defines what each generation thinks and believes about itself and its country.

In a free society, such as ours, there is always an ongoing debate about who we are and what we stand for. This open debate is, in fact, essential to our freedom. But to have such a debate we as a society must have the courage to consider all of the facts available to us. We must have the courage to stand up and demand that before any conclusions are reached, those facts which are beyond question are accepted as part of the debate.

As the fiftieth anniversary of the Hiroshima and Nagasaki missions approaches, now is an appropriate time to consider the reasons for Harry Truman's order that these missions be flown. We may disagree on the conclusion, but let us at least be honest enough to agree on basic facts of the time—the facts that President Truman had to consider in making a difficult and momentous decision.

As the only pilot to have flown both missions, and having commanded the Nagasaki mission, I bring to this debate my own eyewitness account of the times. I underscore what I believe are irrefutable facts, with full knowledge that some opinion makers may cavalierly dismiss them because they are so obvious—because they interfere with their preconceived version of the truth and the meaning which they strive to impose on the missions.

This morning, I want to offer my thoughts, observations, and conclusions as someone who lived this history and who believes that President Truman's decision was not only justified by the circumstances of his time but was a moral imperative that precluded any other option.

Like the overwhelming majority of my generation, the last thing I wanted was a war. We as a nation are not warriors. We are not hell-bent on glory.

There is no warrior class . . .

no samurai . . .

no master race.

This is true today, and it was true fifty years ago.

While our country was struggling through the Great Depression, the Japanese were embarking on the conquest of their neighbors—the Greater East Asia Co-Prosperity Sphere. It seems fascism always seeks some innocuous slogan to cover the most hideous plans.

This co-prosperity was achieved by waging total and merciless war against China and Manchuria. Japan, as a nation, saw itself as destined to rule Asia and thereby possess its natural resources and open lands. Without the slightest remorse or hesitation, the Japanese army slaughtered innocent men, women, and children. In the infamous Rape of Nanking, up to three hundred thousand unarmed civilians were butchered. These were criminal acts.

These are facts.

In order to fulfill its divine destiny in Asia, Japan determined that the only real impediment to this goal was the United States. It launched a carefully conceived sneak attack on our Pacific fleet at Pearl Harbor. Timed for a Sunday morning, it was intended to deal a death blow to the fleet by inflicting the maximum loss of ships and human life.

Hundreds of sailors are still entombed in the hull of the USS *Arizona,* which sits on the bottom of Pearl Harbor. Many if not all, died without ever knowing why. Thus was the war thrust upon us.

The fall of Corregidor and the resulting treatment of Allied prisoners of war dispelled any remaining doubt about the inhumaneness of the Japanese army, even in the context of war. The Bataan Death March was horror in its fullest dimension. The Japanese considered surrender to be dishonorable to oneself, one's family, one's country, and one's god. They showed no mercy. Seven thousand American and Filipino POWs were beaten, shot, bayonetted, or left to die of disease or exhaustion.

These are facts.

As the United States made its slow, arduous, and costly march across the vast expanse of the Pacific, the Japanese proved to be a ruthless and intractable killing machine. No matter how futile, no matter how hopeless the odds, no matter how certain the outcome, the Japanese fought to the death. And to achieve a greater glory, they strove to kill as many Americans as possible.

The closer the United States came to the Japanese mainland, the more fanatical their actions became.

Saipan: 3,000 Americans killed, 1,500 in the first few hours of the invasion.

Iwo Jima: 6,000 Americans killed, 21,000 wounded.

Okinawa: 12,000 Americans killed, total wounded 38,000.

These are facts reported by simple white grave markers.

Kamikazes. The literal translation is "divine wind." To willingly dive a plane loaded with bombs into an American ship was a glorious transformation to godliness—there was no higher honor on heaven or earth. At Okinawa the suicidal assaults of the kamikazes took 5,000 American navy men to their deaths.

The Japanese, through word and deed, made clear that, with the first American to step foot on the mainland, they would execute every Allied prisoner. In preparation they forced the POWs to dig their own graves in the event of mass executions. Even after their surrender, they executed some American POWs.

These are facts.

The Potsdam Declaration had called for unconditional surrender of the Japanese armed forces. The Japanese termed it ridiculous and not worthy of consideration. We know from our intercepts of their coded messages that they wanted to stall for time to force a negotiated surrender on terms acceptable to them.

For months prior to August 6, American aircraft began dropping firebombs upon the Japanese mainland. The wind created by the firestorms from the bombs incinerated whole cities. Hundreds of thousands of Japanese died. Still the Japanese military vowed never to surrender. They were prepared to sacrifice their own people to achieve their visions of glory and honor—no matter how many more people died.

They refused to evacuate civilians even though our pilots dropped leaflets warning of the possible bombings. In one ten-day period, thirty-two square miles of Tokyo, Nagoya, Kobe, and Osaka were reduced to rubble.

These are facts.

And even after the bombing of Hiroshima, Tojo, his successor, Suzuki, and the military clique in control believed the United States had but one bomb, and that Japan could go on. They had three days to surrender after August 6, but they did not surrender. The debate in their cabinet at times became violent. Only after the Nagasaki drop did the emperor finally demand surrender. And even then, the military argued they could and should fight on. A group of army officers staged a coup and tried to seize and destroy the emperor's recorded message to his people announcing the surrender.

These are facts.

These facts help illuminate the nature of the enemy we faced.

They help put into context the process by which Truman considered the options available to him. And they help to add meaning to why the missions were necessary.

President Truman understood these facts, as did every serviceman and servicewoman. Casualties were not some abstraction but a sobering reality.

Did the atomic missions end the war?

Yes . . . they . . . did.

Were they necessary?

Well, that's where the rub comes.

With the fog of fifty years drifting over the memory of our country, to some the Japanese are now the victims. America was the insatiable, vindictive aggressor seeking revenge and conquest. Our use of these weapons was the unjustified and immoral starting point for the nuclear age, with all of its horrors. Of course, to support such distortion, one must conveniently ignore the real facts or fabricate new realities to fit the theories. This is no less egregious than those who today deny the Holocaust occurred.

How could this have happened?

The answer may lie in examining some recent events.

The current debate about why President Truman ordered these missions, in some cases, has devolved to a numbers game. The Smithsonian, in its proposed exhibit of the *Enola Gay*, revealed the creeping revisionism which seems the rage in certain historical circles.

That exhibit wanted to memorialize the fiction that the Japanese were the victims—we the evil aggressors. Imagine taking your children and grandchildren to this exhibit.

What message would they have left with?

What truth would they retain?

What would they think their country stood for?

And all of this would have occurred in an American institution whose very name and charter are supposed to stand for the impartial preservation of significant American artifacts.

By canceling the proposed exhibit and simply displaying the Enola Gay, has truth won out?

Maybe not.

In one nationally televised discussion, I heard a so-called prominent historian argue that the bombs were not necessary.

That President Truman was intent on intimidating the Russians. That the Japanese were ready to surrender.

The Japanese were ready to surrender? Based on what?

Some point to statements by General Eisenhower that Japan was about to fall and that use of the bomb was unnecessary. Well, based on that same outlook, Eisenhower seriously underestimated Germany's will to fight on and concluded in December 1944 that Germany no longer had the capability to wage offensive war. That was a tragic miscalculation. The result was the Battle of the Bulge, which resulted in tens of thousands of needless Allied casualties and potentially allowed Germany to prolong the war and force negotiations.

Eisenhower later candidly admitted about his comments on the bomb, "My views were merely personal and an immediate reaction; they were not based upon any analysis of the subject." Thus the assessment that Japan was vanquished may have the benefit of hindsight rather than foresight.

It is certainly fair to conclude that the Japanese could have been reasonably expected to be even more fanatical than the Germans, based on the history of the war in the Pacific.

And, finally, a present-day theory making the rounds espouses that even if an invasion had taken place, our casualties would not have been a million, as many believed, but realistically only forty-six thousand dead.

Only forty-six thousand!

Can you imagine the callousness of this line of argument?

Only forty-six thousand—as if this were some insignificant number of American lives.

Perhaps these so-called historians want to sell books.

Perhaps they really believe it.

Or perhaps it reflects some self-loathing occasioned by the fact that we won the war.

Whatever the reason, the argument is flawed. It dissects and recalculates events ideologically—grasping at selective straws.

Let me admit right here, today, that I don't know how many more Americans would have died in an invasion—*and neither does anyone else!*

What I do know is that based on the Japanese conduct during the war, it is fair and reasonable to assume that an invasion of the mainland would have been a prolonged and bloody affair. Based on what we know—not what someone surmises—the Japanese were not about to unconditionally surrender.

In taking Iwo Jima—a tiny eight-square-mile lump of rock in the ocean, six thousand marines died—total casualties around 27,000.

But even assuming that those who now *know* our casualties would have been *only* forty-six thousand I ask—

Which forty-six thousand were to die?

Whose father?

Whose brother?

Whose husband?

And, yes, I am focusing on American lives.

The Japanese had their fate in their own hands. We did not. Hundreds of thousands of American troops anxiously waited at staging areas in the Pacific dreading the coming invasion—*their* fate resting on what the Japanese would do next. The Japanese could have ended it at any time. *They* chose to wait.

And while the Japanese stalled, an average of nine hundred more Americans were killed or wounded each day the war continued.

I've heard another line of argument that we should have accepted a negotiated peace with the Japanese on terms they would have found acceptable. I have never heard anyone suggest that we should have negotiated a peace with Nazi Germany. Such an idea is so outrageous that *no* rational human being would utter the words. To negotiate with such evil fascism was to allow it, even in defeat, a measure of legitimacy. This is not just some empty philosophical principle of the time—it was essential that these forces of evil be clearly and irrevocably defeated, their demise unequivocal. Their leadership had forfeited any expectation of diplomatic niceties. How is it, then, that the history of the war in the Pacific can be so soon forgotten?

The reason may lie in the advancing erosion of our history—of our collective memory.

Fifty years after their defeat, Japanese officials have the temerity to claim they were the victims. That Hiroshima and Nagasaki were the equivalent of the Holocaust.

And, believe it or not, there are actually some American academics who support this analogy, thus aiding and giving comfort to a fifty-year attempt by the Japanese to rewrite their own history—and ours in the process.

There is an entire generation of Japanese who do not know the full extent of their country's conduct during World War II.

This explains why they do not comprehend why they must apologize . . .

For the Korean comfort women.

For the medical experimentation on POWs which match the horror of those conducted by the Nazis.

For the plans to use biological weapons against the United States by infecting civilian populations on the West Coast.

For the methodical slaughter of civilians.

And for much more . . .

In a perverse inversion, by forgetting our own history we contribute to the Japanese amnesia, to the detriment of both our nations.

Unlike Germany, which acknowledged its guilt, Japan persists in the fiction that it did nothing wrong, that it was trapped by circumstances. This only forecloses any genuine prospect that the deep wounds suffered by both nations can be closed and healed.

One can only forgive by remembering. And to forget is to risk repeating history.

The Japanese, in a well-orchestrated political and public relations campaign, have now proposed that the use of the term "V-J Day" be replaced by the more benign "Victory in the Pacific Day." How convenient.

This, they claim, will make the commemoration of the end of the war in the Pacific less "Japan-specific."

Some might argue, so what's in a word? Victory over Japan . . . Victory in the Pacific . . . Let's celebrate an event, not a victory.

I say *everything* is in a word.

Celebrate an *event!*

Kind of like celebrating the opening of a shopping mall rather than the end of a war that engulfed the entire earth— which left countless millions dead and countless millions more physically or mentally wounded and countless more millions displaced.

This assault on the use of language is Orwellian and is the tool by which history and memory are blurred. Words can be just as destructive as any weapon.

Up is down.

Slavery is freedom.

Aggression is peace.

In some ways this assault on our language and history by the elimination of accurate and descriptive words is far more insidious than the actual aggression carried out by the Japanese fifty years ago. At least then the threat was clear—the enemy well defined.

Today the Japanese justify their conduct by artfully playing the race card—they were not engaged in a criminal enterprise of aggression. No—Japan was simply liberating the oppressed masses of Asia from *white* imperialism.

Liberation! Yes, they liberated over twenty million innocent Asians by killing them. I'm sure those twenty million, their families, and the generations never to be, appreciate the noble effort of the Japanese. I am often asked was the bomb dropped for vengeance—as was suggested by one draft of the Smithsonian exhibit. That we sought to destroy an ancient and honorable culture.

Here are some more inconvenient facts:

One. On the original target list for the atomic missions, Kyoto was included. Although this would have been a legitimate target, one that had not been bombed previously, Secretary of State Henry Stimson removed it from the list because it was the ancient capital of Japan and was also the religious center of Japanese culture.

Two. We were under strict orders during the war that under no circumstances were we to ever bomb the Imperial Palace in Tokyo—even though we could have easily leveled it and possibly killed the emperor. So much for vengeance. I often wonder if Japan would have shown such restraint if it had had the opportunity to bomb the White House . . . I think not.

At this point let me dispel one of many longstanding myths that our targets were intended to be civilian populations. Each target for the missions had significant military importance—Hiroshima was the headquarters for the southern command, responsible for the defense of Honshu in the event of an invasion, and it garrisoned seasoned troops who would mount the initial defense.

Nagasaki was an industrial center with the two large Mitsubishi armaments factories. In both Hiroshima and Nagasaki, the Japanese had integrated these industries and troops right in the heart of each city.

As in any war, our goal was—as it should be—to win. The stakes were too high to equivocate.

I am often asked if I ever think of the Japanese who died at Hiroshima and Nagasaki.

I do not revel in the idea that so many on both sides died, not only at those two places but around the world, in that horrible conflict. I take no pride or pleasure in the brutality of war, whether suffered by my people or those of another nation. Every life is precious.

But it does seem to me such a question is more appropriately directed to the Japanese warlords who so willingly offered up their people to achieve their visions of greatness. They who started the war and then stubbornly refused to stop it must be called to account. Don't they have the ultimate responsibility for *all* the deaths of their countrymen?

Perhaps if the Japanese came to grips with their past and their true part in the war they would hold those Japanese military leaders accountable. The Japanese people deserve an answer from those who brought such misery to the nations of the Far East and ultimately to their own people. Of course, this can never happen if we collaborate with the Japanese in wiping away the truth.

How can Japan ever reconcile with itself, its Asian neighbors, and the United States if it does do not demand and accept the truth?

My crew and I flew these missions with the belief that they would bring the war to an end. There was no sense of joy. There was a sense of duty and commitment that we wanted to get back to our families and loved ones.

Today millions of people in America and in Southeast Asia are alive because the war ended when it did.

I do not stand here celebrating the use of nuclear weapons. Quite the contrary.

I hope that my mission is the last such mission ever flown. We as a nation should abhor the existence of nuclear weapons.

I certainly do.

But that does not then mean that, back in August of 1945, given the events of the war and the recalcitrance of our enemy, President Truman was not obliged to use all the weapons at his disposal to end the war.

I agreed with Harry Truman then, and I still do today.

Years after the war, Truman was asked if he had any second thoughts. He said emphatically—no. He then asked the questioner to remember the men who died at Pearl Harbor who did not have the benefit of second thoughts.

In war, the stakes are high. As Robert E. Lee said, "It is good that war is so horrible, or we might grow to like it."

I thank God that it was we who had this weapon and not the Japanese or the Germans. The science was there. Eventually someone would have developed this weapon. Science can never be denied—it finds a way to self-fulfillment. The question of whether it was wise to develop such a weapon would have eventually been overcome by the fact that it could be done. The Soviets would have certainly proceeded to develop their own bomb—let us not forget that Joseph Stalin was no less evil than Tojo or his former ally, Adolf Hitler. At last count, Stalin committed genocide on at least twenty million of his own citizens.

The world is a better place because German and Japanese fascism failed to conquer the world.

Japan and Germany are better places because we were benevolent in our victory.

The youth of Japan and the United States, spared from

further needless slaughter, went on to live and have families and grow old.

As the father of ten children and the grandfather of twenty-one, I can state that I am certainly grateful that the war ended when it did.

I do not speak for all veterans of that war. But I believe that my sense of pride in having served my country in that great conflict is shared by all veterans. This is why the truth about that war must be preserved. We veterans are not shrinking violets. Our sensibilities will not be shattered in intelligent and controversial debate. We can handle ourselves.

But we will not—*we cannot*—allow armchair second-guessers to frame the debate by hiding facts from the American public and the world.

I have great faith in the good sense and fairness of the American people to consider all of the facts and make an informed judgment about the war's end.

This is an important debate. The soul of our nation—its essence, its history—is at stake.

INDEX